00015482

This book to be returned on or before the last date below.

0 4 MAR 2004

Sheridan Morley

SPECTATOR
AT THE THEATRE

OBERON BOOKS
LONDON

All reviews first published in *The Spectator*.

First published in this collection in 2002 by Oberon Books Ltd.
(incorporating Absolute Classics)
521 Caledonian Road, London N7 9RH
Tel: 020 7607 3637 / Fax: 020 7607 3629
e-mail: oberon.books@btinternet.com

A catalogue record for this book is available from the British Library.

ISBN: 1 84002 247 7

Cover Design: Jon Morgan

Cover Photograph: Matthew Thomas

Printed in Great Britain by Antony Rowe Ltd, Chippenham.

for Ruth
who shared these thousand or so nights

for Liz Anderson
the best of arts editors

and for James Hogan
without whom this book would not have been possible

Contents

Acknowledgements

The author and publisher wish to thank the editor and publisher of *The Spectator*, where all of these columns first appeared, for their kind permission to reprint here; they would also like to thank the *Evening Standard* and the Society of West End Theatre for permission to reprint the winners of the Olivier and *Evening Standard* drama awards during the decade under review.

Preface

Thanks on this publication to James Hogan at Oberon, this is the fourth collection of theatre reviews which I have been lucky enough to turn from yellowing press cuttings into a book. Like the other three, *Review Copies* (1970), *Shooting Stars* (1980) and *Our Theatres in the Eighties* (1990), it deals with the immediately preceding decade in the London and New York theatre, but as I can hardly expect you to have read the entire sequence, or possibly any of it, a word or two by way of introduction.

I am just sixty, and have been a drama critic for almost forty years. This is not necessarily a good thing: it is arguable that the two best critics of the past century, Bernard Shaw and Kenneth Tynan, were as good as they were at least partly because they only did the job for a relatively short time. Those of us in it for the long haul, largely in my case because I have never been able to think of anything else I really wanted to do, have to fend off the dangers of boredom or repetition, not only for ourselves of course, but for our readers who are the only reason for our existence.

From time to time, theatre people try to tell critics that we have some sort of duty, whether to keep a certain theatre or company from closure, or to foster new talent, or to support a certain actor or director or political line. This is rubbish. A critic's only responsibility is to his or her readers, and they are surprisingly quick to latch onto any specific agenda or special pleading. At that point they lose faith in you as a guide, and you may as well give up spending four or sometimes five nights a week in what the American lyricist of *A Chorus Line*, the late Ed Kleban, once described as 'a large building in the centre of town, where there is a darkened room with a lot of people who have preferably paid a great deal of money to get in.'

Theatre-going was much like that when I started reviewing in the mid-1960s; now of course it is vastly more fragmented, and happens all over the place. This is not necessarily a bad thing, but it does mean (as with television reviewing after the coming of cable and satellite), that you can no longer be entirely sure that what you are writing about is what your readers have actually been to see, or are indeed planning to attend.

Perhaps the other two greatest changes in my working life have been to do with money and spaces. In value for money, theatre-going is now in real terms more expensive than I can ever recall, and to the sheer cost of the tickets has been added a whole set of other problems (parking, restaurant expenses, the collapse of public transport), which means that the ideal West End playgoer is a foreign tourist without family, living in a central hotel and on expenses.

This in turn has made the West End into a theatre essentially designed for those who don't go to plays or musicals very often, and that in turn has led to it becoming often either a desert, or a museum of old stars in old hits.

With few exceptions, anything really intriguing or new now reaches the West End by way of either the fringe or the subsidised companies. Very little starts in the West End any more, and for someone growing up as I was in the 1950s, when Shaftesbury Avenue would regularly offer Christopher Fry, Jean Anouilh,

Tennessee Williams and Arthur Miller, there can be no doubt that it is now a less exciting area of theatre-going, beset also by major decrepitude problems (most West End theatres were built 100 years ago, just after the coming of electricity) and a London that is, in terms of drunks and drugs and nightmarish parking restrictions, rapidly becoming a place you don't want to visit unless you have to.

Which means that anything intriguing in theatre has been edged out to the pubs and clubs of the fringe, tiny studio theatres, or to the safely subsidised havens of the RSC or the National or the Royal Court. But even there, things are changing fast; the RSC has in 2002 effectively abandoned a permanent company and operate, as does the National, on play-by-play casting, which means that any show can be neatly lifted out of the repertoire and parachuted into the West End for profit, thereby avoiding the old cross-casting problems with actors involved in several productions.

One of the saddest aspects of all this is that the last RSC production to come into the Barbican under the old permanent-company system was Ed Hall's 2001 revival of *Julius Caesar*. Ed was therefore effectively (and through no fault of his own) closing down the permanent company which was created exactly forty years ago at Stratford and the Aldwych by his father Sir Peter.

So here we are, starting on a new theatrical century with no permanent companies, and an uneasily mixed economy in which even the National goes for a commercial hit like *My Fair Lady* to boost an apparently inadequate state subsidy. The paymasters here, the Arts Council, are also in a state of some chaos, having recently closed down their regional branches; they are clearly now uncertain of their political or financial role at a time when the Lottery, once promised as the answer to all theatrical prayers, is no longer delivering anything like enough cash.

For the brief time that it was delivering adequately, a number of London and regional theatres were encouraged to expand their spaces at considerable cost; no sooner had they done so than theatrical economy crashed, leaving Lottery winners unable to finance their new buildings and obliged to hire professional administrators rather than artistic directors.

And another thing: those theatres which are surviving on public money are now so deluged with officialdom and bureaucracy that they can no longer get on with their core business of producing good work. Let us be specific, though I need to declare an interest. When, as I noted above, I found myself about ten years ago in danger of boring either myself or my readers as a critic, and was unable to find any other satisfactory way of making a living, I deliberately set about directing plays and even latterly doing a little television acting, whereupon my full interest in reviewing was passionately reawakened, because I now have some personal experience in staging plays.

Does this, I am sometimes asked, make me a kinder critic? Almost certainly not; all it now means is that I can sort out in my own mind rather more clearly whether to blame or praise the writing, the acting, the directing or the designing of a show.

And at least one other mystery was solved for me: for years I have been directing in such fringe spaces as the King's Head in Islington and the Jermyn

Street Theatre, vaguely wondering why it was that so many other shows there which I and other critics loved so seldom made the short journey to the West End. When a production of Noël Coward's *Song at Twilight*, which I had directed, moved from the King's Head to the Gielgud, I learnt something fascinating: the West End producer, as we started rehearsing, took a quarter-page ad in the Sunday Times listing the cast and director. That ad, he later told me encouragingly, had cost him more by itself than we had spent in eight weeks at the King's Head, counting rent, salaries, costumes and scenery. A brief diary of this production can be found at the end of 1998.

In other words, the financial gap between the Fringe and the West End is now wider than it ever has been, and mostly those who make it have to have the resources of a vast subsidised company such as the National or the RSC. The Festival Theatre at Chichester also used to be a regular source of transfers; it has recently taken a small-stage musical, *Song of Singapore*, all of three years to travel the sixty or so miles from there to the temporarily reopened Mayfair.

So what we have now is a state of almost total change and considerable chaos: the RSC abandons its role as a permanent company; the National, in its search of a successor to Trevor Nunn, has found that most of the obvious candidates would rather make Hollywood movies; the twenty-year triumph of the big Cameron Mackintosh/Lloyd Webber musicals is drawing to a close; the West End has just survived a year in which every known plague short of locusts, (floods, rail chaos, foot and mouth, terrorist-induced hesitation) has been visited upon it. Added to that, one of London's most starry and charismatic fringe theatres, the Almeida, has lost its two fine directors.

A generation of distinguished commercial producers from Michael Codron to Duncan Weldon seems either to be moving gently toward a kind of retirement, or to be finding that their old 'angel' backers are dying off at precisely the moment when costs are going through the roof.

Arthur Miller once told me that you could make a killing on Broadway but never a living, and that will soon be true in London; theatre is resilient in the 'fabulous invalid' sense that a hit will always turn up somewhere surprising, but if costs go on spiralling, that single hit will not, as in the past, make up for a few flops from the same team.

Then again, the present government seems deeply in love with cinema and television, but to have precious little interest in live theatre; as always, promises made in opposition have not been realised, and theatre itself seems oddly friendless in high places; why else would it have become so inaccessible for transport and so expensive?

There seems still, it is true, to be general agreement that of all the performing arts, theatre is still what we do best in Britain; I have always felt that to be a drama critic living in London was much like being a wine writer living in Bordeaux. But the French have not made it as difficult as possible to grow wine there, and one wonders why official and establishment Britain has been so hostile to theatre?

Is it for the boringly practical reason that in the evening, when plays usually happen, politicians are otherwise engaged in the Commons and newspaper editors still at work, so that we have no truly influential lobby to fight for us? Is it that Arts Ministers since the great and good Jennie Lee (who built the National and the Barbican in the 1960s) have been either impotent or deeply inefficient? Or has it ever been thus?

We have now also just seen, with the deaths in recent years of Sir Alec Guinness and Sir John Gielgud, the end of the greatest classical generation of actors that the world has ever seen. Their successors are now often happier in Hollywood or on television, or making more money for a morning's voice-over than they can in a month of eight shows a week in an increasingly sordid West End, where they and their audiences now have to climb over used syringes and empty beer cans to get anywhere near the theatre.

I am the third generation of an acting family, and I do not really doubt that London theatre will see me, and maybe even my two grandsons, safely out. It is not about to close. But if it is to stay open, all the above issues have to be faced. Then again, it is often easy for a journalist to start asking the right questions; the problem at the moment seems to be finding anybody out there who has even the vaguest notion of what the right answers might be, or how we set about finding them. We would seem to be in a long winter of general theatrical discontent; I am not suggesting that summer won't come, just that it suddenly starts to feel a long way off.

Sheridan Morley
London, 2002

1991

Around the London theatres in 1991 it has been, to quote the one-time actor and theatre critic Charles Dickens, the best of times and the worst of times. If you happened to be Andrew Lloyd Webber, with five fully sold-out musicals playing virtually all year, or the impresario Cameron Mackintosh, also with five sold-out musicals only two of which were the aforementioned Andrew's, then the boom has come to resemble a bonanza with no foreseeable ending. If, on the other hand, you were any other producer or musical writer in town (not least those who cobbled together *Matador* or *Children of Eden* or *Hunting of the Snark*) then this has to have been the worst box-office year in living memory.

The truth, and it is a scary one, is that the West End is fast approaching Broadway. Not as many theatres may be closed, nor is the theatre district as derelict, nor the unions and national pride as problematic, but we are now for the first time into a hit/flop climate. Until recently, say a couple of years ago, it was quite possible to find at least a dozen shows around the West End that were technically neither hits nor flops. They occupied a safe and often intriguing middle ground, playing for maybe three to six months to around sixty per cent capacity, breaking even so long as they had a small cast and not too ambitious a set. No more: now the hits stay with us forever (indeed 'now and forever' as they say on the *Cats* posters), while the flops and even near-misses are folding their tents before you can even start to spell Recession. It is no longer enough to have a show that some of the people quite like some of the time.

Moreover the multinational tourist economy, while keeping a dozen or more big musicals rich and fat, is masking a quiet collapse of the legit market, so that those in search of a new drama or even a classical revival are now likely to find it only amid the safely subsidised houses of the South Bank and the Barbican or out toward the pubs and clubs of the North and West London fringe.

Nor has this been the best of years for the major established playwrights. Of the new work we were promised from Arthur Miller, Alan Ayckbourn, David Hare and John Osborne, the Osborne failed to materialise altogether (after a rehearsal row with its star Peter O'Toole), the Miller (*The Ride Down Mount Morgan*) emerged, elegant but oddly anti-climactic, the Ayckbourn was in two parts and hopelessly over-padded, and the David Hare (*Murmuring Judges*) proved less successful in its anatomy of the judiciary than his superb *Racing Demon* had been of the Church of England.

All of which left Alan Bennett, at the year's end, to pick up the laurels with his masterly *The Madness of George III*, a play which also gave its star (last year's Broadway-Tony-winner Nigel Hawthorne) more than a reasonable chance of another actor-of-the-year award.

His only real competition there came from John Wood, whose wonderfully quirky King Lear came into the Barbican from Stratford, and Robert Stephens who at Stratford made a memorable return to greatness as the Falstaff of his generation. Among actresses there were the usual front-runners (Vanessa Redgrave for her patchy Isadora Duncan in *When She Danced*, Fiona Shaw for an over-the-top Hedda Gabler), but it was Juliet Stevenson in a brilliantly suspenseful political thriller from Chile (*Death and the Maiden*) who finally scooped the pool.

Revivals of the year were led by *Carmen Jones* at the Old Vic and *A Woman of No Importance,* superbly costumed-and-designed by Philip Prowse at the Barbican. This last production however underlined a major theatre-going problem at the Barbican and the National: hit shows are scheduled, like the flops, for no more than two or three performances a week, sometimes no more than half a dozen a month, and critics on guaranteed first-night tickets are apt to underrate, as are the managers, an increasing fury on the part of theatre-goers unable to get in to the only shows they are told are worth seeing.

With the Barbican closed again this January and February, and the National already sold out for its two great Alan Bennett hits (*The Wind in the Willows* and *George III*), box-office irritation is at an all-time high. Schedulers in 1992, whatever the difficulties of the repertoire and cross-casting system of subsidised companies, will have to work out a better way to let their audiences see their shows if the public are not to be forever alienated.

As always in an election year, the government has been unusually generous to the Arts Council, but the Thatcherite dream of private-company sponsorship has been hard hit by the recession, and cash is still hard to come by if you happen to want to stage a new playwright with a large cast anywhere in central London. There will, over the next few weeks, be the usual West End bloodbath as anywhere between a dozen and twenty shows that were barely clinging on for the holiday season finally put up their notices, but a cooler temperature-taking in about March should give us some idea of the true state of the theatrical economy for 1992. It will not be good, but with luck it may not prove catastrophic either.

1992

What Larks

The Sound of Music (Sadler's Wells)

Romeo and Juliet (Barbican)

In the title song from a Broadway musical of 1959 which became one of the most commercially successful movies ever made, a postulant nun (later to become Maria von Trapp of the Trapp Family Singers) tells us that she wishes to sing through the night, 'like a lark who is learning to pray.' I have long worried about this. Is there, unknown to most bird-watchers, some kind of lark seminary where feathered creatures flap around in training for the priesthood? Could we be about to witness the landing of the first lark Pope?

Other lyrics in *The Sound of Music* are equally disconcerting: 'Edelweiss,' sings the heroic anti-Nazi Captain von Trapp, later still more heroically to take the ex-nun and seven children on world concert tours, 'every morning you greet me.' Austria in 1938 seems to have had a lot more to worry about than the Nazi Anschluss; talking flowers and bird-priests and singing nuns, not to mention a Mother Abbess obsessed with the need to climb every mountain, presumably in order to escape the praying birds and the talking flowers.

And another thing: in what Rodgers & Hammerstein musical does a governess arrive, at a particularly unhappy turning-point in her life, to take charge of several winsome and lovable children parented by a tyrannical and obsessive father-figure who eventually falls in love with the said governess? Well, yes, *The Sound of Music*. Or, as it is also known, *The King and I*, or indeed *South Pacific*.

Rodgers & Hammerstein clearly had a thing about nannies and fathers and children second only to that of J M Barrie: but, as Wendy Toye's new touring revival of *The Sound of Music* at Sadler's Wells admirably demonstrates, the old Broadway hitmen knew exactly what they were doing. The damn thing still runs like clockwork. At the time of writing, Hammerstein was already a dying man and there is no doubt that his lyrics here lack the dark, driving political edge of some of those in *South Pacific* or the lesser-known *Allegro*. But in the end the sheer gala, Gothic inanity of a plot which vaguely suggests that the Trapps escaped the Nazi invaders by singing them into somnolence has a charm all of its own. Ronald Lee's production commendably lacks the cardboard inadequacies of the last Petula Clark revival, and Liz Robertson makes a scrawny girl-guide of a Maria, while Christopher Cazenove invests the Captain with unusual dignity even when required to report on the singing flowers.

~

After a disastrous start last September at Stratford, David Leveaux's RSC production of *Romeo and Juliet* comes into the Barbican with forty minutes mercifully shaved off its running time and a considerably changed cast. One central problem still remains, however, which is that its title players (Michael Maloney and Claire Holman) look as though they should be worrying about their children's school fees rather than their own teenage romantic obsessions. They are a distinctly mature Romeo and Juliet, and the youthful excesses of the plot therefore seem still more daft than usual. Nor is there any real evidence that Leveaux or anyone involved has anything very much to tell us about the play, except that it needs every now and then to turn up in the RSC repertoire. At the opening, against Alison Chitty's magnificently panelled quattrocento setting, the entire cast look as though they were hoping for *West Side Story*; the minor street skirmishes specified by Shakespeare become inner-city battles with thunder and lightning on the soundtrack.

There are a lot of athletics here, but curiously little passion; it takes only Denys Hawthorne as the Chorus, in full melodic flood, to remind us elsewhere of how thin are the ranks of RSC character actors and how uncertain their command of the verse. Long gone are the Stratford days when players like Cyril Luckham and Anthony Nicholls would regularly make of the Montagues and the Capulets strong family portraits, and therefore some sense of the play's parental battles. Here only Sheila Reid as the Scots Nurse and Tim McInnery as a psychopathic Mercutio, achieve any really memorable characterisation, and the moment one best remembers of the entire production has nothing to do with either Romeo or Juliet. Rather is it the moment when Mercutio, stabbed and dying, realises with a sick laugh that none of his apparent friends has even bothered to notice that he is in mortal peril.

Leveaux has one other intelligent notion, which is to have Juliet float through the opening of the Mantua scene like some sort of premature ghost, hovering over Romeo's arrival there as if to warn him of the fatal failure of communication that is about to occur. For the rest, the elements of waking dreams and hot-city nightmares are only occasionally brought together into a coherent statement of what this play might be about, or why we need to keep having another look at it. There is still a style crisis within the new RSC administration, and it shows up most clearly in the most familiar texts.

An Inspector Palls

Murder by Misadventure (Vaudeville)

The Inspector paused on his way out of the stalls bar. 'I think it's a thriller,' he said, 'and it's been dead a long time. Maybe since *Sleuth*. Maybe only since the last revival of *Deathtrap*. These things are difficult to pin down forensically. I blame Roald Dahl myself.'

There was a long silence while he tried to read the eyewitness account he had scribbled on the margins of his programme in the sudden darkness of the first night. 'Unusual for Vaudeville,' he noticed, 'not often you get a death before the interval, maybe two after. Sometimes in the dress circle at revivals of very old musicals, especially matinees. Not usually on stage.'

Only been in the new job a month, and already the Inspector was beginning to feel his age. Back at the old station typewriter, he considered the facts in front of him. Start at the very beginning. Tuesday night, late July. West End a regular bloodbath; fifteen shows gone in less than a month including one of his own. Usual beat, seven o'clock start, report to theatre on Strand. About 300 potential witnesses, well-dressed mob, could be relatives or friends of the victims, investors even, Names and addresses to be taken later. Nothing unusual yet, give or take an agent's hairpiece in the dress circle and a tuxedo in the stalls that seems to have had several previous owners. Check out the ice-creams. Think there used to be more nuts in the vanilla. Unsure of new EEC regulations on this.

Routine briefing in programme lists title, *Murder by Misadventure*, plus four characters. Stars Gerald Harper, a Durbridge man if I'm not mistaken, and Angela Down; also two others listed, but this could be a trap. In *Sleuth* they printed the names of three mythical characters and one of our most promising lads actually reviewed them. Got transferred to the television previewing branch in Sidcup before you could say Shaffer.

Programme also gives location: 'Kent's flat overlooking English Channel.' Thoughtful, that, save a lot of time with the AA Book of the Road later.

The Inspector paused again, this time to consider his life and career in the West End Reviews branch. Fifty this year, hair beginning to recede, usual weight problem, he'd taken the drama beat thirty years ago because it seemed better than fixing traffic lights. Now he wasn't so sure. Night work, it was, often meeting undesirables in dark attics off Shepherd's Bush Green or Islington. Sometimes worse. Sometimes they did plays in Glasgow. Once he'd been beaten up in a pub by a suspect who hadn't much cared for one of his reports. Female dramatists can turn very nasty after a few lagers. When he'd started, back in the 1960s, different world; friendly neighbourhood critics still able to walk dark streets at night without threats from John Osborne. Sometimes even invited in for a drink with Noël Coward around Christmas-time. More plays around then, too, leastways more plays he hadn't already seen. And sometimes, you won't believe this, sometimes they actually put on a musical with new songs in it.

The Inspector went back to his programme notes. Two thriller-writers at the end of their partnership, both want to kill each other, spend all evening doing so. Greg Hicks as possible police inspector does devastating impression of Paul Scofield. This is probably the best thriller in town, given that the other two are *The Mousetrap* and *The Woman in Black*. On the other hand, if I say that they'll quote me on the bloody posters, and all it means is this is a lousy decade for thrillers. End of notes.

Samuel Beckett would have had an entire trilogy out of that lot, not just a drama report. The Inspector typed it up and took it through to his senior officer.

'This it? A week on full pay, entirely alone in Drama division, and all you manage is one halfway adequate thriller down the Strand? What else is there?'

The Inspector thought for a moment. 'Well, up the Barbican they've got an eighty-year-old play by Solomon Anski set in the Ukraine about a woman possessed by the spirit of her dead lover. Probably where they got *The Exorcist* from, but the RSC production just looks like *Fiddler on the Roof* without the songs.

'Elsewhere, not a lot, and August is going to be worse. I find I think a lot about J B Priestley, *An Inspector Calls* and all that. Notions of reality. Am I really here? Does an Edward Taylor thriller halfway down the Strand actually represent the state of the art two thousand years after Aristophanes? Maybe even three. I never did the Greek exam, but I am getting on with writing the books. That never hurt Wambaugh. He was an Inspector too, once. Mind you, he never had to review thrillers in the Strand.'

A Third Great Richard

Richard III (Other Place)

Les Misérables (Palace)

Miss Saigon (Drury Lane)

We are rich in Richards; after the crutch-leaping spider of Antony Sher and the chilly, patrician Windsor Duke of Ian McKellen, a third great Richard III comes to us in less than a decade. At Stratford's rebuilt Other Place, and shortly to embark on a long nationwide tour, Simon Russell Beale gives us a total contrast; a huge evil uncle telling corrupting fairy tales which he then enacts. This is the Charles Laughton version and it establishes Russell Beale in precisely that line of blackly comic classical greatness. This Richard is played for laughs, and becomes in the process all the more terrifying; looking like a bloated, deformed frog, he oozes around a bare stage, casually knocking off the effete, yuppie Clarence (Simon Dormandy) on his way to a crown which he himself is amazed to find so readily available.

If you can recall Laughton controlling the Senate (either Roman as in *Spartacus*, or Washington as in *Advise and Consent*), you will have some idea of what is going on in Sam Mendes brilliantly spare and sparse production, one which allows the golden throne to roll around the stage like some child's discarded toy while all nearby are literally dying for it. This is a manically funny, hugely evil and very black rediscovery of an all-too-familiar text, one which manages to stay just this side of Gothic horror even when Richard drives a walking stick through the neatly brown-paper-parcelled head of Hastings.

Around his murderous charades there wanders the shadow of Queen Margaret (Cherry Morris), present even on the final battlefield to remind him of her curse; elsewhere only an infinitely suave Buckingham (Stephen Boxer) offers even momentarily a challenge to Mr Toad as King. But what one remembers here is manic glee and a kind of wary innocence, as though even Richard himself cannot quite believe how evil he is or what fun he is having at it.

~

Last week there appeared in *Variety*, the American show-business newspaper, a full-page cartoon which, without its caption, would only have been immediately understood by the most dedicated of Broadway historians. It showed the orphan urchin child from *Les Misérables*, familiar from tens of thousands of posters worldwide, only this time she was grinning from ear to ear and seated somewhat mysteriously in the Surrey with the Fringe on Top.

The explanation was of course that *Les Misérables* had just overtaken *Oklahoma!*'s record-breaking Broadway run of 2,212 performances. In London it has been playing for almost exactly seven years, and this seemed as good a moment as any to have another look at it alongside its sister-show (from the same composers and producer) *Miss Saigon*, which has been at Drury Lane exactly three years this month.

I had not seen either show over here since their original first nights, and the news from the Palace is nothing less than wonderful; after something like three thousand performances, *Les Misérables* is looking sharper and fresher and tighter than many West End musicals in their first weeks. The fact that it plays eight shows a week means that its production values are infinitely higher than any you will find in the repertoire systems of Covent Garden or the Coliseum, and *Les Misérables* now bids fair to become the musical not just of its decade but of the century itself.

There is a curious myth, perpetuated by the co-director John Caird on the backstage video of the making of *Les Misérables*, that its initial reviews at the Barbican were universally terrible. In fact they weren't; two or three of us recognised at once that there was something very special going on, largely because of the way in which the producer Cameron Mackintosh had for the first time harnessed the RSC/*Nicholas Nickleby* talents of Trevor Nunn and John Caird to a commercial musical machine.

~

But as *Les Misérables* continues to pour forth its history of nineteenth-century France through the trumpets and drums of a breathtaking Boublil & Schonberg score, it has to be said that their *Miss Saigon*, although four years younger, is already looking a little more dated. The Mackintosh machine continues to ensure that the production is kept in remarkable trim, but the loss of Jonathan Pryce as the Engineer is more wounding to the overall life and energy of the show than any of the cast changes in *Les Mis*. The helicopter still helicopts spectacularly, but the essential problem here is the plot structure. Asked once what separated a good musical from a great one, the veteran George Abbott (105 and still producing) said three things: 'the book, the book and the book', *Miss Saigon* has a score but no real book, unless you count *Madame Butterfly*. *Les Misérables* has Victor Hugo, and it's that simple.

Stop Messing About

An Inspector Calls (National)

Imagine you are the literary executor of the J B Priestley Estate. The National Theatre approaches you. We would, it says, like to revive *An Inspector Calls*. We have, however, a young new director, Stephen Daldry, soon to take over the Royal Court, and understandably keen to make his impression on the play and indeed the audience. He, it seems, doesn't much fancy the front parlour of the Birling home in Brumley, where the play is set in 1912. He quite fancies a beach, possibly Brighton or Blackpool, in about 1945. He also quite fancies adding to Priestley's original cast of seven no less than thirty adult and child actors, who will stand around a lot on the aforementioned beach as silent witnesses to the action. Furthermore, Mr Daldry doesn't just fancy having the house on the beach; he quite wants it to be up on a pier, and for a considerable time at the very back of the set, so the audience can only see or hear what is going on by desperately peering through its upstage windows. Oh yes, and then, by way of a denouement, he quite likes the idea of having the entire edifice crash in on itself, much like *The Fall of the House of Usher*. Apart from those little changes, he plans to do the play more or less as Mr Priestley wrote it. Except, of course, that the Inspector, instead of being the time-travelling visitor to the Birling household, will have to stand around on the beach himself, bellowing his enquiries as if through a megaphone across the sands.

Do you at that point tell the National to go find themselves an altogether different play, possibly an adaptation of Neville Shute's nuclear *On the Beach*, or do you meekly acquiesce in the hope that some of my colleagues, as indeed has happened, will hail 'a radical new insight' into a play that nobody except me seems to think merits un-tampered revival?

The Priestley Estate has chosen the latter route, apparently heedless of any belief that if the author had wanted to write a seashore epic instead of a moral domestic drama he would have done so, and as a result virtually all the impact of *An Inspector Calls* has been defused and diffused by a gimmicky travesty of the original, in which even the great last-act speech ('If men will not live to help each other, then they will be taught that lesson in fire and blood and anguish.') is destroyed by Daldry's sudden lighting of the auditorium, as if he thinks the play is over. Beware, especially when you are dead, directors who wish to 'make their mark'. Richard Pasco and Kenneth Cranham save what little they can from the wreckage.

Nunn Better

Porgy and Bess (Royal Opera House)

In the current Covent Garden programme for *Porgy and Bess* there is an open letter from Jeremy Isaacs in which he thanks Sir George Christie of Glyndebourne for 'the chance to bring Gershwin's masterpiece to Covent Garden'. He might perhaps have moved the apostrophe to allow for Ira's lyrics as well as George's music, but about this being a masterpiece there can now be little doubt, thanks largely to the staging of Trevor Nunn.

And we should not perhaps be too eager to blame the ROH for having taken just sixty years to recognise the masterpiece, given that even in New York the Met only got around to it for the first time in 1957, such has been the deep racial and showbiz uneasiness surrounding the opera since it first appeared in 1935. Yet other questions could well be asked of both the Glyndebourne and the ROH directors. Did it really require six whole years to move this show the fifty or so miles from Glyndebourne to Covent Garden, and would it not have been a great deal better to have offered it to a commercial house such as the Old Vic, where *Carmen Jones* has happily been playing eight capacity performances a week these last eighteen months? To repeat this definitive *Porgy* six years late, for only a dozen performances at £100 a ticket, seems to me to be asking for yet more public frustration at a time when the ROH can ill afford it. But for we few, we happy few, who were actually able to see it (Mr Isaacs will doubtless plead a concert staging in Birmingham next month, and then the chance of television, but these are scarcely the same) the news is nothing but ecstatic.

Nunn's great genius as a director, here as in *Les Misérables* and the RSC *Nicholas Nickleby* and even such flops as *The Baker's Wife*, has always lain in his ability to create a community in which you feel you might almost have lived, and the tragedy of this *Porgy*'s mass unavailability is that it denies most theatregoers something more than just the chance to hear the greatest score written in America this century. Its limited run also denies them the chance to see how Nunn has rethought it, from the way he lifts Porgy out of the usual dogcart and on to crutches, only to have him throw those away too in the final lurch toward Bess and her promised land, wherever that might be. This is the score that showed the way forward to Rodgers & Hammerstein and Sondheim in its great mix of spiritual soul and Broadway big band, and what Nunn has achieved is a reworking and a rethinking of the original, so instead of a faintly patronising white trip down South it becomes a soaring affirmation of the life of Catfish Row and its potential for survival against all odds. The performances here of Willard White and Cynthia Haymon in the title roles, Damon Evans as Sporting Life and Gregg Baker as Crown form the most powerful dramatic and musical quartet in town.

A Musical With Muscle

Kiss of the Spider Woman (Shaftesbury)

Which Witch? (Piccadilly)

Making it Better (Criterion)

Kiss of the Spider Woman is far and away the best thing to have happened to the West End in three long years since *Miss Saigon*. A musical which has the courage to think while it sings and dances, it represents composer John Kander and lyricist Fred Ebb at the very height of their *Cabaret* form and it's the score by which the health of the commercial theatre in London can now be judged. If it triumphs as it deserves, there is a future for dangerously on-the-edge big band shows; if it goes down, stand by for a lot more safe revivals of hits. When I first saw *Spider Woman* at a try-out in upstate New York a couple of years ago, it seemed to me fascinating but flawed; most of those flaws have now been sorted out, and the new Hal Prince staging brings back to the West End musical for the first time in thirty years the great and glorious Chita Rivera, dominating the stage from gallery-high platforms as the vintage movie star who is the stuff of Molina's dreams.

Molina, for those who have never read the Puig novel or seen the film or play, is the gay window-dresser thrown into a South American cell with Valentin, a political prisoner whom he comes to love and for whom he eventually dies. It is a bleak tale, and the Kander & Ebb score in no way betrays that for commercial gain. But the central problem of the show has always been how to co-ordinate the reality of life in the gaol with the fantasy of Molina's dreams of Dolores del Rio.

That problem has now been solved, thanks largely to Prince's versatile staging, the stunning back-projected slides of the designer Jerome Sirlin, and the three central performances of Rivera in the title role, Brent Carver as Molina and Anthony Crivello as Valentin. A musical about love and death, about South American nightmares and Hollywood dreams, about sex and treachery and sacrifice and self-interest, offers us not only one of the last great working stars from the golden era of Broadway but also a rich, dark score, closer perhaps to Kander & Ebb's little-known *Zorba* than to their more recent work. Shamefully abused by most New York critics when it first surfaced over there in try-out, *Kiss* now needs to be sent back to them from here as a reminder of what they missed the first time around. This is a challenging, difficult, dangerous show, but songs like 'Dear One' are going to be with us forever, as is the memory of a haunting, odd-couple prison partnership and a heartbreaking love story about the movies of the mind. *Kiss of the Spider Woman* is nowadays that considerable rarity, an adult musical in which the book (by Terrence McNally after Puig) counts for as much as the score or the sets.

~

The other big musical of the week is *Which Witch?*, about which the only really intriguing question is how it got as far as a first rehearsal, let alone a first night. Described as an 'operamusical', this is a mind-numbing, soul-destroying, achingly amateur, deeply embarrassing, wholly inadequate shambles loosely resembling a musical version of *The Crucible* staged by a Norwegian village institute on a really bad night in 1955. A disaster of epic proportions, it seems to have been devised on the principles of the Eurovision Song Contest in a language best described as Abba-speak, parallel to English (thanks to lyricist Kit Hesketh-Harvey) but full of dire audience warnings such as, 'There's no way to keep it alive.' We are in the far reaches of high Norwegian camp at glacier level, with a dozen leaping nuns chanting 'carnal lust' as though on a staff outing from *The Sound of Music* to a museum of witchcraft. The star, Benedicte Adrian, is during the show possessed of everything but talent, while her co-composer Ingrid Bjornov is to be found in the pit, surprisingly not hiding but conducting the orchestra. *Which Witch?* is an operamusical tobeavoidedatallcosts.

~

And finally, welcome news of the re-opening after three years of the handsomely refurbished Criterion on Piccadilly Circus with James Saunders' *Making it Better*, first seen at Hampstead in the spring. A clenched, bisexual love story in the tradition of Rattigan and Gray, it is elegantly directed by Michael

Rudman and strongly held together by Jane Asher as the BBC radio producer who loses a husband to a treacherous, bouncing Czech (Rufus Sewell). It augurs well for the new Criterion policy of giving a West End home to the best of the London fringe.

The Right Connections

Six Degrees of Separation (Royal Court)

The Rise and Fall of Little Voice (National)

Between any two people on this planet there are apparently in the chain of genetics only six others; hence *Six Degrees of Separation*, the title of a John Guare play which became the snob hit of Broadway three seasons ago and is now in its British premiere at the Royal Court.

Mr Guare's play is about many things, not least the true story of a young black confidence trickster who managed to pass himself off as the son of Sidney Poitier and thus infiltrate several of the glossiest apartments on Park Avenue, claiming that he had been mugged in Central Park and therefore needed a place to stay. The dramatist has subsequently had to fight off a series of legal claims from the trickster that the play has 'stolen' the copyright in his life story, which gives you some idea of the heat with which the embers of the bonfire of the vanities are still smouldering in uptown Manhattan.

But the play is, as it happens, about rather more than just the retelling of a recent high-society scam scandal. *Six Degrees of Separation* takes the temperature of affluent New Yorkers at the end of the Eighties. Well-meaning, liberal, gullible, eager not to appear racist, lonely and deeply insecure, they are principally taken in by the intruder because he promises them walk-on, or rather dance-on, roles in his father's upcoming movie of *Cats* – though why prominent art dealers would wish to be caught up in so improbable a project is never adequately explained.

But central to Guare's thesis here is the idea that everybody, not just the black intruder, is engaged on some kind of hoax: the art dealer selling dodgy masterpieces to his South African client, a white man who notes, 'We have to stay there to educate the black workers, and we'll know we've been successful when they kill us'; his wife who chats to us in the audience, taking us back through the story in the hope that we'll see it all through her inanely non-judgmental eyes; their children, filled with a kind of random hatred of parents endlessly trying to do the right, radical-chic thing in a rapidly disintegrating world.

Guare, as in his much earlier *The House of Blue Leaves*, is writing on the borderline where the American waking dream becomes a nightmarish fantasy: all of his characters are trying to reach out to one another, to make the right connections, that will link up the six degrees of separation, and yet all are digging themselves deeper into pits of isolation and misunderstanding.

His is a minimalist piece, across a no-interval ninety minutes, and it has much in common with the double-sided Kandinsky which hangs over the set in the beginning: you have to stare at the puzzle for a while before it even begins to fall into place. A quirky, impressionistic, off-centre play has at its centre, here as originally in New York, a radiant performance by Stockard Channing, around whom a local cast is now grouped at a respectful distance. She alone, a long-time partner of Guare, has found a way of rounding out his characters so that a woman written in shorthand and sometimes stereotype takes on a vibrant life which transcends the immediate fashionability of her surroundings.

Yet there is still something missing: it is as though Sondheim people, high-rise Manhattan agonised introverts, have suddenly been hurled into a play by Ben Jonson and told to survive as best they can in their new surroundings. Guare asks all the right questions about post-modern New York but doesn't let his characters hang around long enough to sort out any of the answers, 'How do we keep the experience?' asks Channing, and Royal Court audiences may also be wondering about just that. Phyllida Lloyd directs.

~

And then to the National, where Jim Cartwright's *The Rise and Fall of Little Voice* is a curious and somewhat overrated hothouse domestic drama built around the astonishing talent of the actress Jane Horrocks for vocal impressions. She plays the Little Voice of the title, a wan teenager who has lived in an upstairs room for so long with the records of Judy Garland and Edith Piaf that she can even repeat their pauses for breath and, presumably, the cracks in the old vinyl. Her termagant mother, played with manic over-the-top energy by Alison Steadman, conspires with a no-good showman lover to get Little Voice in front of a club audience, where predictably she breaks down, unable to get the voices from her records out of her head and on to a stage. Eventually, as mother's house burns to ashes and true love arrives in the unlikely shape of a British Telecom engineer, Little Voice finds her own voice and all ends happily.

Mr Cartwright has one or two good jokes ('If you are agoraphobical', screeches the appalling mother to her reclusive daughter, 'you can just get out of the house'); but the idea being noised abroad by some of my colleagues that we have here an English suburban *The Glass Menagerie* seems to me to be going it a bit. Sam Mendes directs.

Bang on Target

Assassins (Donmar Warehouse)

The week of an American election is probably as good a time as any in which to consider the death of Presidents, and at the admirably restored Donmar Warehouse in Covent Garden, Stephen Sondheim's *Assassins* does just that. Though not perhaps one of his major works, principally because at ninety no-interval minutes it can never quite decide whether it is a musical or a song cycle, this is nevertheless a characteristically powerful and resonant idea.

Whenever Sondheim writes a new show, said an old 1960s producer, Broadway gets rebuilt; on this occasion it didn't even get to see the show, which opened just off the Great White Way at the time of the Gulf War, was reckoned somewhat unpatriotic and has (as so often with Sondheim) had to await its true acclaim on this side of the Atlantic. Here he has always been reckoned a prophet with rather more honour than in his own country, where they still wish he was more like Jerry Herman and would give them a tune they could hum.

What you hear humming in *Assassins* are the bullets; from its opening fairground gallery number 'Come Shoot A President' through to the final, chilling conclusion in the Texas Book Depository, this is uncompromisingly a show about the thirteen people who have set out, some successfully, to kill American Presidents from Lincoln to Reagan. Why? Because the American Constitution guarantees, among its other eccentricities, a birthright to the pursuit of happiness. Those who are unhappy therefore believe they have a case against the chief executive, and some feel his death to be a suitable punishment for failure to deliver bliss on demand. In one of even his darkest scores, Sondheim and his book-writer John Weidman see assassination as another form of the star-mania that has always gripped America. If you can't be famous as a President, why not achieve an alternative kind of fame as the killer of one? If you have a headache, would like a better world, have to impress a girl, how better than to take on the ultimate star for a shoot-out at the High Noon corral? 'Every now and then a country goes a little wrong,' notes one of the killers, and there's always somebody out there nutty enough to try to put it right with an instant change of government.

Each of these dozen songs is musically and magically of its period, from Civil War marches for John Wilkes Booth through to dreamy Carpenter love songs for the girls who went after Ford. The best number belongs, typically, to the least-known of the assailants: Charles Guiteau, who ended the life of President Garfield because the latter had carelessly failed to make him Ambassador to France, goes out with a song and a dance, a buck and a wing on the steps of his scaffold which is in many literal ways the ultimate Broadway show-stopper. But here too is Booth as an archetypal actor-manager, furious that his killing of Lincoln has turned old Abe's reviews from mixed to raves. Here too is Hinckley, who wounded Reagan in the bizarre hope of marrying Jodie Foster on the rebound, and here too is Lee Harvey Oswald around whom all the others cluster for the Texas finale in 1963, hoping that somehow when he pulls the trigger the profession of assassin will be ennobled to that of saviour.

Time and again, as its score travels from Aaron Copland back to John Philip Sousa, *Assassins* hits all its targets on the shooting line where the American anything-possible dream becomes the usual nightmare of disillusion and decay. It will be argued, as usual, that Sondheim gives us here nobody to root for. The people to root for in *Assassins* are the ones who never fell for that American dream in the first place.

An Evening With Harold

No Man's Land (Almeida)

Our Song (Apollo)

No Man's Land 'will not change or grow old or move – it remains forever icy', says Harold Pinter to Paul Eddington in Pinter's own play, and the line – repeated as the curtain falls – will also serve as a review. For this is Pinter at his most Pinteresque, and the play is a distillation of much of his other work: an evening with Harold, in fact.

As the play opens, an aged, alcoholic man of letters much prone to sudden physical collapse is being visited by a distinctly crumpled poet whom he has encountered on Hampstead Heath, where the latter is wont to indulge in a little light voyeurism when not washing the glasses at a nearby pub. It later transpires, I need hardly tell you, that this is no mere chance encounter: the two men are known to each other, inextricably linked by an unseen wife whom one married and the other lived with, and their relationship is as ambiguous as that of the two sinister men-servants who share a household where the conversation is apt to wander from high drawing-room comedy ('Lord Lancer? One of the Bengal Lancers, is he?') to lengthy discussions of the impossibility of reaching Bolsover Street by car.

What we have here are four characters in search of several answers ('Tell me about your wife – did she google?'), none of which are forthcoming in the tone poem of a play which Pinter has constructed around their uncertainties. When first seen at the National seventeen years ago, the play offered a tremendous opportunity for Gielgud and Richardson to perfect the brokers-men double act they had started to form in David Storey's *Home*, and the result was a dazzling display of virtuoso acting techniques.

David Leveaux's new production at the Almeida is inevitably hamstrung by Pinter's own limitations in the Richardson role, though Paul Eddington (here as in the recent revival of *Forty Years On*) does manage to challenge the memory of Gielgud with an altogether different turn, at once seedier and shakier than Sir John's stunning impression of W H Auden on a bad day. Eddington's Spooner is by contrast an emaciated Mr Chips fallen on hard times, yet in the ritual and inevitable Pinter power game which ensues it is he rather than the thuggish Hurst who often seems more likely to survive the sharks in the harbour. Douglas Hodge and Gawn Grainger as the menservants circle them around Bob Crowley's infinitely elegant all-grey set in a fine display of creepy chic. Never mind the plot, just feel all that menace.

~

The great thing about Peter O'Toole is that he never delivers what you'd expect; give him a major classic like *Macbeth* or *Pygmalion* and he falls all over the place. Give him a really tricky, fragile concoction like Keith Waterhouse's *Jeffrey Bernard* or the current *Our Song* and he delivers performances of such heartbreaking brilliance as to take your breath away. This time he's the old Etonian adman-groper, falling in love with a nubile secretary only to have her drown him in their generation gap.

The story is told to us across the typewriter in a sustained monologue by O'Toole, interrupted by sketchy scenes in which a quite wonderful cast (Lucy Fleming as the neglected wife, Jack Watling as the long-suffering business partner, Donald Pickering as a predatory food guide editor) are left to flesh out the rest of the story in a kind of shorthand before we get back to the central confessional. Determined to deliver a love letter rather than a whingeogram across the empty champagne crates, O'Toole carefully explains to us that where his girl was having *an* affair, he was having *the* affair; like a father at a pop concert, he is left nervously trying not to show his age in a hotbed of rampant youth, and no one plays better the decay that seems to start at the ankles and work its way into the brain. The result is a lyrical account of a doomed affair between creatures from different planets: its only moment of real drama occurs offstage and about thirty seconds before the final curtain, but along the way both O'Toole and Tara Fitzgerald in a stunning stage debut dominate Ned Sherrin's agile, intelligent production with two searing star performances in a touching lament about tears after bedtime, with an ending which O'Toole alone turns from dime-novel to romantic tragedy.

A Fine, Dark Masterpiece

Carousel (National)

Trelawny of the Wells (Comedy)

Written just after *Oklahoma!* but before *South Pacific* and *The King and I, Carousel* is the Rodgers & Hammerstein score that nobody over here ever revives. It has not been seen live in London these last forty years, and perhaps not surprisingly. For *Carousel* is Molnár's *Liliom* transported to New England; a darkly savage tale of a suicidal fairground barker with a fatal grudge against the fishing village that has found him socially unacceptable. It has now been given a joyous, brilliant and breathtaking production by Nicholas Hytner and the late Kenneth MacMillan at the National which re-establishes it as one of the greatest musicals in the history of Broadway.

What MacMillan did in the closing weeks of his life was to take the original dances of Agnes de Mille, celebrate and then improve on them. What Hytner has done is quite simply to put the play back into the musical, so that instead of the sentimental vacuity of the movie we have a fine, dark masterpiece which demands comparison with both *West Side Story* and *Porgy and Bess*. True, it is not perfect: Hytner has unwisely cut the 'Highest Judge of All' number which crucially establishes the barker's sense of social injustice on earth as in heaven, and his central casting of Michael Hayden as Billy and Joanna Riding as Julie sometimes proves dangerously weak. But Patricia Routledge as the clambake-loving old battleaxe, Phil Daniels as the magnificently evil Jigger and Clive Rowe's splendidly black Mr Snow are all definitive, while even the infinitely fey Starmaker scenes, long thought unplayable as written, are given strength and coherence and their central importance to a fine balletic and operatic rediscovery of a lost classic of the American theatre.

Song after song here soars out at you from over the orchestra pit: a dozen of them, from 'If I Loved You' to 'You'll Never Walk Alone', every one carrying the plot forward and every one etched in the memory forever. Ten years ago it was the National which first established that *Guys and Dolls* had a place in the narrow repertoire of what is greatest in world theatre, and they have done it again with *Carousel*: hasten along.

~

The mystery of *Trelawny of the Wells* is why it is the Pinero and not the Julian Slade version: given that the National has already slated the play for next spring, and that the star at the Comedy is Sarah Brightman, it would surely have made more sense to do the musical rather than this shaky version of the play, which two directors (Toby Robertson and Frank Hauser) have brought back to only flickering life. Alongside *Wild Oats* this is one of the first of the great backstage pieces, telling of the decline and fall of the old actor-laddies, the rise of the realist playwrights and of social barriers between green-room and drawing-room finally broken down.

Sir Michael Hordern is in fine harrumphing form here as the diehard old Vice Chancellor suddenly given a heart by his memories of Edmund Kean, and one or two of the other players, notably Margaret Courtenay and Peter Baylis as the outdated old luvvies and Oliver Cotton as the radical young Robertson figure, seem to have worked out what the play is about, which is rather more than can be said for the rest of a large and starry cast led by Jason Connery and Helena Bonham Carter.

Sing Noël

Hay Fever (Albery)

Annie Get Your Gun (Prince of Wales)

Written at great speed in three days when he and the century were in their very early twenties, Noël Coward's *Hay Fever* is a country-house party comedy of appalling manners in which very little happens, but at a tremendous rate. The plot derives from a time when Noël, an impecunious young would-be Broadway playwright, spent several weekends in upstate New York at the home of Laurette Taylor, a formidable grande dame of the period, whose gatherings were mainly notable for impenetrable games of charades at which guests would be ritually humiliated by their hostess and her closest relatives.

Back in the comparative safety of the West End, Noël turned his memories of those weekends into his first great comic success, the one which was also to lead to his renaissance half a century later when Olivier invited him to direct it himself at the National Theatre (the first such invitation to a dramatist) with a cast who could have triumphed in the Albanian telephone directory, let alone one of the funniest plays of all time.

Alan Strachan's splendid new production at the Albery would seem to have two principal aims: to highlight the role-playing which is at the heart of a heartless comedy, and to remind us of the twist that Coward engineers. Here are four perfectly harmless, fundamentally nice people, invited to spend the weekend in Cookham by a family of such monstrous egotism and neurosis that even their mass exodus during breakfast on Sunday morning goes totally unremarked by their hosts, a curtain device that Noël was to borrow from himself five years later for *Private Lives*. Yet by the end of the evening, indeed by halfway through it, our sympathy is not with the guests at all, but with their appalling hosts, so devoted is the author to his family of theatricals and so bored by the sheer normality of the visitors.

Strachan has lined up his players with considerable brilliance: Maria Aitken leads for the home team, swooping around the stage of her home like a demented bat carrying out air-raids on harmless bunches of flowers, while Sara Crowe leads for the visitors, a flapper of such totally imploded social embarrassment that even removing her coat becomes an act of drawing-room rape. Around them are gathered such other Coward experts as John Standing, Christopher Godwin and Carmen du Sautoy, all of whom manage in various and stylish comic ways to explore the deep cruelty of the play which represents Coward at his closest to Ayckbourn and somewhere halfway from Pirandello to the Edward Albee of 'Get the Guests' in *Who's Afraid of Virginia Woolf?*

For all its apparent domestic-comedy safety, *Hay Fever* was for its time a highly subversive attack on middle-class morality, one which suggested to 1920s audiences that merely to be nice and honest and decent folk was not nearly enough. The fact that Noël's sympathies are forever with the players rather than the gentlefolk leads ours too in that direction, and our laughter at their final, frightened departure is therefore not nearly as guilty as it ought to be.

~

Into the Prince of Wales from a road tour for a prolonged Christmas season comes Irving Berlin's *Annie Get Your Gun*, containing seventeen (count them) of the greatest songs ever written for Broadway and one of the worst books ever seen even there. Berlin only took on the score following the sudden death of Jerome Kern, and was writing on commission for Ethel Merman, but the show became only the second in Broadway history to run more than a thousand performances, made a star of Dolores Gray in London and was still being played on the road by Miss Merman twenty years later.

But now what have we got? Songs that could be replaced at any other point in the score, or in any other score, without apparent difference. The book by Herbert and Dorothy Fields was really not even a pamphlet, loosely concerned with Annie Oakley and her attempts to get a man by missing the bull's-eye, and the show itself was precisely what Bernstein and Sondheim were reacting against when they began to suggest, a few years later, that a musical might be made to think while it sings and dances.

Kim Criswell and John Diedrich air their lungs pleasantly here, and so long as everyone keeps singing all is fine; but when the present revival closes, something really does have to be done about that book if the songs are to stay in the repertoire where they so richly deserve a place. There may be no business like show business, but it still needs a little drama.

Winning Oscar

An Ideal Husband (Globe)

Lost in Yonkers (Strand)

Three Birds Alighting on a Field (Royal Court)

The best and worst year of Oscar Wilde's life, 1895, opened on 3 January when Lewis Waller premiered the third of his four major plays at the Haymarket. *An Ideal Husband* was from the start an unqualified triumph; indeed, Wilde uncharacteristically declined to go on taking its curtain calls because he said it would make him feel like a German band. The Prince of Wales was in the royal box and Bernard Shaw, newly appointed drama critic of the *Saturday Review*, in the stalls to hail 'our only truly thorough playwright. Wilde plays with wit, with philosophy, with drama, with actors and with audience'. The future Edward VII agreed, telling Wilde 'not to cut a single word', though *Punch* was a little less enthusiastic ('an interesting play up to the end of Act Three') and Henry James found it 'crude, clumsy, feeble and vulgar.'

But Oscar's real problems were by now close at hand: the actor playing the valet had begun to gather evidence from the rent-boys with whom Wilde and Alfred Douglas were spending much of their time, and there had already been a couple of unsuccessful attempts at blackmail.

So a drawing-room drama dealing with blackmail, imminent exposure and the consequent likelihood of total professional ruin, all of which was to happen to Oscar within months, was never likely to be far from autobiographical, though Peter Hall's sumptuous new revival at the Globe follows usual form by having the Wildean character seen as Lord Goring, who alone of the principals is free of all guilt. But the miracle of the play is its constant topicality, so that now the undertones are of Mellor and Iraqgate rather than anything more historic. Indeed Goring's plaintive cry 'Nobody is incapable of doing a foolish thing; nobody is incapable of doing a wrong thing,' might now usefully be inscribed over the Palaces of Westminster and Buckingham as a warning for all who enter there.

Hall intelligently and sensitively pitches his production roughly halfway from Lyceum melodrama to Haymarket high comedy, heavy on set and costumes and starry support (Michael Denison apparently on loan from the Garrick, Dulcie Gray cascading from the stairs); but it retains an elegantly sinister quality, never allowing us to forget the play's constant relevance to Oscar's own downfall and to the media power politics of the intervening century. David Yelland is a little nebulous as Chiltern, but Martin Shaw is a strongly Wildean Goring, and as the two female furies Anna Carteret and Hannah Gordon are superbly matched.

~

At the Strand Neil Simon's *Lost in Yonkers* has arrived bearing a Pulitzer Prize from Broadway but lacking in my view the tremendous autobiographical strengths of his childhood trilogy, the one that started with *Brighton Beach Memoirs*. Here too we have the suburban New York family facing up to the second world war with a mix of immigrant despair and New World optimism: Rosemary Harris is the battle-axe grandmother; Maureen Lipman, Ron Berglas and Rolf

Saxon the children she has killed with unkindness, Benny Grant and Ross McCall the grandchildren determined to get out from under. All give strong performances, with Lipman at her most touching as the retarded spinster searching for love in cinemas and Berglas very funny as the Mafia hitman still terrified of Mom. But something is lacking here, and it is, I think, Simon's usual ability to find himself in the family snapshot and then act as its guide.

~

Back to the Royal Court, a year or so after its premiere, comes Timberlake Wertenbaker's *Three Birds Alighting on a Field*, the play that does for the eighties art market what *Serious Money* did for the City. The play's thesis ('art is sexy; art is money; art is money-sexy-social-climbing-fantastic') is simple enough: that in the fluctuating valuations put on a painting – even a blank, white canvas – can be seen a metaphor for the valuations we put on society and ourselves within it.

Max Stafford-Clark's fluid, agile, spare staging assembles the characters as figures in a landscape of modern Britain, centred on Harriet Walter's still stunning star turn, and the result (in a tightened and trimmed script, mercifully now without its Greek interlude) is a morality play about the way we lived out the last decade. Hopefully it may also now be an epitaph for the eighties.

Theatre 1992

Against all the economic odds, 1992 was a remarkably strong year except perhaps for major new British drama. Elsewhere, consider: on the musical front we got both Sondheim's *Assassins* and Kander & Ebb's *Kiss of the Spider Woman* from over the Atlantic, both breathtaking examples of how the barriers of music theatre are still being pushed forward to accommodate themes (in these cases the killing of American presidents and a homosexual love affair in a South American jail) hitherto thought inimical to an orchestra in a pit.

Trevor Nunn's production of *Porgy and Bess* after only six years managed to make the short journey from Glyndebourne to the Royal Opera House. At the end of the year came Nick Hytner's wondrous rediscovery of *Carousel* as a dark, suicidal but musically joyous drama of New England revenge and rebirth.

Performances of the year? Again we were spoiled for choice: There was the McKellen/Sher double in *Uncle Vanya*, Simon Russell Beale's toadlike Richard III and Alan Howard's superbly detached Professor Higgins in the National's *Pygmalion.* Not to mention Paul Scofield's ancient-mariner in the Haymarket's *Heartbreak House* with his ever-topical speech about England, our England: 'The captain is in his bunk drinking bottled ditch water: the crew is gambling in the forecastle. She will strike and sink and split. Do you think the laws of God, Sir, will be suspended in favour of this country simply because you were born in it?'

Then again we had Peter O'Toole as always giving one of his major performances in minor material, heartbreakingly heartbroken in Keith Waterhouse's *Our Song*; Jane Horrocks finding her own voice in *The Rise and*

Fall of Little Voice; the Eddington/Pinter double in the latter's *No Man's Land*; Michael Pennington and Judi Dench going blazingly over the top in Shaffer's histrionic *The Gift of the Gorgon*; Stockard Channing confirming her New York reputation in the drama-documentary *Six Degrees of Separation*; Sheila Hancock dismembering an entire family in the haunting, shamefully ignored *Judgement in Stone*.

Major disappointments of the year included John Osborne's return to us and *Look Back in Anger* with the impossibly verbose and under-energised *Déjà Vu*, and *Moby Dick*, which suffered the fatal flaw of having the cast enjoy it more than the audience. Also disappointing were the appalling pretentiousness of Sharman Macdonald's *Shades* and Dusty Hughes' *A Slip of the Tongue*, in which John Malkovich gave one of the worst performances of the year and his career.

In a thin time for new plays about the way we live now, Tony Kushner's *Angels in America Part One*, Timberlake Wertenbaker's superbly scabrous *Three Birds Alighting on a Field*, and the premiere of Doug Lucie's wonderful attack on American evangelism, *Grace*, gave us some hope of contemporary chronicles.

In a rich time for revivals Alan Strachan's *Hay Fever* and his joyous unearthing of the Kaufman/Lardner *June Moon* warmed some chilly nights. The all-star *Trelawny of the Wells* at the Comedy was a depressing clash of acting styles, and the Robert Lindsay *Cyrano de Bergerac* at the Haymarket was woefully undercast in important supporting roles. As against these however, the Peter Hall *An Ideal Husband* at the Globe with Hannah Gordon was a vintage classical delight. Back at the Barbican, the American playwright Richard Nelson had a *Columbus* anniversary drama that was vastly better than any of this year's three movies on the same subject.

In terms of real estate, both the Donmar Warehouse in Covent Garden and the Criterion on Piccadilly Circus came back after two-year refits, the former with an apparent policy of importing hits from elsewhere (the Sondheim *Assassins* and the RSC *Richard III*) and the latter having already reneged on a 'best of the Fringe' policy with a December staging of Stephen King's movie *Misery*.

Talking of the Fringe, all praise to the Orange Tree in Richmond for bringing back John Whiting's *A Penny for a Song* and Rodney Ackland's *The Dark River*, and to the King's Head in Islington for that most touching of AIDS cabarets, *Elegies for Angels, Punks and Raging Queens*.

The issue of the year, though it has yet to achieve much debate, may well turn out to be that of repertoire. Is it or is it not the duty of the National and the RSC to give us a different show on each of their stages each night?

There is nothing in their charters to indicate that, but it has been custom and practice for more than twenty years. This winter however, the sheer size of the *Carousel* staging at the National means an unbroken eight-shows-a-week schedule at the Lyttelton, while Kenneth Branagh's understandable reluctance to sign the usually mandatory two-year RSC contract means that his *Hamlet* performances at Stratford will have to be crowded into a short unbroken season on the main stage there. Is this simply a sensible acknowledgement of new economic and contractual realities for the 1990s, or does it represent a major breaking of at least one plank in the platforms which distinguish the RSC and the National from the commercial theatre? I am not sure that I have the answer to this; what I do know is that I would like to have the question more openly debated.

Marlene Dietrich (1901-92)

Now that I come to think of it, I knew her for almost forty years. Not intimately, certainly not as intimately as some of the relatives and other biographers who are even now racing into the bookshops with their amazing bisexual revelations, and indeed not over the last ten years when she was holed up as an ageing recluse in that Parisian apartment, bitching through the door to Maximilian Schell as he desperately tried to capture her on film one last time.

But yes, I did know Marlene. When I was seven, in 1949, my parents and sister and I were living with my grandmother Gladys Cooper in Hollywood, and Dietrich sometimes used to come in to do the washing up. It wasn't that she had fallen on hard times, or anything like that; she just enjoyed washing up, had a Teutonic fixation about clean dishes, the kind of fixation they now have psychiatrists look at.

In those days in California, it was just regarded as marginally odd, but my grandmother saw no reason to object and was jolly glad of the help, especially as she was in the habit of giving large Sunday tea parties for the rest of that Hollywood Raj of expatriate British character actors from David Niven to Ronald Colman. Garbo also had a thing about helping around the Hollywood houses: nowadays you could probably get some American film school to sponsor a thesis on 1930s European film stars and their housekeeping obsessions.

Anyway, that was 1949. The next time I met Dietrich was about twenty years later. I was writing a biography of Noël Coward and had gone to spend a weekend with him in Switzerland in order to ransack his diaries and scrapbooks. On the Sunday, she arrived for lunch; I seem to recall acres of white fur in the days before that became politically unacceptable, not that she would have noticed, and in her hand a long-playing record which Noël asked me to put on his turntable. The first band consisted entirely of applause. So did the second. And the third. No Lili Marlene, no Lola, no orchestra, no Marlene at all, just the applause. Eventually all became clear. 'The first track,' she said, with a steely glare that denied all irreverent giggling, 'was my applause in Sweden. The next was my applause in Finland. Now we hear my applause in Australia.'

She was big on applause: indeed one of the ironies of the tactful obituaries has been the way they dwelt almost exclusively on a movie career that was effectively almost over by 1930, fully forty years before she stopped working. Sure, she was Lola in *The Blue Angel*: when I decided to write a book about her in the early 1970s, and asked what she had done before being cast by her 'Svengali Jo' von Sternberg in that one film, she replied, 'Nothing,' thereby denying the existence of twenty other movies made in the early 'twenties, at least one of them co-starring the young Garbo.

But within ten years of *The Blue Angel* Hollywood had already begun to turn its back on them both: the fashion for bisexual expatriate sex-smoulderers who looked good in trousers had waned as rapidly as it started, and Dietrich's last great film was the 1939 western *Destry Rides Again*. Within a year of that, she was 140th on the box-office listing of Hollywood stars, and in deep professional trouble.

What saved her was the war: on troop concerts all over the world, Marlene discovered the live audience, and it was thereafter in cabaret that she re-invented herself, no longer the Marlene of the pre-war years but a tougher, lonelier, icier figure who seemed to be carrying on a perpetual and exclusive love affair with the spotlights above her many stages. It was in the theatre that she always worked best: an old German lady with a slight limp, defying the audience not to believe that she was really as ageless as Peter Pan.

Dietrich was her own best invention and contribution to the century, and she was the last of those great solo stars: Piaf, Lenya, Garland, Coward, all traded in her currency, turning apparently bland lyrics into erotic invitations, but Dietrich always did it best: 'They call me naughty Lola, the wisest girl on earth. At home my pianola is played for all its worth.'

'That damn Kraut,' said Ernest Hemingway, one of her more distinguished lovers, with his usual elegant turn of phrase, 'is the best that ever came into the ring.' It took one great fighter to recognise another. Dietrich gave no hostages, took no prisoners, forgave nothing and forgot nothing.

When I published my biography, without her permission, she threatened to reach for the lawyers. An earlier and unluckier author had already been taken to court by her and had his book ceremonially burnt to ashes at the Gare du Nord, Dietrich having characteristically uncovered a little-known Parisian law about the retribution for libel.

I got off more lightly: two years after publication, she wrote to me saying that although she hadn't much cared for some of what I said about her, subsequent biographies had annoyed her even more, so that retrospectively she had become quite fond of mine, and could she please have fifty free copies to give her friends for Christmas? Of course I sent her them, thereby using up almost all the profits I had made on a slender volume. But it was worth it.

For a year or two after that, there would be Christmas cards, even a letter when she approved of something I'd written. And then, in the early 'eighties (hers and the century's), silence. I tried phoning once or twice, usually to hear her in a wonderfully phoney French accent pretending to be her own maid, and regretting that Madame could not come to the phone. I took the hint, as did dozens of her other friends. The real maid had a rougher time, and a notable revenge. Summarily sacked by Marlene for no good reason, she returned to the hall of the apartment block on the Avenue Montaigne, where Dietrich lived, on the following night, when Marlene had arranged one of her last dinner parties. As each guest arrived, the maid sat in the hallway regretting that Madame had developed gastric flu and cancelled the party. Marlene was left alone upstairs, and that was more or less how she remained for the rest of her life.

1993

Beyond our Ken

Hamlet (Barbican)

Cyrano de Bergerac (Haymarket)

Misery (Comedy)

Gift of the Gorgon (Barbican)

Adrian Noble's new *Hamlet* (on the main Barbican stage for the RSC) is the first I have ever seen to star the Gravedigger: not only because in that role Richard Moore gives far and away the most mesmerising performance of a nearly five-hour evening, but also because it is his territory that is centre-stage throughout. Indeed the Ghost of Hamlet's father emerges from it at the outset, and from then on we are deeply into a production which is obsessed by all the forms and ceremonies and after-effects of death.

In the title role, Kenneth Branagh is a natural Horatio or Laertes, maybe even a Fortinbras: but his third attempt at the leading part in the last three years only confirms that this infinitely jolly, boy-scout hero is ill-suited to the melancholy, introspective Dane. When any action is called for, as in the organisation of the play that will catch the conscience of the King, Branagh is splendidly in charge; but the whole essence of *Hamlet* is surely that he is wracked by indecision and doubt and procrastination, all of which are evidently another country and well beyond our Ken.

Nonetheless, this production has several virtues: the extended length makes it far less of a one-man show, with Hamlet offstage for nearly an hour around the late interval and other characters therefore brought more sharply into focus. John Shrapnel as the Machiavellian King, Jane Lapotaire as his house-party hostess Gertrude and David Bradley as a civil servant Polonius all seem at home in Bob Crowley's late-Victorian setting, one which suggests an odd mix of Chekhov and J M Barrie. Ophelia (Joanne Pearce) has a Peter Pan bedroom; trains pull into Elsinore station, and a Christmas tree is set up to cheer the surrounding gloom. All in all a melodramatic, sometimes underpowered but generally sturdy revival, never better than in the theatre of Act Three or the wasteland of Act Five.

~

In contrast, *Cyrano de Bergerac* at the Haymarket has a strong central performance surrounded by shadows: Robert Lindsay makes a fine, buccaneering Gascon, but Stella Gonet and Gary Cady are distinctly lacking in lustre as the lovers and only Julian Glover as an unusually fiery de Guiche manages to suggest that there is much of a supporting cast for Elijah Moshinsky's uncharacteristically pedestrian production, one which only achieves any kind of poetry in the last-act orchard, where suddenly John Wells's new translation comes into its own for a scene of haunting melancholy, exquisitely played by Glover and then by Lindsay himself.

~

Misery at the Comedy is a perfectly adequate but deeply pointless staging of the Stephen King bestseller which became an Oscar-winning movie. In case you missed both, a famous thriller-writer crashes his car into a tree, is rescued and then kidnapped by a barking-mad female fan who chops off his foot when he threatens to kill off her favourite of his characters, and ultimately survives to sell the tale. Sharon Gless, from *Cagney and Lacey*, and Bill Patterson plod through the plot as if hoping it might make for a television series.

~

And the best is last: at the Barbican Pit, Peter Shaffer's *The Gift of the Gorgon* is a flawed but hugely courageous attempt to relate the themes of Greek tragedy to the latterday British theatre. Michael Pennington plays a rogue dramatist in the tradition of the Johns Arden, McGrath and Whiting, who decides to challenge the current stage orthodoxy with plays of relentless social and political violence. Judi Dench is the wife who, unable at the last to restrain him, becomes the unwitting cause of his death. Unwieldy, overwritten, operatic and totally unmissable, *The Gift of the Gorgon* tackles the usual Shaffer conflict between the manic artist and his sober alter ego, the battle that started between Atahuallpa and Pizarro in *The Royal Hunt of the Sun*, ran through the boy and the psychiatrist in *Equus* to Mozart and Salieri in *Amadeus* before finishing up as high comedy in *Lettice and Lovage*. Now we are back to the bleakest of tragedies, but Peter Hall's stunning studio-stage production and the two central performances here come as wonderful reminders of Shaffer's magnificent staginess in a generation of dramatists who have elsewhere fought shy of that particular tradition.

All's Wells

Trelawny of the Wells (National)

The Invisible Man (Vaudeville)

Like its near-contemporary *Peter Pan*, *Trelawny of the Wells* is one of those scripts that everyone hates except the public, and the actors who actually get to play it. Several of those have been lucky in the last few months: after a thirty-year absence from London, Pinero's epitaph for the old actor-laddies has turned up twice, first just before Christmas in a patchy all-star West End revival sadly lacking much direction, and now in a vastly better John Caird production for the open Olivier stage of the National.

The mystery, though, is why he didn't go for the musical: Caird at his best (*Les Misérables*) and at his worst (*Children of Eden*) is a director who, like his old partner Trevor Nunn, knows a very great deal about how to give classical dignity to song-and-dance shows, and rather than just repeat the Pinero it would surely have made much more sense to dig out a brilliant Julian Slade score from the early 1960s, far better than the *Salad Days* on which his reputation still curiously rests, and give us that instead, now that the National has at last begun to realise the true value of the musical theatre, or at any rate the American musical theatre.

What we have, however, is the play, and here, as with the recent *Pygmalion* on this same stage, the National production seems to be straining towards something bigger and better, like a feature film or the full Broadway: indeed the single most breath-taking moment is a scenic one, when the theatrical boarding-house to which Rose Trelawny has returned after her unhappy sojourn in Cavendish Square is suddenly opened out to reveal the bare stage of a huge Victorian playhouse complete with wings and royal boxes.

But the problem with the play is still the problem with Pinero; as Tynan was later to say of Rattigan, he was geographically possessed by the old guard while temperamentally inclined towards the rebels, and as a result Trelawny as character and drama is in severe danger of a broken neck from trying to face in both directions at once.

Written in the 1890s but set back thirty years, the play mourns the passing of the old barnstormers (superlatively played here by Betty Marsden and Michael Bryant: 'I am required to play an old, ham actor.' – 'Oh, but dearest, will you be able to come close to it?') while celebrating the arrival of Tom Robertson (thinly disguised here as Tom Wrench) and his 'cup and saucer realism'. Yet by the time the play was first seen, that too was being thrown out of the green-room by the arrival of Bernard Shaw and even Ibsen, so Pinero is left with a kind of Garrick Club nostalgia trip onto which he has had to patch a conventional love story in the hope of binding it all together without having his audience reel out under an attack of greasepaint fumes.

Everything therefore depends on the playing, and here Caird is superbly served: Helen McCrory, in the title role, perfectly captures Rose's crossover from lovelorn *ingénue* to wounded woman, while Steven Pacey, Kevin Williams and Adam Kotz brilliantly distinguish between the various classic theatrical types who surround her in the boarding-house and backstage.

But the performance of the evening, indeed I suspect already one of the award-winning performances of the year, is that of Robin Bailey as Vice Chancellor Sir William Gower. From his first appearance from beneath a handkerchief in the awful stillness of Cavendish Square, through his horror at the social ineptitude of the players ('Have we no chairs? Do we lack chairs?'), to his heartbreaking conversion at Rose's hands to his own theatrical memories ('Kean? Ah, Kean: he was a splendid gypsy'), Bailey and Caird have wonderfully recognised that this is essentially a play about Gower and his reawakening to the magic of theatre as much as it is ever about Rose's marital problems or Tom's desire to be a playwright. *Trelawny of the Wells* is that curious contradiction, a great play without being a very good one; but for the second time in thirty years the National has shown us precisely how it should be done.

~

At the Vaudeville from Stratford East, *The Invisible Man* is Ken Hill's joyous box of conjuring tricks: the old H G Wells sci-fi thriller turned a century later into a series of stagey conjuring tricks, through which wanders Brian Murphy as an amiable master of eccentric ceremonies: to celebrate the fortieth birthday of Joan Littlewood's Stratford East, nothing could be better or more music-hall familiar.

City Lights

City of Angels (Prince of Wales)

Macbeth (National)

At the Prince of Wales, *City of Angels* is an unusual kind of adult, urban delight: a huge, hit musical put together by what must have seemed in rehearsal an unlikely trio: the writer Larry Gelbart, Broadway's natural successor in caustic wit to the late George S. Kaufman but a man whose last musical triumph had been one of Stephen Sondheim's first, *A Funny Thing Happened on the Way to the Forum*; the director Michael Blakemore who, despite a hugely distinguished career at the National and elsewhere, had never staged a musical in his life; and the composer Cy Coleman who, alone of the trio, had a long run of Broadway musical hits from *Barnum* all the way back to *Sweet Charity*.

Moreover, what they were planning had little to do with the usual expectations of a Broadway musical: no chorus lines, no show-stopping finale, no 'eleven o'clock number' to send them humming out into the night. Instead, a vastly complex double plot centred on Stine (Martin Smith) who writes Chandleresque thrillers in the California of the late 1940s, and Stone (Roger Allam) who is their fictional hero. Stine occupies the left-hand, full-colour side of the stage, either at his typewriter or in constant professional combat with his studio boss about the rewrites. Stone occupies the right-hand, black-and-white side of the stage, acting out the gumshoe thriller that is being written and played before our very eyes.

With me so far? Now, at times the two anti-heroes meet, either for a duet ('You're Nothing Without Me') or to share overlapping characters: Stine's wife (Fiona Hendley) also becomes Stone's sultry nightclub nemesis in Stine's fiction and Stone's bed. And that's even before it gets complicated; where most musicals expect you to check your wits in at the cloakroom with your coat, this one expects you to sharpen them before you sit down.

In that sense, it's the most intelligent and grown-up Broadway show in many a long season, since *Kiss of the Spiderwoman* is only opening there this month; but it is also a joyous celebration of the old Hollywood, where all the heroes looked like Bogart as Sam Spade, all the women were as sultry as Lauren Bacall teaching him to whistle, and all the villains were as megalomaniac as the movie mogul here who (wonderfully taken over the top by Henry Goodman) announces that 'flashbacks are a thing of the past' and that 'nothing was ever hurt by being improved'.

City of Angels is in every respect a rarity: it stars not a singer, nor a dancer, but a director (Blakemore) and a librettist (Gelbart) who have brought very different talents into the studio setting. Blakemore is a genius of stage-management (witness his *Noises Off*) and Gelbart a living history of Los Angeles since the war. What they have created is a company show for at least half a dozen principals, all of whom are primarily actors rather than hoofers, which simultaneously parodies and celebrates all the old Hollywood crime-caper movie traditions, reminding us at one and the same time both of how we were suckered by them all, and of how much we now miss and need them on the wide screen.

The lyricist David Zippel is no less adept at the genre: a line like 'what they write for the screen isn't right for the screen' is brave when designed for the ear alone, and a song about the old nepotistic studio system which manages to rhyme 'nephews' with 'refuse' is one that would not have shamed Sondheim. This is also an immensely classy show, courageous enough to risk losing its audience in the labyrinth of the first-act plot, only to retrieve them in the second half in good time for a stunning studio finale. *City of Angels* is the best box of tricks in town, and it sets up a standard of 1940s Hollywood musicals which *Sunset Boulevard* will have to match.

~

At the National, the Alan Howard *Macbeth* is just that: a showcase for his haunting, haunted talent which doesn't have a lot else going for it, except a spectacular ring of flames on about Gas-mark-6 which is inclined to leap into the air whenever something wicked this way comes. As a stage effect it sure beats pricking of the thumbs, and as he gets older, Howard is getting more and more like his movie-star uncle Leslie, able to find a kind of distant poetry in everything he says and does.

The rest of the cast is a bit thin, with Anastasia Hille looking as if she has just come to Lady Macbeth from a tour of *The Reluctant Debutante*, and Malcolm played, for some curious reason, as a minor aristocrat out of P G Wodehouse. But Robin Bailey makes a superbly querulous Duncan, arriving at the Macbeths in (for some other unfathomable reason) pitch darkness to announce, in tones that would not disgrace Lady Bracknell, that the castle seems to have a pleasant seat, thereby hoping perhaps someone would just show him where it was. Elsewhere, the director Richard Eyre seems to have not a lot of idea as to what the play might be about, except 140 minutes without an interval.

The Importance of Being Maggie

The Importance of Being Earnest (Aldwych)

In a time of considerable commercial peril around the West End, managements are playing safe: a couple of major Wilde revivals, a couple of equally major Rattigans, a couple of Agatha Christies, and if you look a little harder you'll find Graham Greene and George Gershwin and *Cyrano de Bergerac*. Put a time-traveller down in Shaftesbury Avenue tomorrow and he'd be wise to guess the date at sometime in 1954.

The management at the Aldwych are playing it safer still: having landed the catch of the season, Maggie Smith as Lady Bracknell, they've surrounded her with her last *Lettice and Lovage* cast (Margaret Tyzack and Richard Pearson), plus the National's hottest director (Nicholas Hytner), plus a chic young movie star from *Dracula* and *The Player* (Richard E Grant), and the best thing to have emerged from Jonathan Miller's Old Vic (Alex Jennings). The result ought to be an unqualified triumph instead of a mixed blessing, but it's not.

True, Dame Maggie is stupendous: her Bracknell is the only one to challenge Edith Evans this century or at any rate in my lifetime, and it does so by coming from an altogether different corner of the text. The Smith Bracknell is no dominant dowager, cascading from a great social height, but instead an infinitely more neurotic parvenue, deeply uncertain of her own social security and therefore all the more determined not to get caught up with people found in handbags at Victoria Station, no matter the line.

But around this stunning and stupendous comic turn, on stage for barely a quarter of the play, Hytner has oddly and uncharacteristically failed to build a coherent production. True, he has not been much helped by Bob Crowley's wonderfully off-centre set, which suggests not so much Oscar Wilde as Lewis Carroll: with everything at odd angles, one half-expects the Mad Hatter to join Algernon's tea party.

As for Algernon and John Worthing, Richard Grant and Alex Jennings start the evening as a couple of lip-kissing gay young things, an intriguing intellectual idea given the trials of Oscar Wilde's private life at the time he was writing this, but one incapable of being sustained once the girls appear. All through the evening there is the faint offstage sound of theories about the play crashing unfinished into the scenery: only the Dame and her despised Prism (Margaret Tyzack) seem to know exactly what they are doing. The two girls, Susannah Harker and Claire Skinner, are hopelessly out of period, and even the great and good Richard Pearson seems not quite yet to have caught the measure of Chasuble. All in all, a tentative evening.

Juno Forever

Juno and the Paycock (Albery)

The surprising thing about *Juno and the Paycock*, now in a savage and masterly production at the Albery by Joe Dowling and his Dublin Gate company, is how little it turns out to be about its apparent theme. Set in 1922, in the two-room tenement home of Juno Boyle and her 'Captain Jack', the strutting Dublin pub peacock of the title, it was described by O'Casey himself as 'a play about the calamitous Civil War in Ireland, when brother went to war with brother over a few insignificant words in a treaty with England.'

In its final half-hour, this is indeed a play about the original Irish Troubles – but only then. For two preceding acts we have been treated to something altogether else: a comedy of Irish manners centred around the Paycock himself, marvellously played here by Niall Buggy. In his refusal to go out and find work (as if there might be any), in his sudden twinges of mythical leg-pains, in his phoney blustering and makeshift, movable war memoirs, and above all in the love-hate relationship with Joxer, is a character of Falstaffian magnificence.

But Dowling's masterstroke here has been to redefine the double-act with Joxer, who in Mark Lambert's performance is no longer the jovial sidekick of the old Abbey stagings but instead a Beckettian tramp, filled with such loathing of the Captain that he actually spits on the Paycock's inert body as the curtain falls.

It was in the nature of O'Casey's brilliance to realise that neither the Abbey in 1924 nor indeed audiences elsewhere would accept a play of unremitting gloom about the Troubles. Better then to give them a black comedy – '*Macbeth* as viewed from the porter's lodge' – and gradually turn it back on its viewers, so that the laughs would freeze on their lips. And so, seventy years on, they still do.

It is at the end of the second act that it all starts to change: a sudden shadow of a gunman in the doorway, and Juno's already twitching, paralysed son is led away to certain death. Only now do we understand why he has spent the first half of the play in a state of catatonic shock: not just to be the butt of his father's scorn, but because he has betrayed a rebel and is to die.

And that is just the beginning of the end: the legacy which Juno and her Paycock have been counting on to pay for the new furniture proves to be a mirage, their daughter's boyfriend leaves her pregnant and therefore unmarriageable even to the one man who truly loves her, and when the Paycock finally returns from his pub it is to a total ignorance of the fact that his son has been murdered and his wife and daughter have left him in search of a real home for the new baby: 'two mothers are better than one father.'

The Paycock's domestic comedy has become a tragedy of death and destruction, and still he doesn't know it: but this is not your ritual Abbey ending, with the Captain and his Joxer locked together in drunken oblivion. This time the sewer-rat friend is first out the door, and the message of Joe Dowling's production is that *Juno* is forever: the desperation of poverty and civil war that O'Casey captured in Dublin is now that of Bosnia, and Juno's great curtain-speech of hope and regret seems to belong to some altogether other play and century. But that is a small price to pay for the new life that Dowling and his company have breathed into a museum masterpiece. *Juno* has come back to us as a new play for all our times.

Daddy Dearest

Shakespeare For My Father (Helen Hayes, New York)

At the rump end of an undistinguished Broadway season, of which one of the rare highlights has been the return of Julie Andrews in a superb Sondheim anthology concert, alas unscheduled for this side of the Atlantic, another London-born actress long resident in America is currently taking New York by storm. At the Helen Hayes Theater, *Shakespeare For My Father* is a remarkable solo show which mixes classical theatre and personal therapy in a manner only available to an Old Vic actress who has spent the last twenty years in California.

The actress in question is Lynn Redgrave, the father of the title is Sir Michael, and the show starts from her one terrible and terrifying discovery, just at the time of his death, that in a detailed daily account of his life and times he had never even troubled to note the day of her birth, nor in later life had he been much aware of her existence.

At a time when many American writers (and indeed such local talents as those of Jill Tweedie and Blake Morrison) are setting out from the unsafe harbour of a paternal death to redefine their own identities, Lynn's two-hour monologue touches many familiar bases. True, she does not explain the true nature of her father's bisexuality, so recollections of a chilly household are a little hard to fathom: but she does explain at least some of his difficulties as a parent and hers as his child, and soon enough, beneath a symbolically shadowy portrait of the great Stratford hero of the 1950s, she becomes Cordelia to his vanished Lear before embarking on a whole gallery of Shakespeare's other heroines from Ophelia to Viola.

She is not in truth the greatest of Shakespearian actresses, and very often what work best here are the anecdotes of her days at the National in the early 1960s with Olivier and Coward and Maggie Smith and Edith Evans, all natural targets for her considerable comic gifts as a mimic. But what makes *Shakespeare For My Father* so impressive, and the reason I so hope she will bring it to London, is the courage with which she confronts her father's ghost on his own classical territory.

All us children of actors know this landscape: Lynn inhabits the shadows between the footlights and the dressing-room, illuminated in that curious twilight where the only trustworthy reflections are the ones in the dressing-room mirrors. While never attempting to upstage her father, she recalls his career, detailing his disasters, celebrating his triumphs, dwelling on his terrible last illness and never forgetting the appalling cruelty of Olivier when his old rival started to lose his memory at the onset of Parkinson's disease, which was eventually to kill him but not before it had brought him back together with his younger daughter.

Shakespeare For My Father is at once a chilling and a cheering account of what it means to grow up in a family of actors. It has been intelligently and economically staged by Lynn's husband, John Clark, and resonates with courage both theatrical and personal. Miss Redgrave richly deserves the Tony Award for which she has been nominated, and her show deserves to be seen over here for its radiance and its regrets.

The Great and the Grim

Leonardo: A Portrait of Love (Strand)

Sweeney Todd (National)

On the Morley/Richter scale of truly disastrous stage musicals, *Leonardo: A Portrait of Love* at the Strand (or Leonard the Musical as I prefer to think of it, given the defiantly suburban English nature of the casting here) only rates about a five. No scenery crashes to the ground, no actor rushes on stage to announce that Mona is looking pretty damn inscrutable again this morning, and only very occasionally do they suggest that she might have been a man in drag, given da Vinci's sexual uncertainties.

But not even in the great days of the Hollywood Art Class, when Kirk Douglas was hacking off his ear as Van Gogh and Charlton Heston was up there on the ladders fixing the Sistine ceiling, did anyone even think about a life of da Vinci, so uneventful was it, and the Moeller brothers, who are the prime creators of the musical, have the same inertia problem. Nothing happens in the first act of *Leonardo* and then it happens all over again in the second.

A large cast appears to have had a communal charisma bypass in rehearsal, while the actor in the title role, Paul Collis, seems to have won a weekend in fifteenth-century Florence as a prize on a painting-by-numbers correspondence course. For the crowd scenes, several merrymaking peasants have been drafted in from a Palladium pantomime circa 1954, while the songs are of the kind you forget even while they are still being sung.

The result is a kind of Mona Lisa jigsaw for which several of the pieces seem to have been left out of the box. It has all the electric fascination of watching paint dry, and all the vibrant theatricality of a demo-disc for a school concert: but the budget has been raised on Naura, an island rich in bird-droppings, so they must be used to this kind of thing.

~

Attend the tale of *Sweeney Todd*: he served a dark and a hungry God. When Sondheim's bleak, black, masterly musical first opened on Broadway back in 1979 it did so in a huge Hal Prince production (also seen here at Drury Lane a year or so later), which most of my colleagues are now intent on rubbishing in order to praise by contrast the present small-scale studio staging of Declan Donellan at the Cottesloe. But the greatness of *Sweeney* is that it can equally survive and thrive on the grand scale as on the minimalist: the new production is not better or worse than the original, it is just very different, the difference being between that of a landscape and a close-up.

Sweeney is not another cosy Victorian ballad show: no lines of Cockney orphans chanting Bartish pit-a-pat lyrics, no lovable *Annie*-type heroines, no guarantee that when you leave the theatre you will feel anything but worse. *Sweeney* is a jet-black, vicious and vitriolically brilliant musical played at and on the razor's edge. Thanks to its playwright, Christopher Bond, *Sweeney* is no longer the loony barber but the hero of a revenge drama, returning from Australian exile to right his marital wrongs: thanks to its composer and lyricist, we have a semi-operatic construction comparable to *The Threepenny Opera* or *Peter Grimes* rather than any other musical.

When the show first opened, it was alleged that its score was 'unhummable' in the usual Sondheim put-down: nobody now, fifteen years on, could claim that about 'Johanna' or 'Not While I'm Around', and indeed the constant achievement of Sondheim's score is the way that it undercuts and counterpoints and contrasts with what is happening on stage, so that Sweeney's barber-chair murders are in fact accomplished to the strains of a song called 'Pretty Women' which is one of the most lyrically beautiful I have ever heard.

Alun Armstrong now heads a powerful cast, with Julia McKenzie as the definitive Mrs Lovett and Denis Quilley (the original Drury Lane Sweeney) as the evil Judge. For anyone who has ever doubted the greatness of Sondheim or the American musical theatre, or ever felt that a comic song could not be derived from the cooking of shepherd's pies with actual shepherds on top, *Sweeney* is the one to tremble at: it is just wonderful – always has been, always will be.

Past Perfect

A Day in the Death of Joe Egg (King's Head)
Translations (Donmar Warehouse)

In a strong week for revivals of landmarks in post-war theatre, *A Day in the Death of Joe Egg,* the play that made Peter Nichols' reputation, returns for its first major London season in twenty-two years to the King's Head. Originally rejected by everyone but Michael Blakemore at the Glasgow Citizens, usually on the grounds that the autobiographical account of the parents of an epileptic, spastic ten-year-old would not be likely to have audiences rolling in the aisles, the play finally made it to London and Broadway and even the movies as the most heartbreaking of black comedies.

The new production by Lisa Forrell confirms just how much new ground was broken here: Joe Egg's parents and her neighbours and grandmother all chat easily to us in the audience, telling us their innermost thoughts or just what the others don't want to hear, while Joe herself (Katey Crawford Kastin) lolls in her wheelchair, a terrible and constant reminder of the issues of euthanasia and marital destruction that lie beneath the platitudinous surface of the suburban Bristol neighbourhood chatter that goes on all around and about her.

Clive Owen and Elizabeth Garvie now play the parents, while Owen also acts out in gruesome detail the doctors, vicars and psychiatrists who have so signally failed them, thereby neatly proving that every cloud has a jet-black lining. This is a play of dark and terrible brilliance about jokes that can kill the pain but leave the hurt intact: it is also, of course, about our inability to be our neighbours' keepers or to share in their tragedies, and about the ultimate resilience of the human spirit.

~

Elsewhere, we are in Donegal, in the town of Baile Beag, known to the English as Ballybeg and to theatregoers as the capital of Brian Friel country. It is 1833, and a party of initially friendly redcoats has come to chart the countryside and anglicise its place-names. Ireland is to be conquered not by the sword but by the map; there is to be a process of 'erosion' whereby English will replace Gaelic first as a language and then as a way of life. So starts Friel's *Translations* which when it first opened in 1981 struck me as the most important drama politically and historically to have come out of Ireland since O'Casey, and now, in a Sam Mendes revival at the Warehouse, demands no second thoughts.

In a hedge school, one of those secret corners which even at the beginning of the last century were beginning to harbour dissent, a drunken old pedant (Norman Rodway) is leading his pupils back to Greek or Gaelic rather than the dreaded English. A local girl who speaks only Gaelic falls for a soldier who speaks only English; in an infinitely, hauntingly touching duologue they communicate their love only through the alternate place-names of the surrounding hills, she speaking the originals while he intones the translations of the title.

But soon the play itself translates into something very much darker. The soldier disappears, and his captain threatens to lay waste all the surrounding fields until he is found. The apparently harmless group of map-makers has become an invading army, and what began as a John Ford comedy of Irish misunderstanding has become the tragedy which is to last until this very day. *Translations* is an ordnance survey of Irish humanity, in which the present is shaped by the past and the makers of maps have become the destroyers of the land they charted. Zara Turner and James Larkin are the lovers in this powerhouse revival.

Table for Two

Separate Tables (Apollo)

Oleanna (Royal Court)

When Rattigan's *Separate Tables* was first staged in 1954 – and we have had only one revival in London since – it was generally welcomed for the chance it gave two stars to take on massive stellar opportunities and new characters after the interval, while the rest of the cast remained as unchanged as the setting, a private hotel for gentlefolk inspired by the one in Kensington where the author would regularly visit his mother.

This theatrical device is used in no other play I know, and Sir Terence has been given scant credit for it: but then his reputation has only recently been upwardly revalued. In all his time at the National, the present director Sir Peter Hall managed, like his predecessor Olivier, to ignore every one of Rattigan's major works, as always has the RSC. We owe the current renaissance to the Almeida in Islington, which recently went back to *The Deep Blue Sea* with stunning results.

Separate Tables has, alas, not worn quite so well. Two short plays inspired by the 1950s experiences of the model Jean Dawnay and the actor John Gielgud, they are in fact studies in sex and love and loneliness shot through with Rattigan's understanding of the theatre theatrical: his brilliance was in taking stock characters and bringing them startlingly to life, like portrait miniatures suddenly illuminated by thousands of volts of neon.

As we peer through the glass doors of the Beauregard Private Hotel in Bournemouth we find two plays, the first about sexual obsession and the second about sexual repression. Both end happily and hopefully for the two central characters, but around them are gathered an old schoolmaster (Ernest Clark), an overbearing matriarch (Rosemary Leach), an indigent aristocrat (Rachel Gurney) and the lovelorn manageress (Charlotte Cornwell) as terrible reminders of the loneliness which waits out there in these lives of quiet desperation.

These are people who live alone but together, here as in the pages of Maugham short stories, and behind those clipped, tight monosyllables and the sudden outbursts of emotional anguish there lies a whole world of the English upper classes in retreat.

Patricia Hodge is wonderful as the icy Mayfair model of the first play and touching as the repressed daughter of the second; Peter Bowles gets the drunken journalist of the first half spot on, and is only fractionally less successful with the bogus Major who once gave David Niven the role of his entire career. The rest of the evening belongs to Miss Cornwell, with occasional manic interruptions from Miriam Karlin as the old racing biddy who prefers her horses to her fellow-residents.

Peter Hall's production is a little heavy-handed, not least when playing 'Jerusalem' during the final set-change, but this remains Garbo's *Grand Hotel* scaled down to just about the right size for West Hampshire.

~

Last year in New York, this summer in London, David Mamet's *Oleanna* comes bearing flags of warning about political correctness. For this is *Educating Rita* rancid with PC: a professor (David Suchet) spends the first half trying to explain to an apparently dim pupil (Lia Williams) that her right to be taught is only a concomitant part of her ability to learn. Then, in a breathtaking switcheroo during intermission, she gets the upper hand, accusing him of rape, thereby neatly destroying his career and depriving him of tenure and a new house.

The trouble here is that the main turnaround happens during the break in the action, but Harold Pinter's production, infinitely stronger than the off-Broadway original, papers over this crack by suggesting that *Oleanna* may be about something rather more than just contemporary campus terrors. By reverting to Mamet's original curtain, Pinter reminds us that this is in the end a play about who shall be given the power of deciding what things mean. True, Mamet has loaded both dice, his and hers, so heavily that any attempt to treat the evils of PC on a broader level – the level, for instance, on which Miller dealt with the evils of McCarthyism by setting them back 300 years in *The Crucible* – is in the end defeated by the fragility of a drama which thinks it's a debate.

Like Lillian Hellman's *The Children's Hour*, which it much resembles in outline, this is also a play about pupil power and student revenge. 'Teach me,' cries the girl as if it were her God-given right to have her professor's brain drip-fed into hers. When his teaching fails, all that is left is feminist revenge. But *Oleanna* touched an extraordinarily raw nerve in the American psyche, and don't think it can't happen here, because more than the play already is happening here.

On the Wilder Side

Sunset Boulevard (Adelphi)

Much Ado About Nothing (Queen's)

If it ain't broke, don't fix it: one of the major achievements of *Sunset Boulevard* the musical is the remarkable fidelity its makers, Andrew Lloyd Webber, Don Black, Christopher Hampton and Trevor Nunn, have shown towards the original Billy Wilder movie. The recent history of Broadway is littered with the corpses of musicals whose makers thought they could improve on Hollywood originals, and Wilder himself has lived to see two other classics of his, *Some Like it Hot* and *The Apartment*, given similarly dismal theatrical after-lives. But from the moment they use on stage the car chase from the 1950 film, right through to Norma Desmond's final descent of her palatial staircase to an audience of cops, it is clear that this one has been conceived not so much as an original musical, but rather as a play with songs faithfully derived from Wilder. Indeed, all the great moments in the show are Billy's, underscored and very occasionally overscored by Sir Andrew.

The Wilder/Webber marriage works best when one or two great numbers ('With One Look' in the first half and 'Too Much In Love to Care' in the second) soar out of Wilder's dialogue. There are other times when the songs seem a little heavy for the story, and it has to be said that in the ensemble numbers neither Black nor Hampton shows the acutely cynical understanding of 1940s Hollywood which characterised Larry Gelbart's *City of Angels*, set in the same town and the same industry at the same post-war period. But what will save *Sunset Boulevard* from the abrupt West End demise of *City of Angels* is something more than Sir Andrew and a better publicity budget: it is the sheer familiarity of *Sunset Boulevard*, and the likelihood that those who have always loved it will love it even more with songs.

True, certain elements are now missing: when Eric von Stroheim as the sinister butler explained he was also the first husband who had made the career of Gloria Swanson (as Norma) and with it a whole industry of silent pictures, Wilder was treating us to actual Hollywood history as well as movie melodrama: when here a somewhat bland Daniel Bonzali (as the butler) says the same thing of Patti LuPone, we get none of the original shivers of recognition.

What LuPone gives us is the traditional ruined diva, halfway from Callas to Garland and at her best in the final mad scene, which Hampton and Black have wisely conceived as grand opera rather than silent movies. But as a walk on the Wilder side this is still impressive enough, even if Kevin Anderson has trouble fighting his way through the clichés of a role which manages to be simultaneously underwritten and historic: how many other movies or shows have ever been narrated by a man from the bottom of a swimming-pool with several bullets in his chest?

~

Much Ado About Nothing is not in fact the first Shakespeare on Shaftesbury Avenue since the war (as has been claimed by Queen's management), since Gielgud was at the Palace in the mid-1950s, but it is a lively and unusual romp through the Beatrice-Benedick love's labour with the unusual twist that Benedick (Mark Rylance) is an Ulsterman and about half the height of his Beatrice (Janet McTeer). The production by Matthew Warchus goes hell for leather and moment for moment, sacrificing much overall sense for a joyous immediacy which converts masked balls into Wild-Western hoedowns and Italian palazzos into circus tents. As with the forthcoming Branagh movie, the intention here seems to be to introduce *Much Ado* to anti-Shakespearean or non-Shakespearean audiences, and on those terms it works very well indeed, shifting with agility from the broad farce of Dogberry to the dark drama of the 'Kill Claudio' scene.

Hare's Breadth

The David Hare Trilogy (National)
Racing Demon / Murmuring Judges / The Absence of War

At the National, in an all-day sequence of tremendous power and ambition, David Hare has completed his State of the Nation trilogy. It marks two great achievements: first, the creation at the National for the first time of a credible permanent company of character actors who can move from play to play with equal dexterity, and second, the ability of the National to examine the way we live now on a broad political and social canvas such as has not been seen in the London theatre these last twenty years.

The bad news is that the plays function on a sliding scale, with the first far and away the best. This is *Racing Demon*, first seen at the National early in 1990 and still unquestionably the best new play there since Hare's own *Pravda* (with Howard Brenton and Tariq Ali) five years earlier. Set in and around a contemporary South London inner-city parish, it tells of four clergymen in a world where shopkeepers no longer understand why crosses are sold with little men stuck to them.

Here we have the Reverend Lionel Espy, played in the performance of his career by Oliver Ford Davies, a preacher so racked by inner doubt that he can no longer fulfil the job description by spreading a faith he has himself lost. Then there's a bible-thumping zealot (Adam Kotz), a hearty cyclist who believes that God works best on a sports field (Adrian Scarborough) and a suppressed and tortured gay (Michael Bryant), finally exiled by a Sunday scandal-sheet in a tough echo of *Pravda*.

All four clerics are answerable to the ineffably smooth Bishop of Southwark (Richard Pasco), who has decided that the Church temporal and political is of more immediate importance than the Church spiritual. The ensuing battle of wills and weaknesses takes on a Shavian power as the exploration of a massive failure of nerve within the Church of England. This is a play about shepherds who have lost the will to lead and sheep who have no desire to follow, but it is also about the way that the modern Church has become a ghastly, grinning parody of the politics it once managed to avoid. Not since the epilogue to *Saint Joan* have we had a moral thriller of such power about Church versus State.

And so to the law: Hare's second play, *Murmuring Judges*, first seen in 1991, gives us not only judges but barristers, solicitors, convicts, gaolers, corrupt detectives and lesser but more honest coppers, all in a vast semi-documentary tapestry – a tapestry which unfortunately then unravels to reveal at its heart little more than the average plot of a TV cop show in its seventh series.

Hare has clearly done his homework: indeed four researchers are credited on the trilogy and the statistics are chilling. Only three per cent of all crimes lead to a conviction, but if the percentage were any higher there would be nowhere to put the criminals anyway; the only countries with reasonably comfortable or decent gaols are those from which the governments have only recently been released. But the major disappointment here is the way that Hare's breadth of research has denied him depth of insight: what we end up with is the equivalent of a television vox pop, with equal time given to the views of all but the dramatist.

And it is precisely the same journalistic problem which besets the new, last play in the sequence. *The Absence of War* is about yet another crisis of confidence, this one in the Labour Party engine-room during the last general election. John Thaw plays the Kinnock figure, a man whose tragedy it is to have made his party electable for the first time in decades but then to be seen as the one obstacle standing between it and election victory. Figures from the shadow cabinet are vaguely recognisable here, but Hare has his hero brought down by the creakiest of devices (one first used by Rattigan more than thirty years ago), the backfiring of a live television interview.

Like the priests in *Racing Demon*, the politicians in *Absence of War* are destroyed by their own uncertainties: it is the absence of faith that we are faced with all through the trilogy, but only in that first play does Hare seem to care enough to give us great drama as well as cool debate. On the broad Olivier stage however, Richard Eyre's fluent, fluid movement of his troops across Bob Crowley's often back-projected settings is a miracle of stage management.

Kushner's Credo

Angels in America (National)

At a time when our leading home-made dramatists are still on the run from anything which might even remotely touch on the 1990s (David Hare always honourably excepted), we should continue to salute Tony Kushner. But oh, what a falling-off is here: in reviving the first half of his *Angels in America* (*Millennium Approaches,* which won the Pulitzer and most other drama awards last year) and playing it directly before the new concluding half, *Perestroika*, the National Theatre has done him no favours. Where part one, streamlined since its first outing, now emerges as the most important American play of the decade or so since we were first introduced to Mamet, part two is an often unnecessary and desperately overlong continuation of themes that were already adequately treated and debated in the original.

Let us remind ourselves what those were. *Millennium Approaches* is essentially concerned with three things: the remarkable life and death of Roy Cohn, the nightmare of AIDS and the eccentric, ongoing traditions of the Mormons. Nobody, least of all Kushner, says these have to add up to a coherent dramatic whole. 'America is a melting-pot', notes one of his characters early in the eight-hour epic, 'in which nothing ever melts.'

As is now fashionable in most contemporary American drama, Kushner goes time and again for the trailer rather than the main feature. He offers us snapshots of gay New York night-life, glimpses of men ringing their anguished mothers from Central Park pick-up places to inform them of their gayness, blackout scenes, all adding up to the kaleidoscopic conclusion that America has sacrificed the history and traditions of its past to make way for a vacuum-packed, politicised present.

Somewhere here is where the Mormons figure, and Kushner is commendably unafraid of magic realism: he even brings back from the seventeenth and twelfth centuries the survivors of other plagues, ghostly presences around the AIDS bedside to point out that a black death is nothing very new.

Most of Kushner's characters, from the latterday New York gays back to Roy Cohn and his electric-chair victim Ethel Rosenberg, are people whose spiritual cheques are always bouncing; but it is only really with Cohn that Kushner ever gets to grips as a dramatist.

Here, after all, is the best story of the lot: the right-wing demon of McCarthyism, killer of the Rosenbergs, ally of Nixon was himself an AIDS victim who died denying his homosexuality: 'I merely have sex with men – a guy who can get Mr Reagan to answer his calls is not homosexual.' Like all great villains, Cohn eventually takes the play and runs away with it. Like Lambert LeRoux of *Pravda*, he is at once the most terrifying and the most memorable creation, dominating by sheer mesmeric villainy the acres of political correctness in which others seek to lose him. If only *Angels in America* could have been a play focused on the villain in their midst: as it is, in David Schofield's towering performance, Cohn lifts the drama off the floor at every entrance and puts it neatly back there when he departs.

The rest of these honorary citizens of the *Twilight Zone* have rather less claim to our undivided attention, especially as Kushner veers from political thriller to metaphysical fantasy by way of Antarctica and the kind of heavenly debate among the angels which I thought had gone out with early Priestley and Shaw. In the end, *Angels* is about urban terrors and planetary disintegration, and its marathon footnote in *Perestroika* takes the disintegration of the Soviet Union as an all-too-convenient role model for the Chaos Theory. Kushner is singing a blues for the end of the world but, like Cohn, that world is a long time dying, and along the way to the apocalypse we are apt, as is the author, to get somewhat distracted. Where part one now has near-classic status, part two suggests work in progress, swerving uneasily from sex farce to biblical revelation on some demented bus-and-truck tour of universal uneasiness and disease: 'If God does return to earth ever,' says one onlooker, 'sue the bastard.'

Somewhere in this hopelessly overblown, overwrought second half are some of the answers to the questions raised in the infinitely sharper first, but they are buried so deep that even Kushner seems at times to have forgotten where he found them, and is left scoring cheap jokes off better playwrights: 'I have always depended on the kindness of strangers'; 'Well now, that's a stupid thing to do'.

And yet somewhere in this lingering, spluttering, dying bonfire of spiritual and sexual vanities there is the sound of a truly original playwright attempting to clamber out to the top of the heap. Kushner needs to be saluted for his lyrical courage. He also needs to be given a director unafraid of cutting a couple of hours out of *Angels* and leaving us with a five-hour drama about those who grew up in the shadow of Roy Cohn and the American nightmare of identity crisis which he symbolised.

Up The Avenue

Night After Night (Royal Court)

We are in the West End and a lone pianist is about to strike up the overture of a new musical: something by Julian Slade, perhaps, or Sandy Wilson or Vivian Ellis. Songs you have half-heard somewhere before and are going to have no trouble humming in the bath tonight. Nothing to do with phantoms or dancing cats or starving French orphans. Clearly we are not in the theatrical present, but when exactly?

The year is in fact 1958, and we are 'in at the half' – thirty minutes before curtain-up. Neil Bartlett's *Night After Night*, far and away the most inventive and intelligent musical of 1993, takes us back over three decades to an altogether lost limelight. The time and place are personally significant to Bartlett as author and star, since the night in question is the night his father took his mother 'up west' to celebrate the news of his own imminent birth. Mother happens to arrive a little late in the foyer, and to while away the time Bartlett gives us a gallery of ushers, cloakroom attendants, chorus boys and house managers, all of whom (in *Chorus Line* convention) tell us the stories of their lives up to the moment of the starting of the show.

The agenda of *Night After Night* is a gay one, in that Bartlett is eager for us to understand the double standards of homosexuality which then obtained. The vast majority of Shaftesbury Avenue theatre workers on both sides of the 1950s curtains were gay, but never said so even to each other for fear of disturbing the prejudices of a largely non-gay audience – people like Bartlett's parents, in fact, to whose memories the show is dedicated. Bartlett even appears on stage as his own father, looking oddly out of place, rather like Neville Chamberlain at an orgy.

So 'Gay's the Word', to quote an Ivor Novello title of the period, but the word has to be left unspoken: in a tacky, intermittently loving and savage parody of the post-war West End, Bartlett manages to find some of the universal truths of love and loneliness. His show is at once an anthem and a requiem for the old Shaftesbury Avenue, and the wonder is that a man under forty now should have captured it so accurately. I write as one who spent some of his childhood there in those 1950s and, believe me, this is exactly what it was like: a world of deep political incorrectness, full of raging queens and unseen, all-powerful backstage managers, where the kindness of strangers was nowhere much in evidence but the shows went on, night after night, as intriguing for their offstage politics as for anything which ever happened in their plots.

Like Sondheim's *Follies*, Bartlett's *Night After Night* is about the sudden tricks of memory played by stage lighting, and about the shadows in the dressing-room mirrors. What makes it unique over here is that it deals with the front-of-house staff rather than the stars, and that it is aimed at the punters, the innocents out there in the stalls who still thought that Googie Withers might be a warning of frosty weather to come. In his own production, with a score by Nicolas Bloomfield, Bartlett leads a versatile cast of seven on a journey up the Avenue which manages to celebrate and satirise a lost world of backstage bitchiness, suddenly fading into the apparent glamour of a boy-meets-girl musical designed to make a still-post-war audience feel good and never even think about the real lives of the conjurers involved in the greasepaint illusion. If you can imagine a 1950s suburban English *Les Enfants du Paradis*, this, in its own quirky and wondrous way, is it.

Into the Woods

The Wind in the Willows (National)

It is a curious, but infinitely English, realisation that the outstanding, ongoing hit of Richard Eyre's administration of the National Theatre has been not *Angels in America,* not the Hare trilogy, not *Carousel* or even *The Madness of George III* but the story of Ratty and Badger and Moley and Toad. Alan Bennett's *The Wind in the Willows* is now in its fourth consecutive winter season at the Olivier and likely to be a Christmas fixture there annually long after Eyre himself has left the stage.

In taking the *Willows* on stage, Bennett is of course doing nothing new. For fifty years or so, A A Milne's *Toad of Toad Hall* was as regular a West End Christmas treat as *Peter Pan* or any pantomime, and only the 1990 expiry of copyright has allowed it to be superseded by the new version. But what Bennett has done is to return to the original book for a staging that is both darker and vastly more spectacular than the economical Milne version.

A circular drum rises and spins on the Olivier stage to give us the Wild Wood, the river bank and the underground homes of Badger and Moley. Entire choirs of schoolchildren arrive to sing 'In The Bleak Midwinter', and this remains in Nick Hytner's production the most spectacular seasonal treat that London has had to offer since the golden days of Palladium pantomimes just after the war.

But just as Andrew Birkin in *The Lost Boys* deconstructed *Peter Pan* and gave us instead of the old fairytale a complex psychological minefield ploughed up from J M Barrie's own terrors of homosexuality and death, both of which were to surround him in life, so Bennett gives us the full darkness as we go into the woods in search of Badger. All the old childhood magic is still somewhere here, but so too are the territorial imperatives that Grahame hid just below ground. So too is the somewhat gay alliance of Badger and Ratty, crumbling away as they both set out in the subtlest of ways to co-opt and then seduce little Moley.

Bennett's text is full of sly contemporary references: the worst that can happen to Toad Hall, we learn at the last, is not the invasion of the weasels but its conversion to a leisure centre and theme park where actors will be encouraged to give solo shows. Jonathan Miller once told us this was 'a Thames-side tale of old country-house fascism', but in fact it's even more complex than that. It's a social history of Britain, with an Orwellian horse called Albert who has unaccountably strayed from *Animal Farm* and a Ratty straight out of Terence Rattigan. As for Toad himself, he would seem to have delusions of Ibsen's *Ghosts.* 'Give me the sun,' he cries pathetically from gaol, though it's Albert who in the end perfectly captures the Bennett/Grahame mix of plaintive despair: 'I don't mind sunrise or sunset,' he notes gloomily, 'it's what's in between that depresses me.'

Of the original team, only Michael Bryant as Badger survives: but Desmond Barrit as Toad, David Ross as Ratty and Adrian Scarborough as Moley are now into their third winter of what has become the best of theatrical family outings for the nineties.

Bleak Dreams

Wildest Dreams (Barbican)

Aspects of Love (Prince of Wales)

In the Barbican Pit, Alan Ayckbourn's forty-fourth play may well be his bleakest to date: *Wildest Dreams* is the story of four loners who escape their social despair by meeting weekly to play a dungeons-and-dragons game in which they can sublimate their own hopeless characters into such fantasy figures as Alric the Wise and Idonia the Enchantress.

But as so often in bleaker Ayckbourn territory, all it takes is one non-playing outsider to bring the game crashing to pieces and with it most of the players. Here, she is Marcie (Sophie Thompson), a workmate of one of the misfits, and by the end of a short evening she has reduced the others to gibbering wrecks by the simple device of showing up all their shortcomings. No student of Ayckbourn can be surprised by the emotional wreckage that litters the stage long before the last scene.

Wildest Dreams is about the games that people play to avoid facing up to the truth about themselves or those with whom they have been forced, by reasons of parentage or marriage, to share their lives. But Ayckbourn's own production has a tough time convincing us that he has found anything new in his lament for the human condition: if he has a message, the lantern with which he flashes it out to us is flickering very dimly around the Pit.

Brenda Blethyn, Barry McCarthy and Jenna Russell, as the other players, all do what they can with limited resources, but in a play about role-playing, it is ironic that Ayckbourn has in fact written some of his thinnest roles.

~

When Andrew Lloyd Webber's *Aspects of Love* first opened at the Prince of Wales three years ago, I put it to you that it was far and away his most touching, talented and impressive musical, and nothing since, certainly not *Sunset Boulevard*, has caused me to alter that judgment. Now *Aspects* is back at the Prince of Wales for an all too brief Christmas season in a touring production by the Australian director Gale Edwards, and it is looking, if anything, better than ever.

Stripped of the somewhat ornate original sets and costumes and staging, *Aspects* emerges as a cool, adult romance about the little things that people do to destroy each other. As if responding to criticism that he was never going to be another Stephen Sondheim, Lloyd Webber has here written an ice-cold modern coda to *A Little Night Music*, full of soaring melodies, lost dreams and a constant, aching sense of lost love.

Gary Bond, Kathryn Evans and Alexander Hanson lead the new cast, all of them commendably aware that they are in an operetta of remarkable romanticism: 'set down the wine and the dice and perish the thought of tomorrow' may be the anthem at the funeral of the old pretender who heads a complicated household, but this is also a show about lesbianism and prospective incest, as courageous in its sexuality as any musical I know.

But above all there are the show-stopping songs, from 'Love Changes Everything' all the way through to 'I Want to be the First Man You Remember', all with edgy, intelligent lyrics by Don Black and Charles Hart. If you only ever want to see one Webber musical, this is the one to see.

Et in Arcadia Tom?

Arcadia (Lyttelton)

Several ghosts haunt the long dining-table which dominates the set of Tom Stoppard's *Arcadia* on the Lyttelton stage of the National. Many of them we are meant to acknowledge: Lord Byron, who just might have been duelling there in 1809; Capability Brown, whose elegant classical gardens, glimpsed through the tall windows, are being laid low by the coming of the new steam engine; Lady Bracknell, not yet born but hovering over the proceedings already; Lady Caroline Lamb, about whom the latterday researcher of Arcadia (Felicity Kendal) has just published a controversial biography. Then again, there are ancient and modern philosophers and scientists, creators of the Chaos theories and of the computers which add to them. Mrs Gaskell is in there somewhere, and Jane Austen, and Oscar Wilde and Isaac Newton, none of them actually on stage but all gathered in essence, just as in more realistic times Stoppard once gathered Lenin and Tzara and Joyce in Zurich for *Travesties*.

But there are other ghosts around *Arcadia* and they are the more scary ones: the ghosts of Christopher Fry and Jean Anouilh, who in their later dramas (Fry remains of course superbly alive in real life) more or less abandoned activity for arcane debate. The final image of Trevor Nunn's exquisitely measured production is of the four central Arcadians dancing in circles around the table, getting nowhere enchantingly, and it is all too symbolic of the play which precedes it.

Arcadia offers us the terrifying prospect of our most intelligent and referential dramatist finally vanishing up his own brilliance: it is in the end a play about everything and nothing, in which knowledge is all and caring is nil. We are in two time-frames: 1809, when the Byronic escapade might not have happened, and 1993, when its researchers (Kendal and Bill Nighy) come together to ponder its improbabilities as well as those of the Chaos theory and the premature discovery of computer science by one of those elfin spirits (Emma Fielding) doomed, usually by Barrie or Anouilh, to early and tragic death.

This is a word-play of Stoppard's customary skill about the true meaning of life, the nature of existence and the tortoise back from *Jumpers*. It also, at times, resembles a Feydeau farce rewritten by Richard Brinsley Sheridan and at others the desperate erudition of a man painfully unable to make us care about any of his characters. Whole scenes start out as *Hay Fever* or *The School for Scandal*, while elsewhere Stoppard seems to be offering us Enid Bagnold on speed or *The Chalk Garden* rewritten by Stephen Hawking.

In the end, he tells us that history is the last thing ever to be left to people like historians or researchers, and that 'it's wanting to know that makes us matter'. But we also want to know that there is drama here, rather than a hotchpotch of telescoped conclusions. The planting is brilliant: a monkey, inconsequential to Scene Two, becomes central to Scene Five, while a portrait agreed to be a fake in Scene Three is casually authenticated in Scene Six thanks to the miracle of the flashback.

The casting is also superb: not only Kendal and Nighy as the increasingly frustrated researchers but also Harriet Walter, cascading from a great height somewhere halfway between the Ladies Teazle and Bracknell, and Rufus Sewell as her doomed daughter's louche tutor. It is not that these are characters in search of an author, but that the author still seems to be in search of his play, or at the very least its conclusion. Once you have decided that chaos comes from order, rather than the reverse, you have still to clear a path through the trees or what is left of them: Stoppard, like his own researchers, frequently comments on his own play in progress ('Brideshead Regurgitated'), but somewhere along the way he has started to write its footnotes instead of its central text. You won't find a more intelligent evening in town, nor a more maddening one: hasten along.

Molière the Merrier

The School for Wives (Almeida)

Cabaret (Donmar Warehouse)

Jane Eyre (Playhouse)

We may have had to wait until the very last moment for the comedy and the comic performance of the year, but at the Almeida we surely now have them: Jonathan Kent's brilliantly witty ninety-minute staging of Molière's *The School for Wives* offers Ian McDiarmid flapping around the stage like a mad goldfish on speed, dragging back a wondrous farce from library to live performance. Kent has dressed up the old Richard Wilbur verse translation with a production in which actual rain falls on to the town house where Arnolphe is keeping his child bride locked away from her lover. The farcical twists and double-twists of Molière's best-constructed plot are counterpointed with a still-topical debate about the purposes of women and marriage in a male-chauvinist society, and it is the triumph of this revival that it feels the urge neither to mock nor to update nor to realign the original, but simply to restore it to all its long-lost Parisian intellectual glory.

A mix of Malvolio and Mephistopheles, McDiarmid's frustrated would-be husband and gaoler is a gigantic comic and ultimately tragic creation, coolly offset by Emma Fielding's chilly Agnes and Damian Lewis' stud-like Horace. But all the playing here, including that of Linal Haft and Carol Macready as the mad servants and Bernard Gallagher as the only sane figure to figure in Arnolphe's manic scenario, is a tribute to the Almeida's talent for crafting instant company spirit among actors who appear to have been playing together for years. We are unlikely ever to see a better staging: Kent puts a timeless spin on a vintage comedy of appalling manners, and you can't ask a lot more than that.

~

What good is sitting alone in your room? Come to the Cabaret, old chum. Kander & Ebb's classic 1966 musical has always had a curious heritage (Isherwood as Herr Issyvoo by way of John van Druten's *I Am a Camera* and the Brecht/Weill presence of Lotte Lenya in the original Broadway cast transposed to a Liza Minnelli/Hollywood vehicle which had precious little to do with the original Berlin), but it will never find a better home than amid the night-club tables of the Donmar Warehouse.

Sam Mendes' breathtaking new staging abandons the Hal Prince big-band concept for an intimate close-up, no longer *Sweet Charity* with swastikas but instead a plausibly grimy night-club where Jane Horrocks (the best Sally Bowles since Judi Dench) belts out the numbers that link Isherwood's sketchy tale. In a stunning cast, Sara Kestelman as the Mother Courage landlady, George Raistrick as her all-too-Jewish suitor, Adam Godley as the gay English novelist and, above all, Alan Cumming as the epicene Master of Ceremonies all prove that this is a company show, never better than in the final line-up when each of them echoes the political, social and sexual themes that have survived the hurly-burly of the Kit Kat Club.

The score here is an amalgam of numbers from the Broadway, Hollywood and roadshow *Cabaret*, and Horrocks claws it back from Minnelli with a gritty Home Counties resilience. Cumming as the puppet-master host never leaves the stage, and though we have lost the original Lenya link, the show has retained all its Berlin power, never more so than in the title song which Horrocks makes an angry anthem to her own survival; in the last seconds, Mendes pulls a final stunt with the MC which even Hal Prince never thought of, and it makes a chilly, logical sense of the whole show. Go see it again for yourself.

~

It is the curious achievement of Fay Weldon, as adapter, and Helena Kaut-Howson, as director, to have given us at the Playhouse a *Jane Eyre* which puts that novel firmly in the class of *Rebecca* and *The Secret Garden*. For those who like their Brontës on stage, here they all are: Charlotte, Anne, Emily and Bramwell hover around the central action, indulging themselves in minor roles and a little light scene-shifting, while centre stage Tim Pigott-Smith goes memorably over the top as Rochester and Alexandra Mathie drifts wanly around in the title role.

If what you want is a three-hour synopsis of the book, all highlights adequately conveyed with just enough post-modernist feminist updating (largely conveyed by rag-dolls left around the stage and some dolls' houses bursting spectacularly into flames) then this is the *Jane Eyre* for you: rather like one of those talking books on cassette, it gets you painlessly through a digest of the original without ever expecting you to have to think about it too deeply. Bill Kenwright, the manager, is commendably offering all seats at £10 each, and if anything can break the jinx of the Playhouse, at least for the Christmas season, then this is it.

1994

Staff and Stuffing

September Tide (Comedy)
Unfinished Business (Barbican)
An Absolute Turkey (Globe)

Daphne du Maurier's *September Tide*, which ran briefly in the West End just after the war and was intriguingly disinterred at the King's Head a few months ago, has now made it back into the West End much helped by the recent biography of du Maurier by Margaret Forster. It suggested that there might be a coded message in here somewhere about the author's romantic if unrequited passion for Ellen Doubleday, her publisher's wife, and also for the original star of the show, Gertrude Lawrence.

The only problem is that the play itself isn't really about any of that: it's about a mother falling in love with her daughter's husband and deciding on balance not to go to bed with him, and so far as has yet been established that never happened in the du Maurier household at all. Still, the play does bare several other traces of Dame Daphne: a house on the Cornish cliffs, storm clouds gathering, ominous weather forecasts. True, the birds outside all seem remarkably docile, and instead of Mrs Danvers setting fire to the furniture we get a rather more passive cleaning lady content to chat amiably about local climatic conditions to any of the cast who happen to be standing around on stage at the time without much to do, which is surprisingly often.

For in truth this is a pretty terrible little play, but it does have certain back-to-basics values: like *The Age of Innocence* it is essentially Merchant/Ivory with catering, a return to a lost world where lonely widows (Susannah York at her most wistfully appealing) could rely on decent staff and jovial bachelors up the road to take their minds off darker sexual passions. Michael Praed as the artist beloved of mother and daughter does his best to look arty, and my vague hope was that he'd run off with the neighbouring bachelor. Instead he just runs off, and not even a Cornish cliff at that.

~

Michael Hastings' *Unfinished Business* at the Barbican Pit is also in its way about the Staff Problem, though this time with yet more remains of the day. Once again we are at a country house-party somewhere in middle England at the outbreak of the last war. Once again the master of the house is showing distinctly fascist tendencies, and once again the butler has to decide how he should react, if at all. We have, of course, all been here before: as early as 1947 Noël Coward was wondering, in a little-known drama called *Peace in Our Time*, what would have happened to Britain under a Nazi occupation, and the questions he raised then are still the questions of *Unfinished Business* and *Remains of the Day*.

Essentially they are concerned with Mosley matters, the undoubted affection for Germany to be found among upper-crust hostesses not even necessarily related to the Mitfords, and whether in fact a pre-war class system could have opened the doors to Hitler any more effectively than, say, Dad's Army. The ownership of the past is at stake here, and you could if you so wished trace a line back from Hastings through Alan Bennett and the movies of Joe Losey all the way to the Go-Between himself. Hastings writes on the borderlines of self-parody ('Is a Bishop with a sub-machine gun likely to cause comment?'; 'Bad servants are the first sign of a nation in crisis,') but with a poetic intensity well-served by Philip Voss and Gemma Jones as the collaborationist aristocrats, Toby Stephens and Geoffrey Bayldon as the young and old versions of their golden-boy son, and Monica Dolan and Diana Coupland as the women whose lives are casually destroyed by their cruelty in a rambling, haunting timepiece.

~

The Peter Hall Company, currently responsible for just about all the classic revivals in the commercial London theatre, has another winner at the Globe with *An Absolute Turkey*, the bedroom farce that Hall and his wife Nicki Frei have adapted from the classic Feydeau. The translation proves lively enough ('My wife is charming, but she has been charming for a very long time now') but Hall's real triumph here has been to find enough comic misfits to flesh it out. Not since the John Mortimer translations of Feydeau in the earliest days of the National have we had such a vintage company of farce-freaks: Griff Rhys-Jones, Geoffrey Hutchings, Ken Wynne and Peter Cellier all surround the ravishing Felicity Kendal with so many eccentricities of character and voice and manner that the evening becomes a riot of displaced identities.

Hare's Brecht

Galileo (Almeida)
Maxwell the Musical (Not at the Criterion)
By Special Arrangement (Warehouse)

Brecht's *Galileo* has always been a work in progress, first written in 1938, drastically revised with and for Charles Laughton in California towards the end of the war, and again in East Berlin up to the moment the author died in 1956 with the play still in rehearsal. Thus we can hardly blame David Hare (at the Almeida) for having another go at it, especially since he's taken out an unwieldy carnival sequence, made the whole piece accessible for the first time to studio theatres, and knocked the best part of forty minutes off its running time.

Jonathan Kent's production is one that Laughton would certainly have understood and cheered, since unlike the John Dexter staging at the National in 1981 with Michael Gambon (the last major Brecht revival in London, which gives you some idea how the old pirate has gone out of fashion over here), it restores the notion of the one-man show, with Richard Griffiths gargantuan and mesmeric in the title role.

Around him, as is now usual for the Almeida, has been gathered one of the most distinguished supporting casts in the business (Michael Gough, Alfred Burke, Patrick Godfrey, Jerome Willis, Edward de Souza) but they are really only there to prop up, sometimes literally, Griffiths as the charlatan 'inventor' of the telescope who goes on to become the giant martyr in the fight between church and science, giving up the very sight which has enabled him to see the stars. This is a magnificent, unmissable performance in a handy theatrical digest of a sprawling epic.

~

The rest of this column is where you might have expected to read a review of *Maxwell the Musical* at the Criterion, had it not been for the intervention of Sir Nicholas Lyell. Sir Nicholas did not care for the show: he is not a critic nor a producer, nor had he ever actually seen it. He is however Attorney-General, to which office seem somewhat curiously to have devolved some of the functions of the late and unlamented Lord Chamberlain as Her Majesty's Censor in Waiting.

Sir Nicholas took the view that the musical, which was in rehearsal at the time he banned it, might conceivably prejudice the forthcoming fraud trial involving Kevin and Ian Maxwell. The fact that, the way things are going legally, this trial could well not begin until the next millennium seems not to have troubled Sir Nicholas; nor does the fact that you can buy, over the counter of any bookshop, innumerable volumes equally likely to prejudice any Maxwell trial; nor does the fact that there have already been several television enquiries far more damaging to the Maxwell cause than anything in this rather mild satire.

It is one that I happen to have read, not of course since Sir Nicholas banned it (even a reading of the script is now liable to lead to prosecution) but several months ago, when it struck me as a harmless series of patter songs set to the music of Gilbert and Sullivan. Asked for some advice by its creators, I merely suggested that they sub-title it *Moby Dick II* in the light of Mr Maxwell's last sighting at sea.

As it then looked on the page, *Maxwell the Musical* did not actually strike me as very good, so I am not here attempting to defend a masterpiece. I am merely wondering how, thirty years after the abolition of the Lord Chamberlain as censor, which was already long overdue, we have got ourselves back into a position where some bewigged potentate can haul plays off the stage, thereby creating mass unemployment of actors and considerable financial loss for backers. Suppose I now take it upon myself to murder all my children, do I then go to the Attorney-General and ask him to close immediately the Diana Rigg *Medea* on the grounds that seeing it may subsequently prejudice the jury at my trial?

The desire to close things down, often before they can be seen or heard by a paying public, has always been unhealthily strong among British officialdom; we would be unwise not to protest at its sudden rebirth here.

~

At the Warehouse in Covent Garden, *By Special Arrangement* marks quite simply the most dazzling debut in solo cabaret I have ever seen: the actress and singer Maria Friedman has had the intelligent but hitherto unprecedented idea of inviting a dozen or so of the best arrangers in the West End and on Broadway to come up with new versions of classics by Sondheim, Porter, Gershwin and Weill, and the result is a riot of orchestral and vocal treats which deserves to run forever in a larger theatre.

End of the Peer

Peer Gynt (Barbican)

Peer Gynt is the big one: shipwrecks, Troll Kings, madhouses, vast journeys through space and time into the inner soul, confrontations with life and death, childhood and mortality. Nobody, least of all Ibsen, ever seems to have decided how much of it is a dream: at the time of its earliest London staging eighty years ago (when a woman played Peer) the general theory was that he died either in the shipwreck or the madhouse, and that all Act Five is therefore a dream in which Peer's past life was unravelled before him at the moment of death.

Computer games have given the great Japanese director Yukio Ninagawa (at the Barbican and soon on tour) a still better idea: *Peer Gynt* as virtual reality. We start therefore in a video arcade, as the young Peer (Michael Sheen in a brave but too early stab at the role) sets out on the epic search for his own identity. Along the way, in this hugely ambitious and lavish production, we get the screening of film clips which look dangerously like a series of trendy British Airways commercials as they try to convey Peer's flight. We also get a couple of splendid performances from the kabuki actor Haruhiko Joh as the Buttonmoulder, and the Norwegian Espen Skonberg as the Troll King. But a multi-national cast in an Irish translation (by Frank McGuinness) of a Scandinavian classic in a Japanese production is bound to look a little unrooted, and Sheen as yet lacks the sheer charisma to bind it all together. So we are left with a tour of *Peer* as well as *Peer* on tour (Manchester next, then Tokyo): at no point does Ninagawa really seem to have confidence in the text or a clear route map through its complexities and contradictions: but for sheer spectacle, this one will be hard to beat.

Hippy Birthday

The Birthday Party (National)

Pinter's *The Birthday Party*, now on the National's Lyttelton Stage in a dazzling new production by Sam Mendes, did not make much sense to its original audiences in 1958, though I am never entirely certain why they are forever being blamed for this. At the time, Pinter had only recently given up the life of a touring actor, and in one sense his play is a merciless, brilliant parody of all the tacky stage thrillers of the period, except that the Inspector Never Calls.

In another, of course, it changed forever the relationship of playwright to punter: for the first time, Pinter demanded that his spectators do some of the work for themselves, make their own connections, sort out their own puzzles instead of waiting for the dramatist to serve them a neat denouement. Nothing here is quite what it seems, but Mendes has courageously given back to *The Birthday Party* all the trappings of its times: from the bouncy light radio-programme music which introduces it, through Dora Bryan's supremely cosy seaside landlady, to Bob Peck and Nicholas Woodeson as the B-movie heavies, every echo here of the late Fifties gives us the perfect period flavour with which to understand and recall the background against which the play first exploded.

As the unemployed pianist whose body and soul are fought over by all the other characters, Anton Lesser remains somewhat bemused and overshadowed: but as the play moves from boarding-house revue sketch through a long night's journey back to totalitarian oppression, Trevor Peacock wonderfully indicates the price paid by the innocent bystander to the thugs of the state. Best of all, though, apart from Dora Bryan's wondrous return to the height of her comic form, is the moment when the set slides back into a street full of houses just like it: in every window a light, in every room some other kind of nameless terror.

The Bleak and Black

A Month in the Country (Albery)

Beautiful Thing (Donmar Warehouse)

A Month in the Country is the one that isn't by Chekhov: he even claimed not to like it very much, which seems a little ungrateful considering that within forty years he had borrowed most of its plot and all of its characters for several other works, not least *Uncle Vanya*. But Turgenev wrote this one in 1848, which means it is the first modern psychological drama despite the fact that it lay unperformed for almost twenty years and did not fully make its mark until a famous Stanislavsky production in 1909.

Since then, of course, it has been around a good deal, and we have it now at the Albery in a superbly cast and thoughtfully realised Bill Bryden production which brings both Helen Mirren and John Hurt back to the West End after long absences but at the very height of their considerable form. Mirren's Natalya Petrovna is a constant and starry centre for the dozen equally enthralling characters who revolve in her orbit: most are in mid-life crisis or the pangs of unrequited love, and they are of course the creations of a writer who was first and foremost a novelist rather than a dramatist.

So not a lot happens very slowly: Natalya decides, early in the evening, that she is bored of her country life with the faithful if dull husband (Gawn Grainger) and equally bored of her platonic lover (Hurt). Enter, conveniently, a young tutor (Joseph Fiennes, somewhat low in charisma for the role) and exit three hours later virtually all the men in her life, leaving Natalya to reflect ruefully but none too passionately on the problems of loving not deeply but too readily.

Long on languid, romantic boredom, short on the brutal reality of its consequences, *A Month in the Country* allows us to come to terms with Russia in the mid-nineteenth century, or at least the summer-house lives of its ruling classes. In an evening of great performances, any of which would do credit to a subsidised house with a permanent company and twice the rehearsal time that was on offer here, the best of all comes from John Standing as the cynical, self-hating doctor later to be recycled by Chekhov for *The Three Sisters.* Standing has always been a remarkable and under-rated character actor, born out of his stage time, but here his ludicrous, pathetic, opportunist, hopeful Shpigelsky, forever poised on the borderline of tragedy and comedy until he turns his own marriage proposal into a vaudeville routine, is far and away the best supporting performance in town.

Elsewhere we get Polly Adams as the unfortunate object of his affections, and Anna Livia Ryan as the young ward, Vera, whose life is almost casually ruined by Natalya's inability to sort out her own romantic affairs. What Bill Bryden has realised is that this is a company play rather than the star vehicle through which Ingrid Bergman and Michael Redgrave used mournfully to trudge: it is also a bleak and black comedy about people who don't know what they want and don't like it when they get it, and it is the work of a writer who, working in almost constant parenthesis, is happy to go off and explore the life of a minor bystander at just the moment you expect something climactic to happen to his central figure.

As Rakitin, John Hurt turns in a performance of wondrous lethargy and disinvolvement, so that periodically the effort even of speaking seems too much for him; when finally he senses it is time to leave an affair which has never quite managed to become even that, you worry where he'll find the energy to pack. They've all got this one dead right at last.

~

It seems a little early for the Donmar Warehouse to be reviving Jonathan Harvey's *Beautiful Thing,* which had an acclaimed run at the Bush only last August, but I see no reason to alter the verdict I gave you then: this is a sketchy rites-of-passage play about two teenagers growing up on a noisy Thamesmead housing estate to the appalled realisation that they are in fact gay and in love with each other. This does not initially go down too well with a violent father, a chatty mother or the drug-addicted girl next door, but eventually, up on the roof of their tower block, all is resolved in a touching, lyrical 'live and let love' fable which catches the mood of its moment. Hettie Macdonald again directs and in a slightly altered cast the best performance is still that of Mark Letheren.

Johnny One Note

Johnny on a Spot (National)

In six years as director of the National Theatre, Richard Eyre has made very few major repertoire mistakes but *Johnny on a Spot* (Olivier) is certainly one of them. Originally seen for four nights on Broadway in 1942, this is Charles MacArthur's farce about a Southern-state Governor in romantic and financial difficulties running for office on a man-of-the-people ticket; and although the hope may have been for some sort of Whitewater relevance, the truth is that *Johnny* did not close on Broadway so swiftly because of its author-director's alcohol problems in rehearsal, nor yet because Pearl Harbor had just been bombed. It closed because the play itself is a bomb which no amount of frantic stage business can kick into life.

MacArthur without Ben Hecht (with whom he wrote *The Front Page* and other classics) was like Moss Hart without George S Kaufman: only half a playwright, unable to drive his own machine in any meaningful stage direction. The one running gag here is that the candidate has recently died in a brothel, but has to be elected regardless; a group of eccentric larger-than-life misfits are duly assembled as for *The Front Page* but MacArthur alone can never get their fireworks to ignite and the result is about page fourteen, down the column.

There is a wealth of Thirties and Forties Broadway still awaiting rediscovery (sometimes even discovery) over here, from Odets and Behrman through Sherwood and Saroyan to Hellman and Wilder and Philip Barry, which makes it all the more mysterious that Eyre should have turned his considerable talents and a cast of 35 to this dire and derelict farce; *Johnny* just never finds his spot.

Parent Power

Les Parents Terribles (National)
Love's Labour's Lost (Barbican)
The Weekend (Strand)

With its *An Inspector Calls* triumphing both in the West End and on Broadway, it is perhaps not surprising that the National Theatre should have developed a taste for high-camp, director-led revivals of long-lost classics from the 1940s. Thus we now get Cocteau's *Les Parents Terribles* at the Lyttelton, and again we are asked to accept on faith that it would not be enough for a modern audience just to revive the play as written half a century ago. So it now starts behind a cinema screen, with the cast on inadequate radio microphones, and ends (as the current *The Birthday Party* on that same stage) with the set vanishing back into the darkness. Once again we have the designer (in this case Stephen Brimson Lewis working with the artist Ricardo Cinalli) as star, and once again it is the vision of the director, Sean Mathias, rather than the author which is allowed to dominate throughout.

So Cocteau's tight little comedy of incest and appalling relative values becomes a grand-guignol grotesquerie. Sheila Gish and Frances de la Tour camp around as the sisters from hell while Alan Howard peers at them through his mad-inventor goggles and Jude Law and Lynsey Baxter complete the cast as the doomed young lovers.

It is possible that, unlike *An Inspector Calls*, *Les Parents Terribles* is unrevivable as written or originally produced. What is clear, however, is that if you load an always fragile piece with this much director/designer 'concept', it is bound to look overblown and vaguely ludicrous. In an age of director's theatre, however talented, pity the poor playwright now dead and past complaining.

~

Love's Labour's Lost has always been one of those relatively minor Shakespeares much loved of directors wishing to enhance their own reputations rather than those of the author. A thoroughly shaky court romance, it has never really established itself in audience affection, so most spectators remain perfectly happy to have it done under water or in spacesuits according to directorial whim.

Ian Judge, now with an enviable reputation as the man the RSC call in for the 'difficult' comedies, has set this one in and around an Oxford college in about 1912, and the update works a treat. First of all we get the King of Navarre (Owen Teale) and his future Queen of France (Jenny Quayle) leading a team of aristocratic visitors to the dreaming spires; a team which also includes Daniel Massey's superbly manic Don Armado: then we get a home team of eccentric dons and overgrown choirboys (John Normington, Raymond Bowers, Christopher Luscombe).

John Gunter's college settings are enchanting, as are the performances of a cast which seems to be constantly discovering a new period romance and just waiting for Merchant-Ivory to make the movie. Even so, the shadows darken: first the arrival of the messenger with news of a royal death in France and then, infinitely more shockingly, the sudden sound of the guns in Flanders as the men promise to go into sexual hibernation, heartbreakingly unaware that they will be called to die in the trenches before it is over. As the shadows lengthen on the Oxford lawns, something more than love has been lost: even so, Judge manages to end the evening with his ritual musical.

~

Michael Palin's first stage play, *The Weekend* (Strand), turns out rather surprisingly to be *Death of a Salesman* for the Guildford matinee crowd. Richard Wilson, also in a West End debut, recreates his popular television grouch at the head of a somewhat dysfunctional family apparently recollected by its author with a rare mixture of nostalgia and nausea. A desperately thin plot, essentially concerned with little more than the preparation and demolition of a suburban dinner party, flickers briefly to life when father is allowed his Willy Loman speech about the way 'there was once someone alive inside me'. Elsewhere however *The Weekend* comes to a standstill long before Sunday night, with Palin uneasily trapped between Ayckbourn and Bennett in his unsuccessful search for an original voice.

Nicol's Jack

Jack: A Night on the Town (Criterion)

Pericles (National)

Even on the dates when he does bother to show up and play the whole of it, Nicol Williamson's Barrymore solo *Jack: A Night on the Town* (Criterion) turns out to be not so much a night as a rather faltering evening. The idea itself was a great one: Williamson returning to a London theatre where he has been much missed these last fifteen years, and in a stage biography of one of the other great Hamlet hell-raisers of the century.

The trouble, at least as it appeared on the first night, was that nobody had bothered to get anywhere much beyond the idea itself. Although Leslie Megahey is credited as director and (with Williamson) co-author, neither man seems to have done a lot more than trawl through the half-dozen Barrymore biographies for a few old Broadway and Hollywood anecdotes. They haven't even bothered to write an end to the show, so Williamson abruptly departs on the line, 'That's all there is,' giving us no indication of how, where, nor why Barrymore died, or whether this much matters to him or to us.

But it should. Even a cursory glance at Gene Fowler's *Goodnight Sweet Prince*, the best of the biogs, suggests that Barrymore is a classic American tragi-comedy of appalling manners, and one that deserves much better than this. The Hamlet of his generation was a tortured alcoholic, the starriest member of the 'royal family of Broadway' but also a man who could never forget being seduced at fourteen by his stepmother, nor yet the mental-home incarceration of his actor father Maurice. It is a great story, one never yet properly told on stage or screen: merely to use it as a half-built vehicle in which Williamson can warm over his own old Hamlet is a chronic waste of both star and subject. Could nobody involved in this new Criterion management afford the services of a dramatist?

~

A revival of *Pericles*, the least satisfactory of all Shakespeare's plays and indeed the least Shakespearean since there is evidence that whole chunks of it are the work of others, usually means one of two things: Stratford is feeling guilty about having ignored it for a decade or two, or there is some director out there with a reputation to make.

The current revival is at the National, and its director, Phyllida Lloyd, is already reasonably established, so we will have to look elsewhere for the incentive behind this production. It is, I think, that Lloyd wished to see how far she could go, in partnership with a choreographer and a designer, towards taking our minds off the text and distracting us with a selection of rookery nook divertissements, just as though Peter Brook's *A Midsummer Night's Dream* had been rearranged by the Theatre de Complicite.

Thus we get an actress on a pair of stilts giving us a carnival-king Antiochus, while the same actress (Kathryn Hunter, herself a Complicite veteran) later turns up in a breathtaking parody of Barbara Windsor as the bawd of the brothel. References range from the *Carry On* movies all the way to Chinese Opera and Japanese Kabuki, but the most recurrent sight is that of a director desperately signalling across the stage to us that she hasn't the faintest idea what or who this play might be about, but that if we'll just stay in our seats she'll think up something else to divert our attention. Meanwhile, a large cast is left to flounder around the stage, grabbing what they can from the wreckage. The National is at present, on all its stages, dangerously inclined to give star billing to its directors rather than authors and actors: this *Pericles* is typically long on concept, short on actual delivery.

Family Fortunes

Rutherford and Son (National)

King Lear (Barbican)

As I have lately, and in a minority voice, been questioning both the adequacy of the National Theatre's revivalist policy and its passion for director-led extravaganzas often reconstructed at considerable cost to the original text and present casting, I should be the one to shout loudest when the management sticks to its guns but gets them in the right place. On the Cottesloe stage *Rutherford and Son* is a major rediscovery from 1911, and one moreover given a 'concept' production of considerable triumph by Katie Mitchell.

We are in the home of a North Country glassworks' proprietor, in a room cavernous enough to be the factory itself; once upon a time Robert Newton or Wilfrid Lawson would have played him, for we are in the world of *Hobson's Choice* and *Hatter's Castle* and all those domestic drama set around the dark, satanic mills. Our Ibsens they were, the plays that set tyrannical father-figures against pale, hopeless sons, and against daughters just beginning to unfurl the flags of feminism. Here Rutherford either fires or destroys all his own male heirs, and is left at the last to strike a terrible bargain with the only relative who can, or will, stay under his roof and influence: a daughter-in-law who promises him access to the baby grandson who is now his only hope of a dynasty, but only if he will promise not to approach the child for a decade. There is a terrible dramatic and industrial power to Githa Sowerby's writing, though this was the only play with which she made her mark before turning to now-forgotten children's tales. Bob Peck's masterly performance as the brutal, and yet curiously noble, tyrant grinding out lives as his workers grind glass, is wonderfully contrasted with those of Brid Brennan and Phoebe Nicholls as the daughters eking out their lives by inches to the lugubriously deafening sounds of a grandfather clock where there are no grandfathers.

~

The Robert Stephens *King Lear* has come, trailing clouds of his reborn theatrical glory, from Stratford to the Barbican in Adrian Noble's RSC production. Noble, here as in his Kenneth Branagh *Hamlet* and his less successful Derek Jacobi *Macbeth*, is intent on telling the tale. His Shakespeare is not so much the Elizabethan poet as the Victorian novelist, and Noble sets out the story much after the fashion in which 1930s Hollywood directors like George Cukor would tackle the classics, going heavy on the narrative and light on the individual interpretation of character.

Thus Stephens' *Lear* is an endearing old buffer, somewhere between Edward VII and George V perhaps: he strips himself easily of his kingdom and majesty, falls out with his daughters and heads off into the storm, only then to discover he has come somewhat lightly dressed and supported for the inclement weather. This is not, perhaps, a great *Lear* but it is one of the most humane and touching and accessible I have ever seen. Stephens wonderfully suggests a foolish, fond old man: he must be the only actor in the world to have played Falstaff more angrily than he plays Lear.

But around him Noble has assembled a cast all of whom wondrously make you reconsider their characters too: Jenny Quayle is the Regan who can cry even as she punishes her father's vanity; Simon Russell Beale the strange, sinister Edgar; Owen Teale the mad, matinee-idol Edmund apparently in training on the heath for Heathcliff himself; David Bradley a heartbreaking Gloucester. Only when the great globe above the stage weeps sand does Noble get threateningly close to a concept gone wrong. When he leaves it to his superlative character actors to rip up the map of England that forms the stagecloth, this becomes a genuinely gripping yarn.

Down in Tennessee

Sweet Bird of Youth (National)

The Queen And I (Royal Court)

Something is stirring down in old Tennessee (Williams, that is); amazingly we in London have only ever once before been introduced to Alexandra del Largo, the Princess Kosmonopolis who dominates his *Sweet Bird of Youth*. On that occasion, at the Haymarket, she was Lauren Bacall: now, in Richard Eyre's stunning new production for the National, she is Clare Higgins. In the gallery of Williams' great, doomed and ravaged heroines, the Princess has always been a curious mix of Lady Macbeth and the Lady of the Camellias, to which rich mix Miss Higgins adds a fair dash of Cleopatra.

As the local boss's daughter, Emma Amos is rather more Tunbridge Wells than the Gulf Coast in her accent and manner, but Richard Pasco cruelly suggests the massive evil of the old South, while the poisoned treacle of Williams's purple prose has seldom been better poured or more lovingly matured. This is in every sense of the word a truly terrible play, but it has a haunting majesty and aches to be made into a musical. And after the disaster of *Johnny on a Spot*, it comes as a welcome reminder of just how well the National can treat the best of Broadway.

~

Sue Townsend's *The Queen and I* is a staging of her bestseller by Max Stafford-Clark's new Out of Joint company. The story is based on what would happen to the royal family if they were condemned by a new republican government to live in Hell Close, an inner-city housing estate with less than its fair share of modern conveniences.

This was always a painfully thin idea, and feels stretched as a full-length play. Some of the character-sketches work well: both the Queen and the Queen Mother adapt resourcefully to their new surroundings, while Philip takes resentfully to his bed and Charles drifts off to the nearest organic allotment. Princess Diana suffers badly from a lack of local designer boutiques, but Princess Margaret manages to do several deals with the local criminal fraternity.

The other problem is that a small cast are required to play all the royal family and all their neighbours, so most of their energies are taken up with rapid costume and accent changes. Toby Salaman does a wonderful lookalike impression of a hesitant, hang-dog Prince of Wales, but the rest of the cast settle for more thumbnail sketches and are constantly brought up against Townsend's inability to give them anything resembling a plot.

Who Loves You?

She Loves Me (Savoy)

The Tempest (Barbican)

In the history of great Broadway musicals *She Loves Me* (Savoy) has always been something of an oddity: its score by Jerry Bock and Sheldon Harnick dates from 1963, the year before they wrote the infinitely more successful *Fiddler on the Roof* and though it then only achieved brief runs on either side of the Atlantic, it acquired sufficient nostalgia status among lost scores to justify a triumphant New York revival last year.

Its origins are equally unusual: a Hungarian play by Miklos Laszlo which although never seen on Broadway managed to become two Hollywood movies – *The Shop Around the Corner* (James Stewart and Margaret Sullavan, 1940) and *In The Good Old Summertime* (Van Johnson and Judy Garland, 1949). So now we have, at the Savoy, an all-British cast playing an American musical set in 1934 Budapest, and what's more making it work against the odds.

Those odds are high: virtually any song in the show can be taken out, put back in somewhere else or dropped entirely; comparisons of the present score with the 1963 New York and London originals show tremendous changes, though the plot remains virtually intact, such as it is. The central conceit is of two shop assistants (the hugely winning John Gordon Sinclair and Ruthie Henshall, who looks set to become Elaine Paige's only true rival among homegrown West End musical stars), who write love letters to each other anonymously, though what really makes *She Loves Me* work are its many sub-plots. As he was to do still more triumphantly with *Cabaret* three years later, Joe Masteroff has taken almost a dozen characters and given each of them a separate biography as well as a reason to sing about it.

She Loves Me is thus a company show of wondrous lyrical delight: no special effects, no spectacular scenery, just the return to a lost world of style, charm and happy endings.

~

Not often do you get *The Tempest* starring Ariel rather than Prospero, though this is the risk run by Sam Mendes' magical revival newly arrived for the RSC at the Barbican from Stratford. Alec McCowen has rejoined the company after almost thirty years to continue the Robert Stephens/John Wood policy of bringing back the old giants to show the new generation a thing or two about Shakespeare. He offers an oddly muted, schoolmasterly wizard who spends much of his time on the island up a ladder, watching over the rest of the cast from a safe distance.

Simon Russell Beale's Ariel, on the other hand, is everywhere: a portly dictator in a pair of Chairman Mao's pyjamas, he roams the stage in an increasing fury at Prospero's constant delaying tactics to the promise of his freedom. At Stratford last summer he actually spat in his master's eye on the moment of final release, and though he no longer bothers to do that, the rage and the danger are still there. This is no camp fairy, darting about to do Prospero's bidding, but a serious rival for authority who might himself, given luck and a fair wind, have ended up as Duke of Milan.

And Ariel is by no means the only figure drastically reconsidered here: David Bradley's Trinculo has become an end-of-the-pier ventriloquist, forever allowing his dummy to respond to the ills that are heaped upon him, while Mark Lockyer plays Stephano as a refugee from a P G Wodehouse novel.

Even David Troughton's Caliban is a rethink, no longer half-animal but instead a shaven-headed refugee from a Hollywood prison camp, while for the masques a fully-fledged toy theatre descends from the skies. This is, in short, a distinctly quirky production in which every individual idea makes sense but the whole is somehow less than its character parts.

One of its central themes is certainly theatricality: Ariel opens the proceedings by springing out of a skip, and each of the shipwrecked groups arrives like a band of travelling players to explore their new environment. But having abdicated the driving forces of rage and revenge for a kind of melancholy irony, McCowen finds it hard to exert real authority over this band of exiled misfits and the result is a *Tempest* with no real eye of the storm. Its star is still one of the most thoughtful and charismatic of Shakespeareans, an actor who now takes up the mantle of Scofield: but, like Scofield, he rejects the easy routes to stage centre and he has not been helped by Mendes's decision to strand him so far upstage for much of the action. This Prospero is not so much King of the island as its lighthouse-keeper and nightwatchman.

School Play

The Cryptogram (Ambassadors)
Fiddler on the Roof (Palladium)

David Mamet's *The Cryptogram* offers what its title promises: a series of puzzles, one of which is why the producers allowed themselves to be bullied by the Ambassadors Theatre owners into imposing a totally pointless and destructive interval (presumably in the interests of bar profits) twenty minutes into a play which lasts barely another sixty.

The next puzzle is whether or not *The Cryptogram* is autobiographical: an ingenuous programme note suggests the director, Greg Mosher, never bothered to ask, but as the central figure is a small boy in Chicago at about the time Mamet was, the odds would seem strong on memoir. And that is about the best justification for the piece: it is neither a debate like *Oleanna* nor a drama like *Glengarry Glen Ross* but instead a memory piece not unlike Miller's *The Price.*

The boy has a mother (recently deserted by his father) and a gay neighbour: these three make up the entire company, and although there's a fatal lack of dramatic energy, what holds the attention here is the way that everything is seen and heard through the eyes of the boy (Danny Worters or Richard Claxton). He alone still has a handle on the truth, still knows that things not clear now will become clear later if only his hold on the truth can be maintained. The two adults (Eddie Izzard and Lindsay Duncan) have lost that, and are left with the consequences of the lies they have told to keep themselves going.

The Cryptogram is that simple, and that complex: adults deal in bad faith, children will listen. There are haunting fragments here of a boyhood gone horribly wrong, and dreamlike scenes from a family album of despair and distrust. The dark at the top of the stairs is where the boy comes from, and where he returns.

~

In the history of the American musical, certain performances have not only transcended their original settings but also have become the only reason for revisiting them: Topol as Tevye in *Fiddler on the Roof,* Rex Harrison as Higgins in *My Fair Lady*, Carol Channing as Dolly in *Hello Dolly*, Yul Brynner as The King of *The King and I.* Of those, only one started on this side of the Atlantic: Topol as Tevye in *Fiddler on the Roof.*

When he first opened it here he was, amazingly, still in his twenties and straight out of the Israeli army: now, thirty years on, he's about the right age for the role he is again playing at the Palladium and still just wonderful, though the production around him has fallen apart at the seams.

Sara Kestelman is a powerful new Golde, but the rest of the cast and the sets look eerily reminiscent of d'Oyly Carte after about 100 years of low-budget touring: Anatevka is not what it was, though Topol triumphantly still is.

Miller's Crossing

Broken Glass (National)

Lady Windermere's Fan (Albery)

Sometimes I think we don't deserve Arthur Miller, on either side of the Atlantic: in his native America, he gets relegated to short or non-existent Broadway runs while New York occupies itself with yet another ancient musical revival. Over here there are sneers about his 'greatest living dramatist' status: anyone got any other contenders? Attention must be paid, as they said of Willy Loman at his funeral: *Broken Glass*, so far from being the 'bin-end' that my Observer colleague would have you believe, is in fact a breathtakingly brilliant exploration of the paralysis that overtook America in November 1938 as news of the Nazi persecution of the Jews just after Kristallnacht reached their Brooklyn cousins.

Miller has chosen to give this paralysis a living form: a woman (Margot Leicester) suddenly finds that, for no good reason, she cannot move her legs. Her husband (Henry Goodman as a later-life Loman) and her doctor (Ken Stott) eventually understand that the paralysis is sexual and social as well as political and racial: but on the way to that discovery, *Broken Glass* travels through psychiatry, history and geography to give us the analysis of a woman and a world in total moral breakdown.

The eventual cure lies only in death, and not that of the patient: Miller's message here is that forgiveness and understanding are all that we need, though a little love would not come amiss. The waste is of lives in Brooklyn as well as

Berlin, and the destruction is of ourselves by ourselves. In its way, *Broken Glass* is as chilling a play as Miller has ever written; yet unlike Pinter's *A Kind of Alaska*, which it loosely resembles, there is a political heart and soul here. This latest play is a kind of coda to much of Miller's earlier writing: if brings together themes of *After the Fall* and *The American Clock* but sets them for cello rather than full orchestra: once again, his director, David Thacker, has done him proud.

~

Philip Prowse is a director who always designs his own major productions, so for *Lady Windermere's Fan* (Albery) we start with the sets: sumptuous drawing rooms, curtains and carpets so thick that characters seem to be fighting their way through them to us in the audience, and yet perfectly representative of Wilde's already crumbling world, like a greenhouse in decay. This was, just over a century ago, the play that made his name and indirectly led to his downfall: it was also a moral comedy, both socialist and feminist in its own subversive way, and Prowse has rightly seen it as a fable about an aristocracy in anguished ambivalence: Francesca Annis leads a powerhouse cast.

Boy Wonder

The Winslow Boy (Globe)

Henry V (Stratford)

Coriolanus (Stratford)

When I started out as a drama critic in the late 1960s, approval of Terence Rattigan was almost a sacking offence: now that his fortunes have rightly been restored, with a third biography out this year and new stage and screen versions of his *The Browning Version*, it is good to welcome back *The Winslow Boy* as well. This too is the story of a small boy, or rather of the adults around him, and here, as elsewhere, Rattigan took his plot from court records.

First produced a year after the Second World War, but set just before the first one, this is the story about the naval cadet at Osborne falsely accused of stealing a five-shilling postal order. The issue here is the refusal of the Admiralty to bend to common law and have the case properly examined, and Rattigan treats it (as would Galsworthy or Granville-Barker) as a test of England's morality. His somewhat smug conclusion is that a nation which, on the brink of war, can allow its House of Lords to spend an entire day debating the innocence of a naval cadet has got its priorities just about right.

But the characters here are what matter most. Peter Barkworth as the old, ailing father, risking the lives of all the rest of his family to establish the innocence of his youngest; Simon Williams as the icy defence lawyer; Eve Matheson as the suffragette daughter, and Robin Hart and Ian Thompson as her two suitors, all give performances of tremendously clenched dignity. Sometimes the loudest sound in Wyn Jones' pedestrian production is the cracking of stiff upper lips, but though the drama creaks along at a snail's pace, it is still shot through with Rattigan's weary faith in human nature. As so often with this genius, the play is somehow less than its parts.

~

A decade ago Kenneth Branagh first made his name at Stratford as *Henry V*: the RSC is only now returning to the play, and the stars this time around are the director Matthew Warchus and the designer Neil Warmington, both making main-stage debuts. Their idea is simple and dazzling: an Armistice Day *Henry V*, watched over by Tony Britton as a Chorus in a 1914 greatcoat, and set on a field of Remembrance Day poppies which spring to blood-coloured life as the bodies go down into death.

Iain Glen is less than charismatic in the title role (being less than charismatic in title roles would appear to be the main qualification for young actors joining the company this year), but the staging is forever alert, thoughtful and surprising. It goes for neither the jingoism of the warrior-King from Olivier's movie, nor the sullen pacifism of the royal rebel from Branagh's. Instead, Warchus suggests this is far more complex a play, one in which issues of patriotism, cross-Channel politics, kingship, murder and betrayal are variously held up to the light of battle with no easy solutions.

Britton pulls on a massive electric-generator switch to open the show and snaps it off into darkness at the close, thereby suggesting (as of course did the Olivier movie) that we may be all the time in a theatre. But Warmington's sets then open up into dazzling vistas of the vasty fields of France, and as a cast of tremendous energy and versatility clambers over the battlefields of Agincourt, Glen's Henry ages rapidly from rabble-rouser to politician. His eve-of-battle soliloquy 'Upon the King' is rightly where this production comes together and from which it draws its inspiration. Warchus gives equal time to those who, like Pistol and Fluellen, doubt the cause and distrust the King's call to patriotic arms, and in the end this *Henry V*, uncut at nearly four hours, is a memorable national march-past of ideals and compromises, engagements and burials.

~

On the adjoining Swan stage, David Thacker has a new RSC *Coriolanus* courageously set during the French Revolution; next year, presumably, *A Tale of Two Cities* set in Rome around the time of Caesar's assassination. But Thacker is too wary a director to let a gimmick go wrong (remember his Cole Porter *Two Gentlemen of Verona* ?) and this *Coriolanus* makes a certain amount of revolutionary sense, as a populace scrabbles for corn while its leaders try to work out among themselves which one should be allowed to survive. Toby Stephens (son of Robert and Maggie Smith) would have made a better Aufidius than Barry Lynch, but still has some years and experience to go before he is ready for a title role he's been rashly thrown into, rather too early for him, the play or us.

Who's Afraid of Maggie Smith?

Three Tall Women (Wyndham's)

The Merchant of Venice (Barbican)

Edward Albee's *Three Tall Women*, the play that has won him the Pulitzer and this week the London Evening Standard award, tells to some extent the story of his own rejection by a wealthy mother unable to deal with the adoptive child she had signally failed to nurture. But the finest American play of its decade, one which will live in revival long after they have given up trying to preserve the once topical, now already fatally unwieldy *Angels in America*, is about so very much more than personal or familial revenge.

First of all it's about the changing nature of memory: the Three Tall Women are, it transpires during Act Two, just one woman seen at three different moments. As played by Maggie Smith she's a monstrous old dragon getting ready for death by settling her scores with life; as played by Frances de la Tour, she's a middle-aged society hostess wondering what that life might be about; and, as played by Anastasia Hille, she's a debutante already appalled by what the others have told her about the woman she is to become.

When we first meet the trio, the younger two are a lawyer and a secretary come to ease the dowager out of life: but in Anthony Page's brilliantly triangular staging (far better than its off-Broadway original, despite a few shamefully dismissive reviews over here) *Three Tall Women* emerges as a savage indictment of old age and young marriage, as blisteringly brutal as was *Who's Afraid of Virginia Woolf?* but with an icy chill replacing the hot flushes of that earlier dramatic destruct-missile. Smith is predictably just wonderful, Lady Bracknell made over as Martha in a bed-jacket, but Hille and de la Tour also give the best supporting performances in town: you miss them at your peril.

~

The Peter Sellars *The Merchant of Venice*, briefly into the Barbican from the Goodman Theatre in Chicago, is just terrible: living proof of what can come from a director who thinks he matters as much as the playwright, and that it is his mission to make a timeless and ever-topical piece 'mean something' to a contemporary audience. Mr Sellars starts out from the not entirely breathtaking discovery that there is a Venice in California as well as Italy so, hey, let's do the show right there during the recent race riots, let's have a black Shylock because if he's just Jewish I guess it might not show right away, let's have punk rockers and television cameras and just about anything to grab the attention of an MTV audience with an attention span and an intellectual age apparently in the single digits.

Quite apart from the patronising idiocy of all this, it would seem never to have occurred to Sellars or his Chicago team that although the MTV audience is unlikely in the first place to buy tickets to *The Merchant of Venice*, even if it was sung by Madonna to an orchestral setting by Leonard Bernstein, those that do buy tickets are likely to be driven out of the Sellars concept well before intermission. *Othello* is in fact the best Shakespeare for race relations, and for street-fights maybe *Romeo and Juliet*. *The Merchant* is also about many other things undreamt of in Sellars's daft, kiss-me-quick philosophy, and quite why Portia's prenuptial caskets should be turned into coffins is never explained. Like much else here the gimmick is flashy, idiotic, and deeply self-destructive. Sellars' cast stands around a lot looking vaguely unhappy, as well they might: this whole RSC Shakespeare Festival is clearly a plot to make us aware of how much better the home team is than any of the visitors they have chosen.

Wherefore Art Thou?

Romeo und Julia (Barbican)

Coming to the Barbican's Shakespeare Festival is a *Romeo und Julia* from the Schauspeilhaus in Düsseldorf of considerable if bizarre fascination. The first main-stage work of a eighty-year-old director, Karin Beier, who made her name with a German student group which performed Shakespeare in locations ranging from ruined castles to disused garages, this one looks as though its principal influence has been the musical version of *A Clockwork Orange*.

In Düsseldorf ('a city unencumbered by major historical events' says its guidebook enchantingly), this *Romeo* has already caused a certain stir, not least perhaps because the balcony scene is set on trapezes, Juliet is already more than halfway to the madness of Ophelia, Tybalt wears full Nazi costume and the Nurse is a gorgeous young blonde in an evidently lesbian relationship with her charge.

Not to be outdone, Lady Capulet plays the ball scene stuffing a pizza down her face, Mercutio commits suicide on Tybalt's dagger, and Paris is evidently more in love with the mother than the daughter. This is not, then, a *Romeo* for purists: heavily influenced at distinctly different moments by Peter Brook and Michael Bogdanov in unholy alliance, it is clearly designed to grab the eye and the attention of all those who find the original boring or inaccessible.

But a circus presentation which manages to cut about a third of the text and still last three and a half hours tends to run up against its own inconsistencies: on this evidence Beier is hugely inventive but desperately unfocused as a director, veering from an urban-wasteland vision to daft pantomime mugging while her cast frantically tries to keep up the flagging pace.

1995

Prowling Shepard

True West (Donmar Warehouse)

A Passionate Woman (Comedy)

Alice's Adventures Under Ground (National)

A decade after it was first seen over here, Sam Shepard's *True West* comes into the Donmar Warehouse from the West Yorkshire Playhouse in a stunning new production by Matthew Warchus. The story is of two brothers arriving at their mother's Southern Californian home and effectively demolishing it and each other, as they fight out a fraternal battle which is almost biblical in its Cain and Abel intensity. One brother is a smooth Hollywood screenwriter on the make, the other a rough burglar: during two hours they swap roles again and again – and Warchus has had the intelligent notion of having his two leading players take on the two characters for alternate nights.

The performance I witnessed had Mark Rylance as the nervous writer and Michael Rudko as the thuggish drop-out, and Shepard's central joke is of course that in a California where everyone is self-invented anyway, it only takes a couple of conversations for Cain to become Abel. There is a wondrous, raw energy here which even makes much of Mamet look tame by comparison, allied to a brutally funny realisation that the great American frontier dream of self-improvement and self-sufficiency now adds up to little more than the willingness to steal a few electric toasters from complaisant neighbours in the desert.

Marcia Warren as the brothers' bemused mother, and David Henry as a gargantuan Hollywood producer, add cameos of distinction. But this is really a two-man play and as Rylance and Rudko prowl around each other, giving two of the best-contrasted and indeed best performances in town, *True West* seems somehow a much stronger, funnier and more savage play than I recall from its first National outing over here in the early 1980s.

~

At the Comedy, Kay Mellor's *A Passionate Woman* is a fragile maternal and marital fantasy, halfway between Alan Ayckbourn and Alan Bennett, which has been saved from total theatrical superfluity by a breathtaking central performance (Stephanie Cole) and a wonderfully agile production (Ned Sherrin). It is set largely on the roof of a suburban home in Leeds, onto which Cole has clambered in mid-life crisis as her son is about to get married, thereby ending her chief domestic function. Alfred Lynch as a maligned husband, James Gaddas as a ghostly lover and Neil Morrissey as the son, do their best to convince us that this is not just a monologue, but we still haven't really got a play here, just a huge success.

~

Christopher Hampton and Martha Clarke's *Alice's Adventures Under Ground* turns out to be a disappointing trip around Wonderland in which five characters (led by Michael Maloney as a mournful Lewis Carroll) attempt to relate the March Hare to Carroll's hang-ups about photographing pubescent girls. On the Cottesloe stage of the National, it is unlucky to share the NT repertoire with Alan Bennett's rather more confident and competent staging of *The Wind in the Willows*.

Broadway 1995

Passion (Plymouth)

Beauty and the Beast (Palace)

Chauvinism is not enough: sure, the British are still doing well enough on Broadway, with the National Theatre's *Carousel* winning five of this week's Tony Awards, their overblown and overwrought *An Inspector Calls* gaining four, and individual awards to Dame Diana Rigg for *Medea* and Jessica Tandy for longevity – Miss Tandy is indeed so venerable that most people in America have forgotten she's English at all.

But beyond the imports, a far more intriguing battle was being fought for the very soul and survival of Broadway itself. Revivals apart (and that is some distance they accounted for twelve of this year's twenty Tony Awards) the two big musicals in contention were Sondheim's *Passion* and Disney's *Beauty and the Beast*, and this in a year when Broadway took a record 356 million dollars at top ticket prices of $75 each: more money than ever before, but fewer tickets sold than in the middle 1970s.

Passion is a great, dark, brooding and ultimately bloody masterpiece about obsessive love, revenge and regret in a Parma garrison of 1863: as always with Sondheim you take it warts and all, in this case quite literally since two of them disfigure the heroine's features.

Disney's *Beauty and the Beast*, thus advertised presumably to differentiate it from that of the Brothers Grimm who are no longer in touch with their copyright lawyers, is by contrast a super-deluxe 1950s Palladium pantomime complete with breathtaking transformation scenes, peasants gambolling musically on village greens, and a plot that is now more familiar as *The Phantom of the Opera*. It opened to one of the greatest Broadway advances ever, thanks to the movie of the same name, and is currently taking half a million dollars a week at the box-office.

Just next to that box-office you can purchase junior T-Shirts emblazoned 'My first Broadway show' and several hundred dollars' worth of CDs, mugs, baseball hats and other accoutrements: Disney is marketing as only Disney can, the show is essentially on loan from a theme park, and Broadway veterans are treating it as nothing short of a declaration of war on their territory. Hence only one very grudging Tony for costume design: the New York theatre establishment views the coming of Disney much as Disney itself viewed the coming of television in the early 1950s, and their anti-immigration stance would do them proud at Heathrow. *Beauty and the Beast*, one of the greatest Broadway hits ever, has been produced with virtually no help from Broadway itself and almost no New York input: a no-star cast, and a director usually to be found organising the parades at Disneyland.

Passion by contrast earns about a quarter the weekly take of *Beauty*, and without its raft of Tonys might even have had trouble surviving the summer. During a notoriously difficult preview period, even by Sondheim standards, one Broadway observer was heard to inquire 'How much better can it get? The heroine still has warts'; yet this remains one of his greatest and most impassioned scores, not of course immediately hummable yet haunting and virtually through-sung by its central trio, Donna Murphy, Jere Shea and Marin Mazzie. We urgently need *Passion* over here, preferably at the Warehouse and this side of Christmas.

Ludicrously, since they are designed to plug Broadway on television rather than reward New York theatrical excellence, the Tonys could take no account of the best new American play in more than a decade. Off-Broadway at the Promenade is Edward Albee's *Three Tall Women*. Taken together with Arthur Miller's new *Broken Glass*, due at the National this autumn, it proves not only that there are second acts in American lives but also that these two still write the very best of them.

Cowardly Shambles

Design for Living (Gielgud)

John Osborne sometimes threatens the formation of a Playwrights' Mafia, one which would roam the streets at night, fully armed, picking off random critics who had in some way displeased them. I find myself more and more inclined to form a similar organisation on behalf of deceased playwrights: we would wander around disposing of young directors who have decided to make reputations at the expense and in often blatant disregard of those they have been hired to stage.

We have a likely target in Sean Mathias, a talented director oddly obsessed with dirty laundry, much of which was strewn around the stage of his recent *Les Parents Terribles* at the National, and a good deal more of which can now be found littering his *Design For Living*. Whether or not something very nasty once happened to Mr Mathias in a laundrette is unclear: what I do know is that a classic Coward comedy of appalling manners is about a great deal more than can be encompassed within this obsessively sexual but oddly limited reading of the play.

Moving from the Warehouse to the Gielgud, Sean Mathias' *Design For Living* (for it is now rather more his than Coward's) is, like Stephen Daldry's *An Inspector Calls*, the work of a director with apparently precious little faith in the original play and still less in the ability or willingness of an audience to appreciate it. The few liberties taken in the Warehouse staging have now, with a largely new cast, expanded exponentially to the point where in Act Three we get poor vaudeville parodies of the author and, for no textual reason, a female party guest kissing Gilda on the lips.

This is radical gay chic gone raving mad, a desperate designer-concept deconstruction of a once great play in the name of novelty; it is a glossy, magazine-cover event, high on shock value but low on actual content or thought; fashionable without always being fathomable, and functional only if you neither know nor care for the play as written.

The pity of it all is that less intrusive or flashy directors, from Alan Strachan to Michael Blakemore, have frequently and recently shown how to decode Coward and bring him into the freewheeling Nineties without drowning him in self-serving directorial gimmickry. *Design For Living* has always been a study in intensive bisexuality and has frequently and openly been staged as such these last ten years: there is nothing new or revolutionary in bringing it once again out of the closet, but in focusing on the sexuality of the play to the exclusion of all else, Mathias has lost most of what it also has to say about fame and power and love and talent and travel. It is like seeing an old lady relentlessly helped across a road she had no intention of crossing, and although Rachel Weisz is still mesmeric, the posey, posturing performances of Marcus d'Amico and Rupert Graves are disgraceful. If you're a dramatist wanting to keep your work intact, just don't die.

Best Deal in Town

Dealer's Choice (National)

Patrick Marber's *Dealer's Choice* (Cottesloe) is the best first play I can ever recall the National Theatre staging, though there have not been too many and their judgment has always been a little shaky in that area. But this one is an outright winner for Marber as author and director, and if we get a better new play from anywhere in the next few months we'll have had a vintage year.

Like David Mamet, to whom he owes a certain debt, Marber has realised that it's all in the cards: take a small, intense, manic group of colleagues and watch them chance their arms, because somewhere in those poker hands is the key to their lives, their careers, their sexuality, their hopes, their marriages and maybe even their deaths. This is a quickfire, gripping, hilarious and ultimately almost tragic account of what it means to play poker as a way of life. Marber's players are the posh owner of a London restaurant (Nicholas Day) and the staff with whom he has a regular Sunday-night session: among them is Mugsy, a waiter with a dream of setting up his own restaurant in a disused toilet down the Mile End Road, and a quartet of others whose motives, though less immediately giggly, are often no less strange or compelling to their dreamers.

'Has there been much death in his family?' one asks solicitously of a departed colleague, but in truth the outside world holds no reality: it all has to happen around the table, even the son discovering and then rejecting his own father's long-suppressed compulsion to gamble. The energy of Marber's production, set on a slow revolve so that we get to see what each of the players is holding in the game of their lives, and the short-circuit speed and brilliance of the playing, make the rules of the game irrelevant: you didn't have to be an estate agent to appreciate *Glengarry Glen Ross*.

Send Out the Clowns

A Little Night Music (National)

'Whipped cream with knives' was how its first director, Hal Prince, referred to *A Little Night Music,* and the new production by Sean Mathias at the Olivier carefully gives equal emphasis to the cholesterol and the cutting edge. Let's get the objections out of the way first: this particular Sondheim has been seen twice in the West End since it first opened in 1973 and (after *Sweeney Todd* and *Sunday in the Park*) it is the third Sondheim to have formed a part of the National's musicals programme in recent years, leaving *Carousel* as the only other. It might therefore have been better to try something a little less familiar this time round, or at least to put an opera-house piece under the proscenium arch of the Lyttelton rather than allow it to float around, and sometimes off, the vast open spaces of the Olivier, looking occasionally like a huge untethered meringue.

But we're unlikely ever to get a better cast, at least on the female side: Judi Dench sending in the clowns, Sian Phillips recalling her liaisons and Patricia Hodge as the increasingly unbalanced Countess are all definitive, leaving their menfolk (Lawrence Guittard and Lambert Wilson) struggling to keep up. But this is always the show stolen at the final curtain by the maid who sings of marrying the miller's son, and here too Issy van Randwyck fulfils all hopes. Mathias has come up with a commendably ungimmicky revival which mercifully does not seek to impose any point of view, other than that of Ingmar Bergman's original house-party of ill-assorted romantic losers, all drawn from the film which gave this characteristically subversive Sondheim score its inspiration.

But could the National just possibly now give us a musical that we can't sing in its entirety on the way in to the theatre?

Cold War Cold Drama

Cell Mates (Albery)

The spies who came in from the Cold War may now have had their time-codes ruined by the conditional thaw in East/West affairs of state, but they remain of peculiar fascination to British dramatists. Burgess and Blunt found their Alan Bennett, while Julian Mitchell also had a crack at the young Burgess, and Hugh Whitemore went for the Portland couple and Alan Turing of Enigma variations. Now we get Simon Gray on George Blake: *Cell Mates* (at the Albery) is a bleak comedy about his odd-couple partnership with Sean Bourke, the petty Irish safebreaker who alone sprang him from Wormwood Scrubs with a van and a rope-ladder when the KGB failed to bother, and who was for his pains condemned to live with Blake in a Moscow flat.

So far, so promising: but not a lot else happened. Blake betrayed Bourke, as he had always betrayed everyone, in an attempt to keep him in Russia and at his table. But whether this was motivated by a suppressed gay love, or sheer bloody-mindedness, or the conviction that Bourke would be better off in Moscow than Dublin is never really explored or explained. Nor does Blake, who was half-Dutch and half-Egyptian, fit into any of the usual local frames of Cambridge homosexual-intellectual despair, as a result of which nobody bothers to tell us what made him a spy in the first place.

Stephen Fry, in this role, magnificently conveys, in his usual manner, a man so semi-detached as to be unhinged, while Rik Mayall as his bouncy Irish stooge completes the partnership. But, like the play, it never comes together into a coherent study of espionage, or even the etiquette of KGB flat-sharing manners. Their story must be in there somewhere, but it never quite surfaces through this Gray matter, while the playwright's own production is fatally unenergetic.

Attention Must Be Paid

A View From The Bridge (Strand)

Twelfth Night (Barbican)

Though David Thacker's new production (into the Strand from the Bristol Old Vic) is uncharacteristically creaky around the edges, there can have been few greater plays this century than *A View From The Bridge*. While Arthur Miller's native Broadway continues to turn its commercial back on him and is deservedly dying of its own intellectual and dramatic carelessness, London and Thacker have kept him in constant revival as well as finding a home for all of his new work.

This one dates from exactly forty years ago: like Kazan's *On The Waterfront*, which it in so many ways parallels, it is set under the huge, dominant skyline of Brooklyn Bridge and is an immigrant drama framed within the confines of Greek tragedy. Eddie Carbone, powerfully played by Bernard Hill, is the bullish, self-destructive longshoreman unwittingly in love with his own niece: when that love is first revealed and then threatened by the arrival of a Sicilian 'submarine' who has to be kept in hiding while making an illegal living on the docks, Eddie betrays him to the authorities and, in a *High Noon* duel, brings down on himself the full devastation of a moral code he has never fully accepted or even understood.

Eddie goes out like a maimed lion, leaving only the wreckage of a family and a waterfront community that could deal with the Depression and the Immigration but not the Incest. *A View From The Bridge* is about the clash between morality and law, a code of honour and a way of life, but in the end it's only about Eddie. 'I mourn him,' says the play's lawyer-narrator 'but with a certain alarm, because he allowed himself to be wholly known.' This is a mythic and epic play, only now for the first time beginning to show its age.

~

Opening the new Barbican season of last summer's Stratford hits, Ian Judge's *Twelfth Night* is a characteristically show-busy celebration of the play and the town where it was theoretically conceived, so that Illyria is now a district of Warwickshire complete with half-timbered houses; by the end of an enchanted evening one half-expects Orsino to be guiding tourists around Anne Hathaway's cottage.

You always feel Judge wishes Shakespeare had written his comedies as musicals: as a director he is the logical outcome of the RSC process that started twenty years ago, just before *Cats*, when Trevor Nunn used to have Gillian Lynne as his *Comedy of Errors* choreographer for spectacular curtain-calls. But he is also a master caster: Emma Fielding's elfin Peter Pan of a Viola, Desmond Barritt's vast Toad of a Malvolio, Tony Britton's military Belch, Derek Griffiths' burlesque Feste are all performances of careful distinction and insight: nothing here is too familiar, and with *Twelfth Night* that is a considerable achievement.

Away With The Fairies

Under Milk Wood (National)

It is evening in the concrete-bunkered, critic-infested, actor-shouting, scenery-dropping Olivier Theatre. Behold: the backward-spelt village of Llareggub, *Under Milk Wood*, home of all the Dylan Thomas hyphens and their Welsh relatives, all the Nogood Boyos of his drunken-poet, BBC radio, Richard Burton imagination brought to the open stage by Roger Michell in a bedstead-dropping, mouth-gaping, no-expense-spared spectacular which only suggests a wireless, plotless shambles peopled by such legendary characters as Captain Cat having nowhere very much to go but backwards into his memories. Like Wales itself on a wet winter Sunday, look you, and however much money you throw into the wood, somebody still has to find a path through it for actors and audiences: voices are for the airwaves. Listen.

Into the Sunset

Sunset Boulevard (Minskoff, Broadway and Adelphi)

Show Boat (Gershwin, Broadway)

Love! Valour! Compassion! (Manhattan Theatre Club)

The Libertine / The Man of Mode (Royal Court)

So who would ever have thought it? Of the four stars who have tottered down *Sunset Boulevard* as Norma Desmond since it first opened eighteen months ago, far and away the best is the least likely casting. The first, Patti LuPone, played her as a manic diva somewhere halfway from Maria Callas to Gracie Fields on speed; the second, Glenn Close (now to be seen as Norma on Broadway) is perfectly adequate in the role but faintly uncharismatic, as if awaiting the movie version; the third, Betty Buckley (now back at the Adelphi) is hugely efficient. It was only the fourth Norma, our own Elaine Paige (playing the role over Christmas and likely I trust to return to it in the summer) who caught the warmth, the humour and the sheer humanity of the woman. Only with Paige did I feel an audience truly warm to the show, care about its outcome and want her to survive the vagaries of Hollywood fashion and the predatory demands of young screenwriters on the make.

True, the Broadway version is much stronger in its other casting, notably George Hearn as the butler/husband, but it is Paige who has brought the show to its full life, and at the end of a year which she began equally stunningly as Edith Piaf: those of us inclined to balk a bit when her own management ritually bills her as 'the first lady of the British musical' had better start getting used to it: she now is.

~

Elsewhere in a quiet Broadway winter, Hal Prince has directed a new *Show Boat* as though it were *Porgy and Bess*, which makes it both too dark and so top-heavy that it has trouble staying afloat despite the first lady of Broadway (another Elaine, Stritch) as a feisty Parthy and some wondrous sets.

~

Terrence McNally's *Love! Valour! Compassion!* (now transferring to Broadway from the Manhattan Theatre Club) takes more than three hours to say about eight gay men sharing an address roughly what Kevin Elyot's *My Night With Reg* manages to say in less than two, but is wonderfully played and deserves a London life ideally somewhere like Hampstead.

~

One play is just a play: two are an event. The recent history of English-speaking drama, from *Nicholas Nickelby* across fifteen years to *Angels in America*, suggests that audiences like going for the double attraction, especially if the joins are inventive.

For the Royal Court and now his new Out of Joint touring company, the director Max Stafford-Clark has already given us the double of Timberlake Wertenbaker's *Our Country's Good* and the play it is about, *The Recruiting Officer*. Now, in a similarly inspired pairing at the Court, we get George Etherege's *The Man of Mode* and a new play by Stephen Jeffreys about Etherege and more particularly his real-life central character in that play, Charles II's friend and confidant the Earl of Rochester.

As portrayed originally by Etherege in 1676, Rochester was a likeable kind of rogue and rake who had a way with the ladies but remained oddly unpopular with audiences, which explains why the play was largely neglected for about 200 years. As portrayed by Jeffreys now, he is the Libertine: a far more complex and even sinister character, positively eager to inspire audience loathing but always aware that nobody can ever hate himself as much as he does. David Westhead, doubling the leads in both plays, offers a stunning and scabrous libertine: he haunts *The Man of Mode*, lurking backstage while it is first performed to remind the cast that life just isn't like that, rather as though the real Macbeth were to be found wandering around the theatre explaining how little Shakespeare understood what it really felt like to be a murderous King of Scotland in difficult times.

When it comes to the real thing, Etherege's dark Restoration romp, Stafford-Clark's team seems less entirely sure of itself: having given us Jeffreys's gloss on the piece, they are uneasy with its original style. Nevertheless, this is a fascinating insight into the process of period play-making, and the second that Stafford-Clark has given us.

The real Rochester, as exhumed by Jeffreys, was the most dangerous of Charles II's allies and friends: a Royalist who was at the same time radically anti-Monarchist and deeply subversive, an atheist who finished up a born-again Christian, and a lyric poet who traded in pornography, he was a vastly more complex character than Etherege was prepared to write, and Jeffreys has hilariously managed to lift him away from his period, so that we end up with a character out of an early John Osborne tirade, rampaging through the periwigs of an altogether other age and tradition.

Great Gambon

Skylight (National)

The Plough and the Stars (Garrick)

The widely held view of David Hare, for my money unquestionably our greatest topical dramatist, is that he writes public and private plays: in the first category, the studies of journalism and church and state that run from *Pravda* through *Racing Demon* to *The Absence of War*, and in the second such ostensibly domestic scripts as *The Secret Rapture* and now (at the Cottesloe) *Skylight*.

Yet the anomaly here is that it is very often in the private plays that you get the best public statements: way back in 1975, *Knuckle* gave us a Guildford already borderline criminal, and one of the sisters in *Secret Rapture* demolishes Thatcherism far more effectively than any of the official politicians in *Absence of War*. So what we have here, in *Skylight*, is a soaring romantic tragedy which also manages, almost in passing, to nail what has gone wrong with Britain in the Nineties and then to make us love at least one of the guilty parties rather more, in my case, than his apparent conscience.

The plot need not detain us long: to a seedy flat somewhere off the North Circular, so damp that its indoor fog means you can't even tell whether the one-bar electric fire is on or off, comes a distraught young student whose father has sunk into cranky depression at the death of his wife after a long and painful cancer. The reason their son has come is because the thirty-something occupant of the flat, a dedicated slum-schoolteacher, once lived in their family, once indeed had an affair with the father.

What the boy wants is some sort of reconciliation, and hot on his heels comes the father, also in search of something: Hare's talent is also for suspense, so it takes us most of the rest of the evening to work out just what that is. A quick return to sex, certainly, but also forgiveness for his sins, and even an apology for the manner in which the girl left him.

But the sorrow and the pity, the end of the affair, the betrayals and the compromises, are only one aspect of the view through *Skylight*, underlying an uneasy, brief re-encounter is a whole moral debate as to whether it is better to love people as she does, in buses and classrooms and principle, or to love one woman as he does, and let the rest of the world go to hell in its own handbaskets.

This is not the English *Oleanna*: sides are not taken, the man is by no means a villain, and the girl is by no other means a heroine: only at the last does Hare begin to cop out, and on a very simple plot issue. The man, it transpires, has deliberately left her love letters for his wife to find: for this he is branded a destructive egotist who could not let the affair survive on its own terms. The idea that he was so wracked by guilt that he wanted the wife to divorce him, and had in the end to hand her the evidence, is never considered, although I have to admit that it is precisely what I did at the end of my first marriage. But to write that would be to give him the end of the play, and Hare wants it reserved for the girl and a Chekhovian breakfast scene of new beginnings.

Yet this is not a fatal flaw, and so stunning is the performance of Michael Gambon as a man who can see no crime in working hard and living well, who believes memorably that 'listening is halfway to begging', and who does not think he was put among mankind in order to save anyone but himself and those he most loves, that *Skylight* would be unmissable were it a solo show. It is not. Lia Williams as Kyra matches him scene for scene, speech for speech, and when she finally lights up with love, or at least the recollection of how she wrote of it, a priggish and smugly self-appointed angel of mercy suddenly becomes the most romantic and enchanting of creatures. Brilliantly directed by Richard Eyre, *Skylight* is far and away the best play in town.

~

To the Garrick after a long regional tour comes Joe Dowling's all-Irish revival of *The Plough and the Stars*. Dowling, about to take over the Guthrie Theatre in Minneapolis, has a distinguished track record in O'Casey and this production brilliantly reminds us of the play's roots in Shakespeare, that feeling of the tavern as focus for debate and brawl, with Eamon Morrisey as the Fluther-Falstaff figure, there to underline the ironies of good men dying for bad causes.

True, this is O'Casey in resignation rather than rebellion, wearily counting the injured and the dead and wondering whether any of it has been worth the candle, let alone the national honour: but a vintage cast, precisely the one the Abbey has been lacking this past half-century since John Ford took the best of them off to Hollywood, does the debate justice and then some.

Squeak and Bubble

Pippin (Bloomsbury)

Spring Awakening (Barbican)

Certain Broadway musicals have, on this side of the Atlantic, always been more honoured in the breach than in the observance. Sondheim's *Anyone Can Whistle* (never seen in London), Herman's *Mack and Mabel* (about to open this autumn for the first time, some twenty-one years after it was first seen in New York), and Stephen Schwartz's *Pippin* (now in the National Youth Theatre revival at the Bloomsbury) have always attracted more backstage anecdotes and original-cast-recording addicts than actual audiences. And in the case of *Pippin* it is not hard to see why.

The score has one of the best opening numbers ('Magic To Do') in the history of the American theatre: it also comes from the composer of *Godspell*, and has the same kind of maddening optimism. You feel that the only other possible author would have been Lord Baden-Powell. And yet we are talking here of a show which ran to 2,000 Broadway performances back in the mid-1970s, won five Tony awards and launched the careers of, among others, Jill Clayburgh, Ben Vereen and Betty Buckley.

But in 1973 the London premiere survived barely six weeks despite a cast headed by Patricia Hodge and Elisabeth Welch; by then we'd already had Tony Newley stopping the world and wanting to get off. And *Pippin* is also a carnival show about personal identity, albeit rather more ambitious. We are in the era of Charlemagne, and it is his title-character son who rejects world dominance in favour of the simple life on the farm, rather as though Hitler had gone into a tour of *Oklahoma!*

In truth, all this show ever really had was Bob Fosse, the most inventive and remarkable choreographer in showbiz history; without his presence in the rehearsal room, *Pippin* will never make sense again.

~

In the repertoire of the Barbican Pit, Tim Supple's new production of Wedekind's *Spring Awakening* is a masterpiece of intelligent rediscovery. Ted Hughes's new version gets us away from the dustiness of the original, and by using schoolchildren of the right ages Supple wonderfully illustrates the tragedy of parental incomprehension and prejudice without ever resorting to caricature or pre-judgement. What is so good, and so terrible, about this staging is that it all makes perfect sense, right down to the suicide rate in German boys' boarding schools in the 1880s of the play's first production.

Krays for You

Gangster No. 1 (Almeida)

The Steward of Christendom (Royal Court)

In a remarkably rich time for new writing and star performances, *Gangster No. 1* at the Almeida is something rather more than North London Tarantino. True, it echoes a fashionable concern with the underworld of violent crime, which for British dramatists seems inextricably linked to a nostalgia for the 1960s: *Krays R Us* could be the overall title for a whole season of recent plays and movies over here.

But Louis Mellis and David Scinto have come up with an immensely powerful morality tale of crime and corruption, sudden death and slow salvation. Jonathan Kent's brilliantly spare production on a skeletal set spotlights, in B-movie fashion, five archetypes of the genre: two master-crooks, a bent copper, a squealer and a good-time gangster's moll, all of whom tell us their stories in isolation, coming together only when the stories merge into one.

The performance of the evening, and of his career, is Peter Bowles as the smooth and sinister killer who degenerates before our eyes into a world-hating, self-hating wreck, the Archie Rice of Soho whose violence finally implodes at the point where there is nothing left to destroy but himself. There are other great performances here too: Richard Johnson as the rival thug, finding an amazing redemption through prison and then in the arms of Sharon Duce as the club dancer; Kenneth Colley as the wearily corrupt cop and John Cater as the squealer have all understood the writer's curious mix of love and loathing for London at its most fashionably violent.

Gangster No. 1 does not romanticise violence: but it does go some way towards explaining its hugely theatrical appeal: if you can imagine Osborne's *The Entertainer* soaked in blood rather than bathos, that is what is on offer here.

~

At the Royal Court, *The Steward of Christendom* is Thomas Dunne, last head of the Dublin Metropolitan Police before it was disbanded in 1922. No Catholic had ever risen higher working for the English in Ireland, and few ever paid a higher price; by the time we meet Dunne a decade later, he is a mad old man living out his time in a mental home, tortured by memories of his own and his nation's past.

Sebastian Barry, writing the fifth in a series of plays about his own ancestors, clearly sees a lot of Lear in his grandfather; the man has three daughters, is driven over the edge by a mix of ingratitude and sudden self-awareness, and yet yearns for a time when he still had the right to wear a uniform and call the shots – or rather call them off, since Dunne was nothing if not a peacemaker. But Barry is not only concerned with the Shakespearean parallels: Dunne also had a son, killed in the first war, who comes back to visit him as the child that he too once was. This is a complex time play about memory and madness, about national identity and personal betrayal; but it is shot through with a love and lyricism which genuinely and uniquely allows us to salute Barry as a new O'Casey; for he too has found the key that links the Irish wars to the homes in which they were often fought.

In Max Stafford-Clark's tense production for Out of Joint, Donal McCann in grimy long-john pyjamas roams the stage ransacking his faulty mind and memory for clues as to how it has all gone so wrong; Ireland, his family, his career, his life, all torn apart by civil wars and an uncivil peace. There is still a terrible topicality here, as well as a timeless tragedy.

Block's Boys

Not A Game For Boys (Royal Court)

More by accident than design, the National Theatre studio for young dramatists has happened upon a rich new seam of playwriting: first we had Patrick Marber's *Dealer's Choice*, successfully transferred to the Cottesloe and now the West End, and it is followed by Simon Block's *Not A Game For Boys*. Both are by first-time dramatists, both have all-male casts and both are about a game being played for the dreams, hopes and even lives of the players.

In *Dealer's Choice* that game is poker; in *Not A Game For Boys* it is table-tennis. Three cab drivers are gathered for the tournament that will either leave them, just, in the premier league or relegate them to the indignity of the second; but as in *Dealer's Choice* there is a great deal more at stake. Peter Wight's dour Oscar is just back from a funeral at which he has seen one of his fellow players prematurely laid out. Intimations of mortality are crowding in as he decides to leave the game and settle for something more restfully senile, possibly bowls. Christopher Fairbank's Eric still dreams of leading his trio to victory, however, if only as an escape from the awfulness of a marriage to which we are only introduced via a series of increasingly unhappy phone calls home.

And then there's Neil Stuke's Tony, third member of the team and the one who really doesn't give a damn for any of it. Richard Georgeson's studio production wonderfully isolates each of these men in their own breakdowns, bringing them together only when the tournament, never seen, is going well enough or badly enough to demand attention for its own sake. We have of course been through this game of life before: it is not unknown to David Mamet. But *Not A Game For Boys* is lethally good.

Dying for a Laugh

Dead Funny (Savoy)

Peer Gynt (Barbican)

Suitably enough it was the producers of *The Rocky Horror Show*, creators of the notorious 'Time-Warp', who have pioneered what is now an increasingly popular West End fashion. That show never officially opens or closes, it just hovers like a spaceship above Shaftesbury Avenue, alighting whenever it spies an empty theatre and staying there until something better comes along. In an increasingly shaky West End economy, other producers now seem to have seen the merits of instant revival: the two biggest hits of 1994, *Three Tall Women* and *Dead Funny*, are back with revised casts; it must be reckoned that there are still more people wishing to see them than risk buying tickets to anything that might have happened since.

Dead Funny, now at the Savoy, is still directed by its author Terry Johnson, the man who brought Dali and Freud together for *Hysteria* and who engineered the meeting of Marilyn, Einstein and Senator McCarthy for *Insignificance*. That Johnson is the most agile comic manipulator of his generation is beyond doubt – he is Ray Cooney with a triple first in history, psychology and politics. Here his concern is the weekend of 1992 when both Benny Hill and Frankie Howerd were found dead in their flats, and for the Dead Comics Society, of which most of his cast are members, this is a rare opportunity for mourning and mimicry.

One member is a doctor specialising in hysterectomies but unable to touch his own wife, another is a mother-obsessed gay, and two others are sexually challenged neighbours with one of whom the doctor has had an unwise affair. All the makings of French farce and English domestic tragedy are here, as Belinda Lang and Kevin McNally lead a new team in this bitterly brilliant analysis of people who will die for a laugh but cannot live for a relationship.

~

When John Barton's *Peer Gynt* first opened at Stratford last year it was in the immediate wake of Ninagawa's vastly misconceived epic at the Barbican, and was therefore chiefly applauded for its still, small, soft focus. What is clear now, as the production has a brief London run in the Pit, is that it is also a work of stunning poetry. The translator is one of our greatest living playwrights, Christopher Fry, himself shamefully ignored by both the RSC and the National of late, and what he has achieved here is the reduction of Peer to his minimalist essentials.

A cast of less than a dozen double and redouble the other figures in Peer's life (so that Haydn Gwynne is both his mother Aase and his wife Solveig) but Fry's Peer is essentially the Playboy of the Northern Isles, an ever-youthful Alex Jennings making it clear that all his travels are essentially taking place inside his head.

This is the chamber version of one of the greatest plays ever written, one like *Hamlet* that defies the definitive. What we are missing this time is a real sense of drama, since Fry goes resolutely for the Celtic twilight; but we learn far more of the inner nature of Peer as he goes round and about and on to the next crossroads for his final meeting with the Button Moulder.

Not only has Barton discovered an unknown additional scene for Peer and Solveig and her father from the original manuscript, he has also (with this Fry version) re-established the huge folk-poem that was Ibsen's original intent.

Alex Jennings plays Peer as an ageless Irish peasant, refusing even in the central acts to age or costume him to suit the scenery: this is a spare, spartan but hugely haunting evening.

Ackland Fit For Heroes

The Maitlands (Orange Tree)
Rat in the Skull (Duke of York's)
The Master Builder (Haymarket)

Anybody who cares, no matter how remotely, about the British theatre of the 1930s owes a tremendous debt of gratitude to Sam Walters out at the Orange Tree in Richmond. At such better-endowed addresses as the National, revivals from this period generally depend on the whims of a currently hot director or player, and are then usually subjected to that director's 'vision' of what the play can be made to say to a 'modern audience'.

Walters does things mercifully differently: he discovers plays that work for an entire and often largely unknown cast, and then directs them as they would have been done at the time, without the ghastly, trendy overload of a '90s perspective'. First he gave us, long before the BBC or the National, the rebirth of Rodney Ackland: now, in *The Maitlands*, he gives us Ackland's no less important or intriguing contemporary Ronald Mackenzie. Here was a dramatist, killed in a car crash just before his thirtieth birthday in 1933, author of only two titles: this one and *Musical Chairs*, both of which originally considerably enhanced the career of John Gielgud.

Like Ackland, Mackenzie was an English Chekhov. In *The Maitlands* he deliberately portrays the drunken professor, bungled suicide, lovelorn old man, hopeless youth, yearning young woman and the old housekeeper, but translates them to an English seaside village. This hugely influential script, neglected for sixty years, is the bridge from Chekhov to Rattigan: it's about people unable to live apart or together, destroying each other out of love and loneliness in a country run by 'men with the souls of cuttlefish'; in short, a masterpiece of national and personal self-hatred, brilliantly staged and played.

~

To open a season of Royal Court Classics at the Duke of York's, one might have expected a play with a particular debt to that theatre, or one centrally associated with the history of it. In fact, Ron Hutchinson's *Rat in the Skull* would always have worked just about anywhere and perhaps best of all on television. It's a taut, tense four-character power play set in a London police station at the height of the Irish bombings a decade ago, and it seems at first deliberately perverse of the director Stephen Daldry to have ripped out the stalls of the theatre and put up a set (designed by William Dudley) reminiscent of the sound stage of a Spencer Tracy prison movie from the 1930s.

And sure enough, for the early scenes, that set is the star: but gradually Rufus Sewell (as the suspect bomber Roche) and Tony Doyle (as the specialist investigator from the Royal Ulster Constabulary) come together as the two faces of Ireland, locked into a ritual and tribal war of territory and attrition going back not just decades but centuries. Hutchinson's genius here has been to write a police thriller and a history of the Irish troubles that plays for less than two hours: 'we are about to land in Belfast, please set your watches back three hundred years', as the play's best joke neatly has it.

Daldry's determination to make what was once an intimate confrontation into an epic event sometimes backfires, as our attention starts to wander to the gantries and flashing lights that surround the set. But such is the dangerous power of Sewell and Doyle, joined at the hip by Ireland's psychic death-wish as the two British coppers watch them with a characteristic weary cynicism, that the focus always returns to the centre of this nation-baring bearpit.

~

At the Theatre Royal Haymarket, Peter Hall's revival of *The Master Builder* is a curious disappointment: true, it gives us a powerful star turn from the newcomer Victoria Hamilton as the destructive, charismatic Hilde Wangel, but in the title role Alan Bates seems somehow absent, as though (like his director) he had decided that this might be a good play to do but then in rehearsal couldn't for the life of him remember why.

Pottering About

Son of Man (Barbican)
The Way of the World (National)

Death, as Gore Vidal once observed of Tennessee Williams, as well as many others, can often be a wise career move for a playwright; and sure enough this year, the Royal Shakespeare Company, having never paid too much attention in their lifetimes, have decided we should have another look at John Osborne and Dennis Potter.

Dennis Potter originally wrote his *Son of Man* for television in 1969, when it caused a considerable if now largely incomprehensible furore for daring to portray Christ as a more or less ordinary bloke caught up in an unfathomable mystery, though writers like Dorothy L Sayers had in fact been suggesting as much for decades, albeit not in front of millions of viewers.

Now the RSC gives the script to Bill Bryden, a charismatic stage manager far too long away from us in Scots television, but who made his name soon after this play was written with a series of epic Mystery cycles in the Cottesloe. True to his own pop-theatre traditions and to Potter, Bryden duly imports songs and has the audience join in the crowd scenes: sure, there's imminent danger of *Godspell* here, but a strong cast led by Joseph Fiennes as Christ and John Standing as a weary, elegantly confused Pontius Pilate consistently avoids it.

With his sure grasp of group playing and character acting, Bryden reminds us of what our subsidised stages have for too long been neglecting: the power of sheer, unashamed theatricality as, in this case, a way of expressing Potter's eternally simple belief in the strength of love over law.

~

At the National, Phyllida Lloyd's *The Way of the World* (which I saw at its last preview) is a considerable joy despite the fact that it seems to require a fashion consultant rather than a theatre critic. Characters are gorgeously costumed in an eccentric mix of ancient and modern, each entrance getting more confidently grotesque until Geraldine McEwan (in the performance of the night and her career) comes on looking like an ostrich which has mysteriously been crammed into a tambourine lined with fresh flowers.

She also seems to be running a remarkably myopic household, since her entire staff comes on wearing spectacles; little house jokes like these make one (for a while) suspect that the director has lost confidence in her author, but thanks to the highly intelligent, thoughtful Millamant and Mirabell of Fiona Shaw and Roger Allam, Congreve eventually wins through. A play once perceived and played as a kind of Restoration romp now emerges as something at once funnier and darker; against the increasingly frantic farce of Wishfort, we get the other two principals trying to set out a whole new (and for its time dangerously revolutionary) pattern of marriage and peaceful sexual co-existence.

The perennial modernity of *The Way of the World* may not need all the help that Lloyd and her designer Anthony Ward have given it, with their background of London's trendiest art galleries and the notion of Wishfort ending up as a bag lady locked out of her own front door. But in here somewhere is an intelligent reappraisal of the play that raised the curtain as well as the alarm on a whole new artillery charge in the battle of the sexes; what Lloyd has done is show us the way forward from Congreve to Coward.

Take Courage

Mother Courage (National)
Mack and Mabel (Piccadilly)

The miracle of the National Theatre's new *Mother Courage* is that nobody in rehearsal ever seems to have used the word Brechtian. David Hare's new adaptation, like his recent *Galileo* for the Almeida, cuts through the undergrowth of apparatus and footnoting that has grown up this half-century around the German dramatist and gives us a brisk, cool version committed to no pet scholastic or political theories as to what the play might really be about.

Similarly, Diana Rigg in the title role takes the straight showbiz route: recalling perhaps that Brecht himself once suggested either Ethel Merman or Mae West as his perfect Broadway casting for the lady with the cart, she gives us a legendary survivor of all known war, unafraid to twist the knife or tug the heartstrings as the moment and her survival demand.

The director, Jonathan Kent, has also surrounded her with some of the best character actors in town (we even get a fleeting visit from Michael Gough as the Very Old Colonel), so what usually becomes a one-woman show is, in fact, filled out with all the personalities of an epic. But precisely because she is not confined within a single thesis, Rigg's power here is immense: dragging her followers across the world in pursuit of the wars that provide her only livelihood, she is at once comic and tragic, terrific and terrible in her Yorkshire accent and her timeless belief that God only helps those who help themselves to anything they can lay their hands on.

A new score by Jonathan Dove evokes Weill and Sondheim in equal measure, and a play whose previous history at the National (and indeed the Barbican) has never been a happy one suddenly comes to brilliant British dramatic life for the first time.

~

The problem with Jerry Herman's *Mack and Mabel*, at the Piccadilly in its long-awaited London debut, is exactly what it was on Broadway more than twenty years ago: great score, pity about the book. Unlike Herman's other musical classics, from *Dolly* through *Mame* to *La Cage aux Folles*, this one has no original novel or play or movie to fall back on. Instead, it relies on the two characters of Mack Sennett, the silent-film pioneer, and his star Mabel Normand; they were not individually an attractive pair, and there is historical evidence that they were only ever a love match in very limited terms.

Accordingly, the late Michael Stewart, in writing the original book, and now Herman himself, in trying to patch it up, have had to take considerable biographical liberties with Mack and Mabel's lives, ages and general relationship, and yet we still deep down don't really care about either of them the way we cared about *Mame* or *Dolly*.

As a result, we are left with a sequence of show-stopping numbers that have no show to stop; Paul Kerryson's production, in from Leicester, is also disastrously underfinanced, so that when Herman's lyrics refer to dozens of beautiful girls or crowds of slapstick policemen, we look up to see about a dozen actors desperately trying to fill out a big set. You always need to throw money, and then a lot more money, at a Herman musical because they are essentially pageants of great showmanship in a tradition that goes back through Irving Berlin to George M Cohan: Kerryson's low-budget treatment works better with a Sondheim or Kander & Ebb.

The casting is also a little uncharismatic: neither Howard McGillin nor Caroline O'Connor make you want to love them or them to love each other, and without that all we have are those great songs.

Country Matters

The Country Girl (Greenwich)

King Lear (Hackney Empire)

The Shakespeare Revue (Vaudeville)

At Greenwich, something seems to have gone horribly wrong with *The Country Girl*. Written in 1950 by Clifford Odets, one of the greatest and most shamefully neglected (on both sides of the Atlantic) of all American dramatists, it was originally seen over here forty years ago as *Winter Journey* with Sam Wanamaker and Michael Redgrave, whose son Corin now takes on the role of the ageing, drunken actor trying for a Broadway comeback.

But nowhere in Annie Castledine's makeshift and elsewhere very undercast new production is there any sense of the American theatre in the 1950s, or just what it meant to have a New York opening night hanging over your hangover. The tension, the sense of terror and waste and loss, and possible private and public redemption, are all reduced to some little local difficulty backstage at some singularly underprivileged local English seaside repertory company, and as a result we are never brought face to face with the issues that Odets raises about the price of fame and the destructive yet seductive power of the footlights.

Nor, more surprisingly, can Corin Redgrave yet approach the sense of wasted majesty that was his father's stock-in-trade: as though deliberately avoiding such comparison, he reduces Frank Elgin to an adequate character man in a little temporary alcoholic setback, rather than the Barrymoresque giant we need to glimpse if we are ever to understand what this play is about.

The rest of the company are so uncharismatic as to be forgettable even while you watch them, and a great backstage tragedy has thus been thrown away, probably for another forty years until someone has the courage to play it full out instead of in this half-hearted, almost apologetic and shambling fashion. 'Odets, where is thy sting?' unkind critics would ask, and this gives us no answer.

~

Warren Mitchell's *King Lear* (into the Hackney Empire from the West Yorkshire Playhouse) is patchy but powerful. Though by no means natural casting, Mitchell manages moments of great magic and leaves you and others wishing he'd gone for the more obvious Shylock. Like Mark Rylance's recent Greenwich *Macbeth*, though nowhere near as bad, Jude Kelly's is a production so full of ideas that there is no room or time for even one of them to take control or make sense of any of the others. True, she has had the unenviable task of building this first for the ultra-modern Playhouse in Leeds and then for Hackney, arguably the last and most perfect of all Frank Matcham's red-plush, chandeliered Victorian music-halls.

So, half-ancient, half-modern is understandable; there are machine-gun-toting terrorists here, but Mitchell himself wanders around like a displaced Santa Claus, and the Victorian special effects at Hackney allow real rain to fall during the storm. At one moment spectacular and at the next penny-pinching, this is a *Lear* for all seasons: somewhere in there you'll find the one you really want, but there seems considerable uncertainty as to which is the director's ultimate choice. Yet Mitchell, one of our most underrated and perennially powerful players, does achieve with the blinded Gloucester a scene of immense brilliance as two old men with a catalogue of personal and political losses wait, if not for Godot, then at least for some kind of explanation as to what their suffering might all have been about.

Elsewhere, the cast seems ill at ease with the verse and the play, as time and time again Mitchell is left to kick-start it back into action on some altogether new track.

~

One of the perennial myths of the modern British theatre, like the theory that the coming of John Osborne at the Royal Court made Rattigan and Coward unplayable and unnecessary, is the belief that after *Beyond the Fringe* you could never get audiences back to intimate revue. Happily, Michael Codron, one of its most consistent impresarios in the 1950s and early -60s, still loves the form and makes his Vaudeville Theatre available to it whenever possible.

At that address in the last couple of years, we've had *Kit and the Widow* and a good Cole Porter songbook, and now (from the RSC at Stratford and the Barbican) we get *The Shakespeare Revue*, a joyous words-and-music anthology in loving mockery of the Bard.

Some of the material here goes back half a century and is none the worse for that. There is a brilliant sketch of a courtier returning to Elsinore just after Hamlet's death and enquiring as to the health of his immediate circle, and also (in the week of Robert Stephens' death) a heartbreaking musical lament for Falstaff. Other songs and sketches work much less well, but that's the great asset of a revue: there'll always be something better along in a minute.

Baby Doll

Break of Day (Royal Court)

Hysteria (Duke of York's)

We drama critics are an ungrateful lot: we complain, with some justification, that, even in a year as strong as this for new stage writing, the obsessions have been with Soho gangsterdom, poker-playing and other such all-male pursuits behind closed doors. Where, we ask, are the State of the Nation plays, the ones that David Hare might recognise as dealing with the broad issues of Britain as we fall towards the end of the century?

In her new *Break of Day* (at the Royal Court), Timberlake Wertenbaker offers us an entire shopping-list of social ills: designed surely to play in tandem with Chekhov's *Three Sisters*, her script tackles childlessness among the achieving classes, the troubles an actor has in choosing between his art and his overdraft, the collapse of public education and healthcare these last five years, the exploitation of Eastern Europe as a baby farm and, at the last, the right any of us have to echo Chekhov's fall-of-the-curtain optimism about a better tomorrow.

Any of these issues might have made a play: the problem here is that all of them don't, which may be why Wertenbaker, once the most fashionable of Sloane Square dramatists, has had an unjustly rough ride from most of my colleagues. It is quite true that her first act uneasily resembles one of those BBC radio mid-morning chat shows, at which a trendy debate is cranked up around a table of professional psychiatrists and welfare workers and social healers intent on making a living out of the age-old worry that we ought to be healthier and richer and happier than we ever are.

But then, after the interval, Wertenbaker homes in on just one of these agonies, the inability of two middle-aged, middle-class media couples to have babies, and it is then that her play does catch fire.

One couple (Nigel Terry and Catherine Russell, as the actor and the feminist magazine editor) elect to go through the agonies of induced fertility to no avail; the other (Brian Protheroe and Maria Friedman, as a record producer and his one-time star singer) choose Eastern Europe, by the look of it Bulgaria, and the complex possibilities of adoption. This is where Wertenbaker moves brilliantly into Michael Frayn territory, as a couple of well-meaning if desperate Brits have to be taught the arts of bribery and corruption by ex-communists now willing to sell anything that moves, even at a crawl.

Along the way we also get some desperately inadequate sub-Sondheim songs, to cover scene changes, and the lurking shadow of Chekhov since there is also a third 'sister' here, a disillusioned schoolteacher angrily played by Anita Dobson. Nobody much wants to go to Moscow any more, but Wertenbaker does, I think, want us to know that we too are at the end of an era and the collapse of a regime. But which? Capitalism? State benefits? The right of women to work as if they were husbands rather than wives? The belief that no woman is complete without a baby? All of this gets aired, as at a nightmarish Chelsea dinner party for the chattering classes, but, as there is no real solution or radical addition to any of it, Wertenbaker just moves on to another issue without ever making us care about any of these people for more than about ten minutes each.

Max Stafford-Clark's production is suitably chilly and fluid, but would have looked a lot better were it to be played in tandem with *Three Sisters*, the way that on their last collaboration *Our Country's Good* played in partnership with *The Recruiting Officer*. That, surely, was the original idea here and it seems wilful to have abandoned it, presumably in the cause of economy.

~

Feminism, or at any rate the female-first movement, is also getting an uncharacteristically rough mauling from the Royal Court Classics season at the Duke of York's: where is Caryl Churchill now she is most needed? The three 'classics' chosen for transfer offer a total of almost forty roles for men and just one for a woman, the avenging daughter who comes to wreak havoc on Freud in the first transfer, Terry Johnson's *Hysteria*. Since this was first seen at the Court only a couple of years ago, 'classic' may just mean a show for which they still had the set in storage and hadn't managed a transfer first time around.

Soho Stories

Absolute Hell (National)

The Hot Mikado (Queens)

The rediscovery of Rodney Ackland, first in the 1970s by my distinguished predecessor Hilary Spurling, and then by the Orange Tree director Sam Walters, was what first began to challenge the current critical orthodoxy that nothing worth recalling had happened on the West End stage in the fifteen years or so before the now-discredited revolution at the Royal Court in 1956.

But since the National Theatre has finally caught up with Ackland (and could they soon please start thinking about N C Hunter and Wynyard Browne?), certain truths need to be established about his masterpiece *Absolute Hell* (National). No, it is not 'English Chekhov': it fits instead into a quite separate tradition, the one that runs from Vicki Baum's *Grand Hotel* through Coward's fascinating if still unknown *Semi-Monde* to Rattigan's *Separate Tables*, whereby you set a large number of representational types in a hotel or nightclub and then tell their separate stories as a pattern of the times through which they are struggling to stay afloat.

The time here is that of the Labour election victory of 1945, and Ackland's people are the flotsam and jetsam of Soho at the end of the war – literary critics, film producers, alcoholic barwomen, suppressed gays, all trying to work out how to survive the peace now that they have, just about, survived the war.

Marshalling a cast of almost thirty across John Gunter's symbolically self-destructing set, Anthony Page's epic production allows Judi Dench to rampage around the bar as the mistress of these semi-suicidal revels: the reason for Ackland's unpopularity, especially with this 'libel on the British people' as Binkie Beaumont of Tennent's condemned it, was that he saw all too clearly that having won the war was not enough: if we were not to lose the peace, we would have to learn to live with each other, and that we clearly still weren't going to manage.

~

Perhaps because, by its very weird Japanese-Victorian nature, the *Mikado* is already a parody, it has always lent itself to others: over the last century we have had Black Mikados, Cool Mikados, Rock Mikados and now, from Ford's theatre in Washington to the Queens, we get *The Hot Mikado*, this one updated by the director-choreographer David Bell and the orchestrator Rob Bowman to somewhere in the Broadway 1940s.

Thus we get Ross Lehman doing a remarkably accurate impression of Bert Lahr as KoKo, and Sharon Benson suggesting what Ethel Merman might have been like as Carmen Jones: their duets are the highlight of an otherwise rather patchy and uncertain revamp, though the tap-dancing of the Mikado himself (Lawrence Hamilton) is also a reminder of vintage Broadway talent long gone elsewhere.

Always Sorry, Always Grateful

Company (Donmar Warehouse)

Rosencrantz and Guildenstern Are Dead (National)

In comes *Company*: Stephen Sondheim's 1972 musical arrives at the Warehouse looking as strong as ever, all the better in fact (like so many of his shows) for being given the small-stage studio treatment rather than the original glitz. This is the high-rise Manhattan apartment revue about the little things you do together, children you destroy together, people you annoy together. It's the one about the ladies who lunch, and the air hostess not going to Barcelona, the one that defined for the very first time what we really mean by a Sondheim show: acid satire, heart-stopping acknowledgments of unrequited love, and the realisation that not only is every man an island, but most of them are under enemy occupation.

The star here is New York itself, where another hundred people just got off the train and where you're always sorry-grateful about people who will marry you a little; but a quarter of a century down the line, *Company* has acquired a curious kind of pre-AIDS innocence. It is still, in its own quirky way, a show about safe sex and unsafe relationships; the fears are of marriage and loneliness, not of sudden death or permanent loss, and Sam Mendes, the director, has wondrously understood that the strengths of *Company* are in all of the company. This is a team effort in which not even Sheila Gish in the old Stritch show-stopper gets star billing: a cast of fourteen all get their moments in a score which sounds at its best as if Noël Coward and Cole Porter had been asked to turn Schnitzler's *La Ronde* into a Broadway hit.

Adrian Lester has the uneasy task of holding these short stories together with nothing more than his own indecision about whether or not to get married, but in his curtain-call plea for someone to make him alive, ruin his sleep, force him to care, vary his days is one of the great anthems to urban and personal unrest.

~

Rosencrantz and Guildenstern Are Dead made Tom Stoppard's name at the Edinburgh Festival and then the National Theatre at the Old Vic back in 1967, but is only now getting its first National revival, in a strong new staging by Matthew Francis. The idea of *Hamlet* seen through the eyes of two of its least substantial characters was never a new one; W S Gilbert had tried it back in the 1880s, though what made it work for the first time here was Stoppard's brilliant realisation that they could stand for all of us, and for the absolute certainty of confusion. His Rosencrantz and Guildenstern are a deeply endearing couple; tetchy, certainly, bewildered by a universe in whose arrangement they have been allowed no part, only gradually aware that every exit is really just an entrance somewhere else and that actors are the very opposite of people.

A good many of Stoppard's later philosophic and philological concerns can be seen starting here, not least the notion that death simply constitutes an unusually successful vanishing act. A detailed knowledge of *Hamlet* scene by scene is certainly a help but by no means essential: R & G are a double-act, with Simon Russell Beale as Hardy to the Laurel of Adrian Scarborough, desperately trying to make sense of Elsinore in crisis. The brilliance is all in the conjuring, from the flipped coins at the outset through the appalled realisation of eternity ('Where's it going to end?') through to a *Pirates of Penzance* finale which Shakespeare unaccountably forgot to write. This way, rather than in his two throwaway lines, we do at least finally get to understand what happened to two of his most forgettable and forgotten characters and their demon king, brilliantly hammed by Alan Howard.

1995: the Year in Review

So what kind of year have we had in the London theatre? Violent for a start: the most influential director around has been neither Sam Mendes nor Stephen Daldry but Quentin Tarantino, who without leaving California has managed to condition a whole generation of young British playwrights. It is hard to believe that without him we'd have had *Mojo* or *Bruises* or *Blasted* or far and away the best of them all, *Gangster No. 1* by Louis Mellis and David Scinto, two young first-time dramatists who gave Peter Bowles the role of his career in a Soho shootout that I cannot believe will be much longer in transferring to the West End, and then I'd guess Hollywood, thus rounding the vicious circle that began there with Tarantino himself.

Two of these plays (*Bruises* and *Blasted*) were the work of women, but elsewhere it has been a blokish sort of a year with at least two plays (*Dealer's Choice* and *According to Hoyle*) entirely set around poker tables, and many others devoted to the joys of bashing the living daylights out of your nearest and dearest.

When Timberlake Wertenbaker tried for a more elegant and, some would say, feminist social debate about the price of parenthood versus the cost of careers (*Break of Day*), she was rapidly dismissed by critics, leaving the field to such male counterparts as David Edgar (*Pentecost*, dealing with art versus communism) and Ronald Harwood (*Taking Sides*, art versus the Nazis and then the Americans in 1945 Berlin).

Tom Stoppard's lyrical farewell to the Raj, *Indian Ink*, was much underrated while *The Steward of Christendom*, despite Donal McCann's brilliant performance, struck me as a character in search of a play. Michael Frayn also came up with a new play, *Now You Know*, vastly more intelligent than my colleagues would allow, though if I had to choose a single script of the year it would undoubtedly be David Hare's heartbreaking love story *Skylight*.

Musicals were in unusually bad shape. So, as usual in times of crisis in the pit, it was back to Sondheim whose *A Little Night Music* at the National gave us a new group of Supremes (Judi Dench, Patricia Hodge, Sian Phillips), while his *Company* came into the Warehouse at Christmas to prove itself the revival of the year.

Gay theatre had a good year, with new plays by Jonathan Harvey wherever you looked and David Greer's *Burning Blue* which faltered at the Haymarket but triumphed in smaller venues as a homosexual rethink of *A Few Good Men* or *The Caine Mutiny* for the nineties. The National continued to triumph under Richard Eyre, who perhaps announced his 1997 departure rather too early thereby creating a needless vacuum of almost two years; but the RSC under Adrian Noble seemed to be in continuing midlife crisis, with a catastrophic decision to pull back from the Barbican for half of every year.

Villain of the year was, as usual, John Major's government, which persisted in clawing back from the arts whatever the lottery had bestowed on them, so that we are now in the ludicrous position of having millions of pounds floating around for capital projects that nobody really wants to build, and less money than ever for the companies which will have to inhabit them.

Performances of the year included the aforementioned McCann and Bowles, the great Gambon in *Volpone* and *Skylight*, Daniel Massey as a haunting, haunted Furtwangler, Simon Russell Beale as Stoppard's Guildenstern and Jonson's Mosca, and Terry Johnson was undoubtedly the director-dramatist, with no less than three of his shows playing in London.

Among the women were Maggie Smith back by popular demand in *Three Tall Women*, Zoë Wanamaker definitive as the mother in Tennessee Williams' *The Glass Menagerie*, Maria Friedman in a stunning solo concert at the Whitehall,

Fiona Shaw and Geraldine McEwan in *The Way of the World* while Shaw went on alone to a memorable *Richard II*, Diana Rigg as Mother Courage, Sheila Gish in *Company*, Dench in *Absolute Hell*, all as close to perfect as makes no difference.

An unusual number of theatre companies are now on the move because of restructuring at home base, not least the Royal Court, which will occupy the Ambassadors and the Duke of York's for the whole of 1996; but we still have a real-estate situation around the West End where not nearly enough theatres are owned by producing managements, and unless we start paying some attention to the state of our commercial rather than subsidised theatre, Shaftesbury Avenue will be just another outpost on the Broadway map.

1996

Broadway 1996

The New York theatre starts the new year in better shape than anyone can remember it this decade: the new plays by Terrence McNally, Steve Martin, Richard Nelson; the return to Broadway after twenty or thirty years of three legendary leading ladies (Carol Channing, Julie Andrews, Carol Burnett), and a general if somewhat amazed feeling that, yes, folks, this really is the Great White Way lit up once again. The fabulous invalid, as Broadway has always been described, is sitting up in bed and even taking a little nourishment.

True, we are not talking London here: only twenty-five theatres open on Broadway as against forty in the West End, and of those barely a dozen offering anything other than musicals between five and fifty years old. The collapse of *Racing Demon* is being taken as a sign that New York theatre-goers really prefer our National Theatre when it sends them *Carousel* rather than serious dramas, but on the other hand Patrick Stewart in a Caribbean *Tempest,* Jason Robards in Brian Friel's *Molly Sweeney,* Frank Langella in *The Father,* Uta Hagen in *Mrs Klein* and Athol Fugard in his own new *Valley Song* hardly argue for a theatre totally given over to showbiz. We may have to start rethinking our smug assumption that play-going is always better in London, as New York at last begins to climb out of the decade of dramatic despair brought about by the triple threat of inner-city blight, union expenses and the AIDS plague that has decimated its theatrical community.

Heading the renaissance is Zoë Caldwell, an Australian actress long resident in the classical American theatre and currently giving an amazing performance as Maria Callas in McNally's *Master Class* (John Golden Theatre). This is, in all but name, a one-woman show: Callas comes on stage to take a series of master classes as she indeed did in real life; McNally then uses these to trace her own operatic life in and out of the theatre, so we get the barefoot student in wartime Athens, the bitchy diva ('Sutherland? I won't hear a word against her, but a twelve-foot Somnabula? What was she supposed to do, stoop her way through it?') and the rejected mistress of Onassis. Only in the last forty minutes is there real evidence of the greatness of this recital, and it's unlikely that in the 1950s Callas would really have said 'Go for it' to a trainee tenor about to hit a tricky B flat. All the same, the sheer power of Caldwell's obsessive, manic performance has to be seen over here and soon.

Victor/Victoria (Marquis Theatre) is the musical that brings Julie Andrews back to Broadway for the first time since *Camelot* all of thirty years ago, though she was of course off-Broadway just last year in a rather better score, Julia McKenzie's Sondheim revue *Putting It Together*. This one could hardly be described as new: Andrews herself filmed it fourteen years ago, and Jessie Matthews did it as *First A Girl* back in 1935, but it has always been a good story – that of the chorus dancer pretending to be a man so that she can become the best female impersonator in the business. The problem this time around is the late Henry Mancini's score (lyrics by Leslie Bricusse) which is redolent of the worst *American-in-Paris* numbers of the MGM 1950s. But Blake Edwards' production recalls some of his best *Pink Panther* farce routines, and is strongly played, not only by Andrews but also by Tony Roberts and Michael Nouri as the men in her somewhat confused life.

Ken Ludwig (he of *Crazy For You* and *Lend Me A Tenor*) has a new backstage farce, *Moon Over Buffalo* (Martin Beck Theatre), which owes a good deal to such English forerunners as *Curtain Up* and Rattigan's *Harlequinade*. It's the old story of a tacky repertory company in all kinds of backstage trouble, not least when the leading man gets so drunk that he comes out to play the balcony scene from *Private Lives* under the impression that it's the night for *Cyrano de Bergerac*, false nose, codpiece and all. Philip Bosco is hilarious here, but opposite him Carol Burnett satisfies her television audience with some prolonged facial mugging which adds about twenty unnecessary minutes to what should be a quick-fire farce.

I have saved the best till last: Carol Channing is back where she belongs, as Dolly Levi at the Lunt-Fontanne Theatre, and the fact that her audience remains on its feet cheering through most of a three-hour show is the very least they can do in the circumstances. After Ethel Merman, Ray Bolger, Alfred Drake, Mary Martin, Channing is the last surviving star of the old Broadway: when she, probably way past her centenary, eventually stops starring in *Hello Dolly!* nobody will ever know quite what the Broadway musical was like at its stellar best. Her arrival at the Harmonia Gardens at the top of that staircase is what a coronation always ought to look like and somehow never does: see her now, and tell your grandchildren.

Side By Side By Betjeman

Betjemania (King's Head)
The Duchess of Malfi (Wyndham's)

When *Betjemania* first opened at the Orange Tree in Richmond exactly twenty years ago, it was, alongside the near-contemporaneous *Side By Side By Sondheim*, a pioneer of what we now know as the 'songbook show' in which a single writing talent (more usually that of a composer or lyricist than of a poet) is celebrated in the old revue format by a small and usually dinner-jacketed cast.

John Gould and David Benedictus have now revised their show to take account of the best of Betjeman's newly published letters, but essentially *Betjemania* remains what it always was: a joyous celebration of the Poet Laureate as teddy bear for those who loved him, and a maddening reminder of his Victorian Gothic eccentricities for those who did not.

Since the first production we've also had the Jim Parker settings of Betjeman to jazz, which inevitably overshadow Gould's quiet palm-court work at the piano, and we also have the problem of a cast mostly unborn when Sir John was at the height of his fame and popularity, who seem now a little uncertain of tone: is he to be parodied, annotated, explained, apologised for or simply enjoyed?

Betjeman was always, of course, a showman, with an avowed love for the Crazy Gang and the Max Miller music halls of the 1920s; he was also joyously politically incorrect, obsessed by his own mortality ('old and ill and terrified and tight'; 'I am thirty summers older, richer, wickeder and colder') and worried about a lack of sex ('a little lech never really hurt old Betj'). Yet there is a curious modernity about all his writing; the description of a middle-management achiever 'basically viable from ten o'clock till five' could have come from the 1990s rather than the 1950s, and like only his friend Noël Coward he was uniquely able to love England while sending the old country up rotten.

~

There's been a lot of 1920s fascism around the classics of late: first, the newly filmed Ian McKellen *Richard III* and now Cheek by Jowl's touring *The Duchess of Malfi* (Wyndham's) which again takes us into what appear to be the private chambers of the Duke of Windsor at a time when the court playwright must have been neither Webster nor Shakespeare but an unusually sinister Pirandello.

Coming into the West End off the back of one of their usual whirlwind international tours (New York last month, Hong Kong next), the director Declan Donellan and his designer Jonathan Ormerod are inevitably in their usual minimalist mode: the programme cover just tells us *Malfi*, crediting neither Duchess nor author, while on a chessboard stage the only real furnishings are some drapes and the occasional table. In the title role, Anastasia Hille is remarkably like a young Maggie Smith, archly swooping her way around a set full of death and disaster as though involved in some high-camp court charades; when given the severed hand of her lover, she merely pops it into the wastepaper basket with a look of mild distaste. She also remains on stage as an observer long after her death, thereby heightening the chilly impression that 'these wretched, eminent things' are really no more than court jesters.

Donellan's rich production is about arrogance and loneliness and betrayal, but time and again it substitutes psychiatry for the full theatricality of Jacobean melodrama; we are so cool here that sometimes the deep-freeze anaesthetises any hope we may have of real involvement in the gothic awfulness of these people's lives and loves and lusts: the daggers have been replaced by pistols, and inevitably we are therefore now at a distance.

Tell Me A Storey

The Changing Room (Duke of York's)

Valley Song (Royal Court)

When I was a small boy (everything in life is relative), I remember being dragged away from a book and a warm fireside, dressed in shorts, and sent out to a muddy frozen field in the middle of which lay a brown leather ball. I was then ritually humiliated by not being chosen for somebody's team, made to run around in circles for about three hours, scratched, grazed, bumped and otherwise wounded, and then marched back, congealed with cold and blood and misery, leaving the brown leather ball exactly where I had first seen it. I couldn't see the point then and I still can't. I thought of it this week when the Royal Court's classic series brought a new production of David Storey's *The Changing Room* into the Duke of York's for a nostalgic twenty-fifth anniversary look at male bonding on, or rather off, the field of sporting endeavour, circa 1971.

Set in the eponymous changing room of a northern rugby club before, during and after a game on a gelid Saturday in winter, in the days when all rugby was amateur and those who played it were hard men, it exhales the blood and dirt and general discomfort rather than making a convincing argument for the nobility of sport. Seventeen men take off all their clothes and with them their individual identities as they suit up and turn into a team.

What strikes me twenty-five years later is that in admiring Storey's economical prose and poetic simplicity in 1971 I had singularly failed to notice that nothing at all happens in this play, give or take a broken nose, and a series of character sketches including a jack-the-lad whose idea of a joke is to pee in the communal bathwater.

The cast seems to be having an awfully good time; the problem is they don't want to include us. In 1971 there must have been more to *The Changing Room* than 'boys will be boys' highjinks but, on this showing, I'm damned if I can remember what.

~

Some subsequent season of Royal Court classics should, if there's any justice, include *Valley Song*, the elegiac, elegant, new play by South Africa's prophet and playwright Athol Fugard. Set in a village too small for maps, it is poised, like South Africa itself, in a world struggling from apartheid to Mandela. Fugard, who directs and plays two of the three characters, demonstrates definitively that his playwright's voice is still clear and true as the chronicler of his country, in the good times as well as the bad. He was a prominent white voice against apartheid, but, now that battle has been won, he still ruminates onstage as to how the adjustment will affect those least able to argue for themselves.

His protagonists this time are coloured, a septuagenarian grandfather and his talented granddaughter. All the other members of their family are dead and the survivors love each other with a fierce protectiveness. Buks (Fugard) ekes out a meagre living on a few acres he doesn't own but is connected to by generations of farming them. Now, in this post-Mandela world, a white writer buys those acres and Buks' world is threatened. His best defence, he reckons, is to appease this frightening new entity. But Veronica, full of songs and energy, refuses to wash the white man's floors as her grandmother did; instead she wants to escape to Johannesburg and learn to be a professional singer.

Valley Song is a tone poem for two actors, a meditation on change, on the natural transition from youth to maturity, the balancing act between the old and the new, the root and branch disruptions of a universe suddenly and irrevocably different, from the old order that may not have been fair, or modern, or equitable, but was known, into a more democratic future still being invented, where all the old signposts are missing.

The new South Africa gives Veronica choices. Buks wants her to choose the past, his past, but knows he must let her go, while she is looking towards a future that will leave his world behind forever. Veronica (a luminous Esmeralda Bihl, a young South African in an irresistible performance) craves his blessing. Their confrontation is deeply moving as Buks struggles to understand what Veronica strains to explain. *Valley Song* is an illustrated short story, told by the third character, the white writer (played by Fugard on his welcome return to the London stage after thirty years) in language of rare simplicity and compassion, the unresolved conflicts of both the people and the country bound together in mutual love.

Simon Says

Chapter Two (Gielgud)

At the Gielgud with a cast led by Tom Conti and Sharon Gless (of *Cagney and Lacey* fame), we have the first West End production of Neil Simon's *Chapter Two*, a Broadway hit from 1976. This was in some ways the turning point for Simon, the moment when he started to use his own life as something more than an excuse for a gag-fest. It was written as a tribute to Marsha Mason, his second wife, and her tolerance with his long-lasting grief over the death of his first wife, so the shadows are beginning to darken around the edges of the autobiography.

There is something very painful here, in among the gags, about a man trying to come to terms with death rather than a new life, and in David Gilmore's admirably unsentimental production Tom Conti (in a curious wig but a very strong performance) catches the grief as well as the mirth. When we first meet him, he is newly returned from the European vacation he has taken to get over the funeral. It was not a success: 'London was bankrupt, Italy on strike, France hated me and Spain was still mourning Franco,' he notes in a kind of Michelin guide to woe, which is a fair indication of the shape of the dialogue to come.

This is a comedy about death and despair and rebirth, and its desire to make us laugh through tears ought not to blind us to Simon's very real achievement in starting down the path that led to his later autobiographical trilogy. Conti is especially good on this borderline of emotion, and in her first stage comedy Sharon Gless is long-suffering and often very touching as the next Mrs Simon.

Cry the Beloved Country

*Observe the Sons of Ulster Marching
Towards the Somme* (Barbican)
Tommy (Shaftesbury)

Frank McGuinness's *Observe the Sons of Ulster* is in a new RSC touring production briefly at the Barbican; only eight years after its London premiere at Hampstead, the revival was sadly conceived to celebrate the all-too-short IRA ceasefire.

Like Sebastian Barry's award-winning *The Steward of Christendom* this too is a memory play digging deep into the Irish past in an effort to explain its present; but where Sebastian Barry takes us back to the Troubles, McGuinness goes a few years further back still, to the Flanders battle of the first world war. In that sense, what we have here is the Irish *Journey's End*; eight soldiers, all of them ghosts, come to their only surviving comrade, now himself dying, to take us through the agonies of the first war as it affected the Irish, whose Ulster Protestants offered themselves like lambs to the slaughter in a war which technically was not theirs to fight. Through their overlapping, sometimes contradictory memories an awful beauty is born: the beauty of McGuinness's bleak poetry, reminiscent sometimes of Eliot or Christopher Fry, which takes the place of action ends up by giving us what is often more of a poem or novel than a play.

The action is strictly limited, and though these sons of Ulster are afraid, it is not just of the war: they fear for their homeland and buried deep somewhere here are the seeds for the conflict of these last eighty years.

~

Even within the often chaotic history of stage musicals, The Who's *Tommy* (now in its London premiere at the Shaftesbury) has an eccentric past. Written twenty-five years ago by Pete Townshend, it has been a record album, a rock-opera concert, a Ken Russell film; it was also the first pop musical ever heard at the Metropolitan in New York, and picked up five Tony Awards when it finally hit Broadway a couple of years ago.

So now that we finally get to see it in London, what is it? Essentially still a rock-opera in the tradition of such contemporaries as *Hair* and *Jesus Christ Superstar*. But where they both enjoyed plots of a kind, and some sort of dramatic force in book and lyrics, *Tommy* stubbornly refuses to make any real concessions to Shaftesbury Avenue musical traditions.

True, it has a couple of great songs in 'Pinball Wizard' and 'See Me Touch Me', but the plot such as it is remains often unfathomable, and the Broadway director Des McAnuff seems to have decided that the more the show resembles the Planetarium, with lights darting all around the stage and overhead, the less we'll be aware of the great hole in the heart that lies at the centre of *Tommy*.

The real problem is that there's nobody here we much care about, least of all the title character who goes deaf and dumb and blind on seeing his father kill his mother's lover, and then is miraculously restored by his addiction to pinball machines. One of these explodes in a neat metaphor for the second half of the show itself, especially after the interval when not a lot happens several times.

Kim Wilde as the mother and Paul Keating as the adult Tommy do their dramatic best to clamber over the gaps in the narrative and make out we have a halfway coherent show here, but the rest of the cast look as though they'd have been happier supporting the original Who for a gig at Wembley Stadium.

Sondheim's Passion

Passion (Queen's)

Harry and Me (Royal Court)

In his native New York this has not been the best of times for Stephen Sondheim, who this month opened the thriller it has been his life's ambition to write only to have it close within a week, a casualty to some of the worst reviews since Pearl Harbor. *The Last of Sheila*, the one he wrote for the screen, has been curiously neglected these last twenty years, but displayed his passion for mysteries and his intelligence in solving them. We will never know whether he's lost his touch or just his audience for straight plays, since a thriller with a Broadway life of five performances rarely makes it across the Atlantic. It might find an audience here, though, because in London, like Arthur Miller, his work is revered as nowhere in America, and we currently have three of his musicals playing simultaneously. At the risk of losing such Broadway friends as I have left, it needs to be noted that all are looking vastly better now than on their first New York outings.

One of those is *Company*, about which I have raved quite enough already; the other two are the National's *A Little Night Music,* such a hit that in an unprecedented move it will play every single night throughout August instead of the usual repertory system, and his latest, *Passion*, with which it shares some intriguing and hitherto unreported similarities.

Though written twenty years apart, both musicals derive from cult art-house movies: *Night Music* comes, of course, from Ingmar Bergman's *Smiles of a Summer Night*, while *Passion* comes from the largely unknown 1981 Italian movie *Passione d'Amore*, itself based on a still more obscure 1869 Italian novel by Tarchetti. So comparisons are not so much odious as largely unavailable; if *A Little Night Music* is about six mismatched lovers in some long-lost tale from the Vienna Woods, *Passion* is about one woman so hideously ugly (and brilliantly played by Maria Friedman) that her obsessive love for a Guards Officer (handsomely played by Michael Ball) starts by being ludicrously impossible and ends through the arc of the show by becoming inevitable.

I am not convinced that the director Jeremy Sams is right to have added an interval, since *Passion* works best as a kind of symphony, its score haunting and progressive and as obsessive as the title. Every time Sondheim writes a new show nowadays, it is the West End that gets rebuilt; I can think of no other living composer who would have even attempted to score this dark, difficult piece but Sondheim, as usual, makes it soar. And no, you can't hum the songs as you leave the theatre; what you can do is buy the CD, live with it for a while and only then be made aware of the genius of this tricky, ultimately wonderful piece. Yet again Sondheim has pushed out the barriers of the musical; this time I fear so far that other composers are going to need a passport and a road-map even to find the territory, let alone reclaim it.

~

At the Royal Court, Nigel Williams' *Harry and Me* is cruelly disappointing. Williams is a good comic novelist and a distinguished maker of arts documentaries for the BBC; he has combined both talents to give us the story of a derelict chat-show host, his producer and researcher, in an office all too familiar to those of us who have ever worked in arts broadcasting. Most of the staff have left in disgust, the show itself is falling fast through the ratings floor, and the star is so drunk and depressed that he can barely make it through the office door. Ron Cook is just wonderful as the manic producer with telephones clipped to every orifice, and Sheila Hancock does a brilliant series of impressions as the put-upon researcher. For the first ten minutes I thought we had that comparative rarity, a brilliantly funny new comedy. But it quickly becomes clear that Williams has not the faintest idea where to go from this start; he has essentially written a revue sketch which the desperately hard-working cast have to play and replay to make up the two hours' traffic on the stage. Were Williams even half as good at plots as he is at the one-liners (though many of these will only make sense to media workers), then we might have had a play here instead of a few good television gags.

Song of War

Martin Guerre (Prince Edward)

For the third time in little more than a decade, or so it would seem from all but about two of the first dozen reviews, Alain Boublil and Claude-Michel Schonberg have written a great and classic musical which nobody likes except the public. When they come to write the history of our theatre in the second half of this century, and in the process to rewrite first reactions to it, they will, I now firmly believe, come to realise that one team outclassed in ambition and sometimes also in achievement even that of Lerner & Loewe or Rodgers & Hammerstein or Rodgers & Hart.

What Boublil & Schonberg give us, at five-yearly intervals, are the operettas of our time: great soaring scores, heartbreaking books and lavish stagings which bring to rich theatrical life moments when French history at home or abroad was on the turn.

But overwhelming, epic emotions on the broadest of scales are oddly unfashionable in a minimalist age; when *Les Misérables* first opened at the Barbican eleven years ago and I suggested that it was the musical of this half-century just as securely as *Porgy and Bess* was of the first, I was told that it was, on the contrary, too long, too French, too obscure in plot and intention.

A decade and fifty world-wide productions later, I have surely the right to remind you of how misguided those early notices were, and of the ludicrous way we are now being told that *Martin Guerre* is 'not as good as *Les Mis*' when that opened to equally dismissive notices. *Martin Guerre* is as much a masterpiece of musical magic and mystery as that earlier score, and you can bet your life that whatever Boublil & Schonberg write in the year 2006 will be similarly dismissed as 'not as good as *Martin Guerre*.'

Once again the setting is their native France but this time in the Basque borderlands of the Middle Ages. We are somewhere in the sixteenth century, and a man has returned from religious wars to a small village claiming to be the Martin Guerre who left it and a young wife several years earlier.

This much will be familiar to anyone who has seen the French or American (*Sommersby*) movie versions, but there all similarity ends; Boublil & Schonberg have transformed *Martin Guerre* from an identity thriller to the story of an isolated, incestuous community in social, familial and ecclesiastical turmoil.

The new story, lighter and brisker than *Miss Saigon* and still richer in plot and character than *Les Mis*, is again the story of a community in transitional historical crisis, and again told through the trumpets and drums and cellos of an orchestral masterpiece under the guidance this time of Jonathan Tunick.

Sure, there are times when *Martin Guerre* resembles an unholy wedding of *Brigadoon* and *The Crucible*: the echoes of Arthur Miller and the choreographer Agnes de Mille are everywhere. Elsewhere, there are echoes of *Don Giovanni* as a Commendatore returns from the grave, and even of *Macbeth* as three old crones foretell the troubled future of their hero.

But, in the end, *Martin Guerre* belongs to nobody but itself. Declan Donellan as director wondrously brings his own intimate experience with his Cheek by Jowl and such other revolutionary small-scale touring companies as Theatre de Complicite and Shared Experience to recreate the tensions of an isolated village community, just as Nunn and Caird used the RSC *Nicholas Nickleby* experience to meet the massive demands of *Les Mis*. In a jokey tribute to that famous predecessor, Donellan even has his full company do the famous RSC race to the footlights.

Yet there is a great deal more going on here, not least a mystical sense of war and religion, death and rebirth, deception and redemption. A cripple sings a most haunting love song to a scarecrow, even as the misfits of mediaeval history try to come to terms with an outcast woman whose unborn child may yet prove the saving of the community.

The lyrics of Edward Hardy and Herbert Kretzmer and Boublil himself wonderfully counterpoint the soaring strings of Schonberg in Tunick's breathtaking orchestrations; a song like 'All I Know' will become a classic wherever great show songs are sung, and as the ghosts of all the great story-tellers of world history gather around this legendary folk-tale, as the putative Martin Guerre is christened, already in the crucifix position, a Protestant in a very Catholic community, we begin to understand that this is something even more than a *Devil's Disciple* set to music.

Donellan's intelligent staging, and Cameron Mackintosh's hugely loving production ensure that whenever spectacle is needed we get it: the village goes up in flames as satisfactory as those which burnt Scarlett O'Hara's Atlanta. But in the end this remains an intimate tale of prejudice and passion, love and other loyalties, and if its central casting is a little uncharismatic (neither Iain Glen nor Juliet Caton quite yet manage to rise to the huge vocal and dramatic demands) we are more than compensated by a supporting cast of rare brilliance led by Michael Mateus as the holy fool who acts as crippled narrator to these terrible events.

Vanya Victorious

Uncle Vanya (Chichester)

John Gabriel Borkman (National)

Back in 1962 it was *Uncle Vanya*, in that legendary Olivier/Redgrave production, which effectively saved the first Chichester Festival and therefore all others after a catastrophic start consisting of *The Chances* and *The Broken Heart*. It is no exaggeration to suggest that it was therefore the production (revived in the following season) which made it possible for Olivier to lead his company on to the Old Vic and thereby become the first ever National Theatre of Great Britain. The least they could have done, in West Sussex as on the South Bank, was to erect a statue to old Anton though, of course, they have done nothing of the kind.

Thirty-four years after that immortal *Vanya* we have the next best. At the Minerva, there is a Bill Bryden revival of Chekhov's masterpiece which is the only one in my experience of three decades' reviewing to challenge the Olivier original there. The casting alone is about as spectacular as you can get nowadays: Derek Jacobi in the title role, Alec McCowen as the Professor, Peggy Mount and Constance Cummings as the old ladies, Trevor Eve as Astrov, Imogen Stubbs as Yelena, Frances Barber as Sonja and John Normington as Waffles.

Arguably neither the National nor the RSC could muster such a cast nowadays, least of all for a production scheduled to last less than a month in a two hundred-seat theatre. But what really matters about Bryden's production is its quiet confidence, its utter refusal to truck with any specific contemporary theory about the play but simply to celebrate it in Mike Poulton's sturdy but unobtrusive new translation.

What could simply have become a gallery for star-spotters has been turned into an exquisite ensemble piece, in which each character finds at least one moment of perfect partnership before having to acknowledge that this too must end in futility. A haunting, brooding gloom is softened by the infinite elegance of much of the underplaying, as though the entire household was simply breathing one last sigh of rejection before the coming political storm. These scenes from country life have never been better painted nor more thoughtfully composed, and the result is a little masterpiece.

~

For those of us who believe that if Gielgud is our greatest living actor then Paul Scofield is our greatest working one, there is considerable cause for rejoicing at his return to the theatre for the first time in almost five years. Scofield as *John Gabriel Borkman* (Lyttelton) may lack the manic intensity of Sir Ralph Richardson, who last played the role at the National twenty years ago, but what Scofield substitutes is more poetic, more touching and infinitely more haunting – a man who has gazed into the abyss and seen there only his own reflection. Eileen Atkins as the ice-cold wife matches him in scene after desolate scene, though the great final act of death on the snow-covered hillside is not much helped by Vanessa Redgrave (as Ella) who bizarrely elects to play the finale in full hunchback cape and stick.

But the wasted majesty of Scofield is, rightly, what Richard Eyre's production is all about, and it has the added benefits of Felicity Dean as the flame-haired temptress of the younger Borkman, and of Michael Bryant, the National's longest-serving player, as the genial neighbour never happier than when describing how he has been run over by his own daughter's sleigh.

I am not entirely convinced that Eyre has got the transition from downtown parlour to snow-covered hill totally right on Anthony Ward's set, for on the first night at least the snow seemed suddenly and mysteriously to be gusting through the living room as though a roof had been removed from Scofield's attic. But this is a minor complaint about a major revival, one which only serves to remind us that we now have nobody left to challenge Scofield at his most sonorously ghostly and cadaverous.

The White Knight

Voyeurz (Whitehall)

Promises Promises (Bridewell)

The Lights (Royal Court)

Like the Habsburgs, producer Michael White forgets nothing and learns nothing; thirty years ago he brought us *Oh! Calcutta!* which, while admittedly earning a cool $30 million or so world-wide, did a certain amount of damage to his reputation as an otherwise intelligent and honourable impresario, and a great deal more damage to the reputation of Kenneth Tynan who, far and away the best post-war drama critic on either side of the Atlantic, never really recovered from the accusations of sleaze and soft-porn which the show brought him as writer and deviser.

Believe it or not, here we go again: at the Whitehall, *Voyeurz* is a porno-musical of breathtaking inadequacy, impotent in every theatrical art and limp even in its nudity since the cast are of such stunning hideousness as to make even their costumes look defensible if only by comparison. Midway through the first number, most of us not otherwise engaged in leaving the stalls were yearning for a revival of *Which Witch?* or even *Fields of Ambrosia*, and as for the star lesbian band Fem 2 Fem, though they will doubtless soon be taking part in a new and improved Last Night of the Proms, neither their talent nor their looks suggest that they are deserving of anything more than a stiff letter of excommunication from the Lesbos Tourist Board.

In an evening of such dire awfulness, of use only to the manufacturers of rubber sheeting and those sad social and sexual misfits who have drifted a few yards south of Soho in the misguided belief that the Whitehall has something to offer which wasn't largely abandoned by Paul Raymond circa 1965 and Hugh Hefner circa 1950, I can only report that the ice-creams still come very nicely wrapped, unlike the cast, and the whole misbegotten, misguided, misogynistic shambles only lasts about ninety minutes. That is still, however, an hour and a half too long.

~

At the Bridewell, an interesting summer of 'lost' American musicals gets off to a shaky start with *Promises Promises*, the Burt Bacharach & Hal David Broadway hit of 1968 which has seldom, if ever, been seen over here since. Its interest is now essentially for Broadway historians, as this was quite clearly the show which bridged the gap from *How to Succeed in Business* (1961) to *Company* (1970) in its cynical, high-rise, urban intensity. The source was Billy Wilder's movie *The Apartment* as adapted for the stage by Neil Simon, and, though some of the numbers (notably the title song and 'I'll Never Fall in Love Again') are indeed show-stoppers, their problem is that they could have stopped any show of the period at any point in the action.

The score is thus oddly distinct from the book, though very much stronger, and I doubt that even a production more impressively cast or expensively staged, (on this one the shoestring seems to have broken somewhere early in rehearsal), could have done much to breathe new life into so rapidly dated a show. The lesson here is that it was not the classics of the 1940s or 1950s that Sondheim rendered obsolete, but those shows which came immediately before his in the 1960s that he made to seem both lazy and sloppy by the relatively simple process of injecting real thought and emotion into their story-lines and characterisation.

~

About to close for a two-year period of redevelopment (during which its mainstage shows will occupy the Duke of York's and its Upstairs plays the Ambassadors), the Royal Court is going out in a blaze of reconstructional glory by having its last audience sit on the stage and its last play, *The Lights*, happen all over what was the auditorium. Howard Korder's 1993 script (first staged by the South Coast Repertory Theater in California) is an impressive addition to the range of unnamed-urban-angst dramas we have lately been getting in considerable numbers both from the Court and Hampstead, this one set in the usual nameless city of dread across which two apparent innocents abroad have to make their way unmolested, as in some Manhattan board game of peril and potential.

Korder is essentially school of David Mamet with an equally filmic eye for the menace inherent in random street corner meetings: his heroines are a couple of shop girls (Emily Mortimer as the softly touching one and Deirdre Harrison as the harder-boiled broad) who encounter a couple of seducers and a drifter and then have to make their way back to some sort of social and sexual safety in a city where 'nothing matters and everything sucks'.

O, What a Lovely War!

War and Peace (National)
By Jeeves! (Duke of York's)
The Odd Couple (Haymarket)

On the Cottesloe stage of the National, Nancy Meckler and Polly Teale have a four-hour staging of *War and Peace* which is little short of a masterpiece. I have in the past had my doubts about their Shared Experience habit of staging classic novels; in the first place anyone who does that still has the RSC *Nicholas Nickleby* of twenty years ago to contend with, and in the second the feeling of a staged masterpiece is often akin to the one you get from the increasingly popular books-on-tape: the plot is all there but somehow none of the sense.

All such doubts are destroyed here: for the first time since *Nickleby*, unless of course you count the even greater job that was done on *Les Misérables*, a thousand-page narrative has been brought to the boards with all of the intensity of its feeling still intact.

Helen Edmunson's masterly dramatisation brings us the characters rather than the chronicle: like a great David Lean movie, this *War and Peace* roams around the battlefields and banquets of the epic novel, zooming in on its most intriguing characters and then following them through Tolstoy's history of a nation and an entire continent in turmoil. A cast of fifteen doubles and redoubles 100 characters over an almost-bare stage.

~

By George, by Jove, by Jingo, *By Jeeves!* (Duke of York's), they finally did it; fully twenty-one years after Alan Ayckbourn and Andrew Lloyd Webber's attempt to make a musical of P G Wodehouse's classic country-house comedies first thudded onto the stage of Her Majesty's like two tons of condemned British beef, they have at last got the show as nearly right as it will ever be. From the outset, almost everything had been stacked against it: Tim Rice walked off the project in its earliest weeks, reckoning, understandably, that if Wodehouse, himself no mean lyricist and the creator with Kern of at least a dozen other scores, had wanted to make a musical out of his most famous literary partnership then old Plum would have done so. The first director had taken to the bottle long before opening night, David Hemmings played Bertie Wooster as if he'd already lost the plot, Michael Aldridge played the ineffable Jeeves with the look of an actor who'd read the rest of the script, and was actually denied a song to himself, a decision roughly analagous to building a movie around Esther Williams and then shooting it on dry land.

But neither Lloyd Webber nor Ayckbourn have in their intervening two decades ever had to suffer flops on such a massive scale, and their determination to get this one right at last is understandable; intriguingly, they have turned the show around by the simple device of moving it back from a massive musical (Webber had just come off *Jesus Christ Superstar*) to a small-scale play with songs. Ayckbourn thus now becomes the senior partner: instead of trying to encapsulate several of the best-known Wodehouse plots, as originally, he has now thrown out the aunts and the pigs and all the other apparatus of Plum's eccentric imagination and given us instead a plot of his own concoction, vaguely reminiscent of the amateur-dramatic-society chaos of his *A Chorus of Disapproval*.

In this new scheme of things, Lloyd Webber simply provides a dozen songs, wisely retaining 'Code of the Woosters' and 'Banjo Boy' and the enchanting 'Half a Moment' from the original, but taking as his model the local two-piano style of Vivian Ellis or Julian Slade or Sandy Wilson rather than anything more operatically or transatlantically ambitious.

The result is a little treasure: shaky at first, certainly, and vaguely miscast with Steven Pacey's Wooster and Malcolm Sinclair's Jeeves altogether too alike in age and manner for the paternal master/servant relationship switch which lies at the heart of the jokes. But swiftly and surely Ayckbourn's own staging (from his Scarborough theatre-in-the-round) builds to a dazzlingly joyful second half, one which opens with one of the greatest title songs I have ever heard in a British musical.

~

And, briefly, to the Theatre Royal Haymarket for a three-month season have come the veteran Tony Randall and Jack Klugman in a staging of *The Odd Couple*, Neil Simon's classic comedy of flat-sharers run amok and the one they have been playing on television these last thirty years. Logically, therefore, they are both about thirty if not forty years too old for the roles of the male divorcees thrown together in a nightmare replica of married life, but queues around the Haymarket would suggest that we are here into Hall of Fame country: see your favourite television stars live in their original roles. Proceeds are, however, going to Randall's admirable if thus far doomed attempt to set up a classical theatre company on Broadway just like the ones in which he starred before the war with the Lunts and Kit Cornell. You can only admire his tenacity and wish him luck.

Big Ben

The General from America (Stratford)
The White Devil (Stratford)

Closing the current RSC season of new productions at Stratford before the director Adrian Noble awards himself an unprecedented personal season of his own *The Cherry Orchard* and *A Midsummer Night's Dream* running alone there all through October, Richard Nelson's *The General from America* is a rich, rare and remarkable triumph on the Swan stage. One of the RSC's more intelligent decisions, in a regime now racked by redundancy fears at the Barbican and a curious kind of lassitude at Stratford, is the continuing adoption of Nelson as its American house dramatist.

In play after play for them, Nelson (like A R Gurney in the United States) has established himself as that contemporary stage rarity, a civilised, urbane, literate, acidic ironist in an age of urban thuggery. *The General from America* is in fact Benedict Arnold, that nation's most infamous traitor, played here by James Laurenson in a major-star performance. In a time of hypocrisy and double-bluff as the War of Independence dragged into the stalemate of 1779–80, Nelson gives us the paradox of an Arnold who is the only fundamentally honest man in a colony of time-servers and crooks.

Around him are ranged Corin Redgrave's disappointingly low-key George Washington, Stephen Boxer's acidic Kemble, and John Woodvine as the less familiar Sir Henry Clinton, commander of the British forces in North America and deeply in love with the young major whose unfortunate capture is the undoing of Arnold. Howard Davies' wonderfully subtle, large-cast production gives us not just a pageant of American history at one of the great turning-points of the war, but also a domestic tragedy involving Arnold, his wife and sister caught up in an act of fatal but now all too understandable betrayal. *The General from America* is far and away the best new play I have seen all year, richly deserving a long London run.

~

Also on the Swan stage at Stratford, (which like the Minerva in Chichester always seems to have more interesting work than the neighbouring main stage), is a virtually uncut production by the Australian Gale Edwards of Webster's *The White Devil*. Again we get a very powerful character-acting cast (led this time by Richard McCabe, Ray Fearon, Philip Quast, Jane Gurnett and Caroline Blakiston) working their way through the thicket of Webster's plots and sub-plots and only leaving one wishing they had tackled his infinitely more rewarding *The Duchess of Malfi* instead.

For the truth about *The White Devil* is that it never really engages our pity or terror the way the *Duchess* does: a series of spectacularly violent scenes do not somehow add up to a plot, though Edwards leads us briskly and coolly through all of them, underlining the constant theme of man's infinite corruption and women's equally infinite capacity for suffering.

Mercifully this is not a concept production: it lays out the play for us on an often semi-bare stage, allowing only McCabe as the wonderfully sweaty, lustful Flamineo the chance to take the audience into his confidence as he goes deeper and deeper into a conspiracy of his own making. As for the others, Princes of the Church and their unlucky consorts, the production achieves strong contrasts nowhere greater than when four grieving women rise from the earth to visit retribution on their murderous menfolk, a concept that might almost have been lifted from the Shakespearean Queens to Richard III.

Edwards still doesn't convince us that this is a major tragedy: but she does find a route-map through to its bloody end, and along the way manages to isolate some contemporary themes of sexual struggle.

1997

On Broadway

After thirty years in which the 'fabulous invalid' seemed to be in intensive care if not actually deceased, Broadway has been of late coming back to life, with this season almost a dozen new musicals and plays, roughly as many as were notable there throughout all of the 1980s. New work from David Mamet and Neil Simon, not to mention new big-band shows on themes as diverse and sometimes implausible as the Titanic, Siamese twins, and a vicious double murder in the gang wars of Hell's Kitchen forty years ago: all are surely symptons of a healthy present and perhaps even future.

Maybe we should start in the Kitchen: *The Capeman* is Paul Simon's first ever musical, and it still has a month in previews before press night, so these comments are based on one of its very first public performances. Simon (he of 'Bridge Over Troubled Water') is co-author, lyricist and composer, and, if backstage rumours are believable, he has treated the project as a one-man show; true, there's a cast of seventy under the ballet master Mark Morris' direction, but like Disney's remarkable *The Lion King* (just opened to a record $28 million advance, such is the movie, television and theme-park marketing power of old uncle Walt), *The Capeman* is regarded by old Broadway hands as an outside job, unimproved by, and maybe unanswerable to, any of the ancient laws of the American musical.

In the first place, it is controversially and unusually journalistic: where *West Side Story* (its most obvious and immediate model) was about unnamed and non-specific gangs of ethnic hoodlums, *The Capeman* is about one specific killing in 1959 of two young men whose families are still very much around and understandably indignant that their tragedy is being sold to theatre audiences at $70 a ticket.

The killer, who came to be known as the Capeman, was a Puerto Rican youth of sixteen who became the youngest criminal ever to be sentenced to the electric-chair; three years later he got lucky, at the time of Eleanor Roosevelt's anti-capital punishment crusade, and after several more years in prison he was released, only to die quietly at home of a heart attack in 1986. Not perhaps the most likely subject for a musical, but then you could also argue that of most of Sondheim's classics; and before we dismiss some of *The Capeman*'s clumsier and more obscure choral moments we need to recall that its co-author is Derek Walcott, who now joins T S Eliot of *Cats* as the second Nobel prizewinner to have a show on Broadway at this time, not an achievement the West End has ever been able to claim as its own.

The Capeman has a vibrant and vital stage energy not always matched by Simon's score, which wanders all over the place in search of urban and ethnic inspiration; on a very filmic set by our own Bob Crowley, it ends up as a series of tableaux, not all of them very *vivants*, but it certainly doesn't deserve premature dismissal. Like the *West Side Story* towards which it so often looks for inspiration or approval, *The Capeman* is alternately touching and terrifying in what it has to say about the chaos of urban violence: as it turns out, the victims were not who their killer thought they were, and their deaths were as random and incidental and yet heartbreaking as much of this haunting score.

Like *The Lion King* which comes from the mask-and-puppet queen Julie Taymor, *The Capeman* is largely the work of Broadway newcomers and there are many more of those waiting in the wings; Barry Manilow has a show called *Harmony* for 1998, Randy Newman is working on a *Faust* musical and the country star Garth Brooks is planning the old Alan Ladd *Shane*. It's all a long way from Rodgers & Hammerstein (though the old survivors have a *The Sound of Music* about to open yet again, this time presumably on ice or under water), but we are I believe in at the birth of a whole new Broadway musical generation, the first perhaps since the war to be this radical and so diverse in its interests.

Even the new Neil Simon, shamefully underrated by most local critics, is something new, neither a gagfest of one-liners nor yet another chapter of his early autobiography; rather *Proposals* is a weird and wonderful piece set somewhere between *The Cherry Orchard* and *A Midsummer Night's Dream*. We are in a house in the Pennsylvanian woods around forty summers ago, and an old black housekeeper (unusually for Simon, the central character) is recalling just one Sunday lunch party at which a group of wildly ill-assorted guests came together in search of love and understanding, or at any rate some kind of a working relationship. Lovers divided, lovers coincided, something for everyone, a comedy tonight: or at any rate half a dozen brilliant character-actors in search of a plot, especially Peter Rini as the Mafia son who goes out to fish with a shotgun, and Suzanne Cryer as the girl torn between the love and lust of at least four men, one of whom is her dying father. *Proposals* is lyrical, achingly nostalgic, and deserves like *The Capeman* to be seen over here with all possible speed.

Off Broadway, *The Last Session* is a curious and courageous account of a rock singer turned composer who, dying of AIDS, assembles his ex-wives for one last recording session before he takes his own life; what might so easily have become mawkish or macabre is turned, in Steve Schalchin's musical, into an oddly hilarious show in which the sudden arrival of a born-again Baptist, torn between his God and his recording career, suggests a good bet over here for Dan Crawford's King's Head, always assuming we manage to keep it alive.

As so often in New York, the single starriest evening I spent was not at a theatre but an auction house: Sotheby's are selling off the contents of Leonard Bernstein's apartment, and as a preview to the sale they assembled his three children plus such old Bernstein hands as Betty Comden, Adolph Green, Lauren Bacall and Isaac Stern to recall the maestro and a few of his Broadway songs. Celebrity auctions are clearly here to stay, and they now provide some of the best shows in town.

Greater Loesser

Guys and Dolls (National)
Listen to the Wind (King's Head)
Marry Me a Little (Bridewell)

It is generally reckoned that the production which assured Richard Eyre's future as Director of the National Theatre back in 1982 was his *Guys and Dolls*, and there is therefore a certain logic to having him start his farewell season with a revival of it on the same set. On the Olivier stage we now get Clarke Peters, Joanna Riding, Imelda Staunton and Henry Goodman in place of Bob Hoskins, Julia McKenzie, Julie Covington and the late Ian Charleson.

Most of all we miss the late David Healy as Nicely-Nicely Johnson; talented though Clive Rowe is, he cannot begin to approach the show-stopping way in which Healy told us to sit down we're rocking the boat, and when John Normington, sole survivor of the original cast, goes into the breathtakingly quiet 'More I Cannot Wish You', it comes as an uneasy reminder of the sheer class of the original and the absolute adequacy of this revival fourteen years on.

Guys and Dolls had always been Olivier's dream in his own initial management of the National, and it says something for our changing attitudes to Broadway that he was forbidden not only by ill health but also by a strong feeling on the part of his governors that the show was, well, not quite National material. As one of the classics of the American theatre it is ideal National material, but it remains a curiously intransigent show to stage; its songs are its plot, its characters are its action, and in the end it lives or dies by David Toguri's breathtaking choreography and the company's understanding of the original three-cent opera convention.

The filmic opening titles on a screen unwisely beg comparison with the great Brando/Sinatra movie of 1955, but this is a production in which the whole has always been greater than its parts: it is a tapestry of small-time losers and big-band numbers, and, though I still think Eyre's production goes a little soft around the edges of Runyon's acidic original tales of Broadway jungle, the brassy sound and tacky soul of Times Square is in there somewhere.

If there is now the faint feeling of a second company inheriting the show after a long run, that is perhaps inevitable: we also have to recall that this was the National's virtually first-ever smash-hit musical, since when they have given us a lot of Sondheim and Rodgers & Hammerstein under the Cameron Mackintosh grant. If we are now more demanding about National musicals, they have only themselves to blame for giving us so much else that has been as great if not greater than this old war-horse.

It's far too early to assess how, if at all, the National policy on musicals will alter under Trevor Nunn, though this year's choice of *Lady in the Dark*, a famously difficult Ira Gershwin/Moss Hart/Kurt Weill score which has only ever really worked once and then in the early 1940s with Gertrude Lawrence and a young Danny Kaye, suggests that they are already moving into bolder territory.

~

Two other musical treats over the holidays: at the King's Head, a charming low-budget staging of the last score written by Vivian Ellis (and the one he was still revising when he died at ninety-one this summer): *Listen to the Wind* is that comparative rarity, a musical for and about children. Written in 1954, it has the charm of an altogether different period, that of late Victorian fairy tales as a gang of rowdy cousins and their prim leader get caught up with pirates and mermaids and the magical wind people. *Listen to the Wind* owes a lot to *Peter Pan* and a little to Enid Blyton's Famous Five; but Dan Crawford has given it a loving, seductive staging for all those who still complain that children's theatre isn't what it was in their day, just as long as their day was about 1896.

~

And finally, to the Bridewell for the least familiar of all three Sondheim anthology shows. The other two are of course *Side by Side by Sondheim* and *Putting It Together* which Julie Andrews did off-Broadway a couple of seasons back and over here was taken to Oxford but nowhere else by Diana Rigg: we urgently need to see that one in the West End, but in the meantime there's *Marry Me a Little*, a wonderfully characteristic Sondheim title for this two-character anthology songbook of all his early Manhattan numbers, many of which pre-date *West Side Story*. The double act of Clive Carter and Rebecca Front admirably catch the bitter-sweet spirit of these early numbers, in many of which can be heard the outlines for later, better and more familiar Sondheim classics.

The Kindness of Strangers

A Streetcar Named Desire (Haymarket)

The School for Wives (Piccadilly)

Considering that she made her name on screen being clutched in the paws of King Kong and has since won a brace of Oscars, Jessica Lange is perhaps the most surprising contemporary actress to have requisitioned Blanche DuBois in Tennessee Williams' stage masterpiece about dependence on the kindness of strangers, *A Streetcar Named Desire*.

Yet here she now is, at the Theatre Royal, Haymarket, tackling the role for the third time in a decade in Peter Hall's new production, one of the most hugely fascinating, enjoyable and entertaining misreadings of a classic text that I have ever seen.

First off, if, as she says, 'the dark is comfortable to me', this Blanche seems a little unlucky to have been caught in the full glare of a lavish Technicolored epic, not so much *Miss Saigon* as Miss Psycho perhaps, but certainly a setting where Lana Turner or Joan Crawford might have been the more obvious casting.

The only two areas of show business where Hall has never really achieved commercial success or acclaim are movies and musicals, and, as though to repair that gap, he has bizarrely chosen to make this *Streetcar* far more Hollywood than anything even Miss Lange has ever been involved with hitherto. At moments of high emotion, Stephen Edwards' offstage score comes crashing in like a tribute to Dmitri Tiomkin or Eric Wolfgang Korngold; a set worthy of *Porgy and Bess* slightly defeats the claustrophobia and intimacy usually associated with this script, and all through Hall pulls lighting and sound effects of the kind much needed in Williams's later and more flawed work, but not really essential here.

Not that I really object to this: Miss Lange is much better here than she was on Broadway five years ago, and the idea of *Streetcar* being hijacked by a driver determined to make it into a glossy epic is certainly something new. Toby Stephens is adequately Brandoesque as Kowalski, Imogen Stubbs is perhaps still a little local for Stella, but an impressive supporting cast boasts Sandra Dickinson (now there's a Blanche I'd love to see) as Eunice and Christian Burgess as the gentleman-caller, Mitch.

Williams himself, a melodramatic old showman, would have just loved the glossiness of all the high drama, as well as the sound and fury; high camp and neon have replaced the usual low-light despair, and I just wish they had gone the whole hog and done it as the musical which this production seems so itchy to become.

Not since Pinter gave Lauren Bacall the all-stops-out superstar treatment in *Sweet Bird of Youth* has a Williams script been handled with such a sense of period stardom. What the production lacks in sheer dramatic energy (largely because Miss Lange is a highly efficient performer desperately lacking Vivien Leigh's unique ability to give us a woman on the verge of a total nervous breakdown and manic depression, which was precisely what she was undergoing at the time in reality) it makes up in grand guignol, so that we are subtly shifted from Williams to Lillian Hellman's neighbouring estate.

The result is mega-showbiz night, on no account to he missed: just don't expect it to resemble any *Streetcar* you have ever seen before. This one is the full VistaVision and the streetcar is only taking full-fare, first-class travellers with a nostalgic desire for melodrama.

~

Out of London the best news of this new year is that the producer Bill Kenwright has brought the Theatre Royal, Windsor, England's longest-surviving non-subsidised regional playhouse, back to life with an impressive new schedule; clearly just as his only real rival impresario, Duncan Weldon, now uses the Minerva in Chichester as the starting grid for all his West End transfers so Kenwright intends to upgrade Windsor, and his opening production (about to move into the Piccadilly) is also by Peter Hall, though in a very different mood. Molière's *L'Ecole des Femmes* (1662) has never been as popular over here as *Le Malade Imaginaire* or *Tartuffe* but Ranjit Bolt's new translation makes a joyous little parable as *The School for Wives*.

Essentially this is still a one-joke play about a man falling in love with a teenage girl and trying to ensure her virginity which is, of course, lost all the sooner, but Peter Hall has given it a cool, elegant staging built around the wondrous double-act of Peter Bowles as the gullible prospective husband and Eric Sykes as his malevolent valet. Sykes, one of our last great vaudeville talents, has never been funnier than as the resentful, irritable, incompetent manservant with the manic, lethal sense of humour in distress; early days I know, but if we see a better comic turn on stage this year, we shall be more than lucky.

Paper Tigers

The Shallow End (Duke of York's)

Who now recalls Lambert LeRoux? The question is, I hope, purely rhetorical; twelve years ago, LeRoux was the demon newspaper proprietor of Brenton and Hare's *Pravda*, one of the greatest and most charismatic villains in all post-war British theatre and the character who set Anthony Hopkins back on the road to his present stardom.

But the question arises because those of us still idiotic enough or maybe just innocent enough to believe in the redemptive power of great drama are amazed to this day that, after the arrival of the dreaded Lambert, nothing in the British press actually changed, at least not for the better. Somehow I thought that nothing would ever be the same again after *Pravda*: that no newspaper, or newspaper conglomerate, would ever dare to behave in the way so mercilessly and brilliantly satirised by the play which told us of life and sudden death in the newsroom of the Daily Victory.

Unfortunately, life doesn't work like theatre: the only discernible after-effect of *Pravda* was that real-life press barons behaved even more like the charismatic Lambert, as if eager to prove that Brenton and Hare in their wildest nightmares could never conjure up anything so appalling as what was actually going on in the British press even then.

So now we have another great play about newspapers, making three this century if you start as we always should with Hecht and MacArthur's *The Front Page*. True, journalists will always warm to a play about journalists, even one which holds up a mirror so horrible to our current trade that by the end of it you are seriously wondering whether you are young enough to take up some altogether different and more honourable profession, such as estate agency.

For what, in essence, Doug Lucie's unmissable and unbeatable *The Shallow End* tells us is that not only has nothing got better in this particular rag trade since *Pravda*, but it has all got even more horrible. His frame is simple and stunning: we are in a lavish country-house attending the wedding of a multinational newspaper proprietor's favourite daughter to the son of some equally powerful media baron from the world of television. But we never get to meet the happy couple, nor even their proud parents; for, behind the scenes, an all-powerful British Sunday newspaper is being remodelled for the millennium, a remodelling which involves wholesale bloodshed in the newsroom and the arrival of a team of marketing murderers out for the skins of every decent journalist still to be found lurking anywhere in its pages.

In what may sound a rather familiar scenario, Lucie rings some subtle and witty changes; the one truly noble character turns out to be an Australian, and it is Jane Asher, at her most vulnerable, who as a deserted and forlorn newsroom widow articulates the play's central thesis about the utter corruption of politics, journalism and hence the nation over the last ten years. *The Shallow End* belies its own title; it is a cynical, thoughtful, vicious, witty and brilliant hatchet job on a newspaper empire, and through that on the society which we still take a lunatic pride in calling civilised. Robin Lefevre marvellously spotlights a company of the best character actors in town led by Asher, Julia Ford, Nigel Terry and James Aubrey. I doubt we shall get a better new play this year, and we sure as hell won't get another one this decade which demolishes the new Wapping with such assured stilettoed savagery.

Fine Fiennes

Ivanov (Almeida)

American Buffalo (Young Vic)

Cardiff East (National Theatre)

One explanation of the supremacy of the British theatre could just be this: where else in the world would you walk into a 150-seat fringe playhouse and find, even as you take your seat, an actor alone on stage reading a book – an actor moreover who is being paid less than £200 a week, despite the fact that he has just received his second Oscar nomination?

The actor in question is Ralph Fiennes, and the production is *Ivanov*, an early and usually rather unsatisfactory Chekhov here given a blazing new lease of life by David Hare as the adapter and Jonathan Kent as director. What the new version establishes, and for the first time, is that this is not some sort of early dry run for *Uncle Vanya*; instead, it is a play about a man in deep depression, having a suicidal nervous breakdown several decades before Freud began the programme of analysis which would give it a name.

Chekhov was himself a doctor, and it becomes clear that he is writing here of symptoms all too familiar to him, either from within his own character or those of some of his patients. The title character thus, instead of the usual failed Hamlet, becomes a figure of considerably more fascination engaged effectively in a race against death the result of which we learn only in the very closing moments.

But Chekhov's first play was never a solo star vehicle, and one of the great highlights of this production is the hilarious vodka-and-cards sequence in which three of the best character actors in London (Oliver Ford Davies, Anthony O'Donnell and Bill Paterson) offer a master class in competitive playing which should be caught by every drama student in town. And that's not all: Diane Bull as the appalling heiress, Ian McDiarmid stepping into the role of yet another obsessive card player, and Collin Tierney as the puritanical doctor are all at the very top of their form, as is Harriet Walter as the dying wife. Hare has realised that this is not a failed first attempt at tragi-comedy but rather a vibrantly successful mix of moods, in which the energy of the writing has at last been matched by both staging and editing in translation. This is a production which does more than deserve a long West End and Broadway season; if it fails to get one, either for economic reasons or because of the lunatic intransigence of unions both here and in America who are making actors the very last species of worker unable to cross the Atlantic at will, both London and New York will be considerably the poorer.

~

Over at the Young Vic, Lindsay Posner has a revival of David Mamet's *American Buffalo*, the play which twenty years ago shot several thousand volts through the American theatre and started us on the long, bloody march to Tarantino. I'm still not convinced of this as a great play, but it does have an immense theatricality which is why presumably it has always appealed to such stars as Al Pacino (who has played it here) and Dustin Hoffman (who made the movie); the script turns if not on a dime then at least on a nickel, that being the Buffalo of the title and at the centre of an elaborate if ever more circular series of power games revolving around three small-time losers and a possibly valuable coin.

The star performance in Posner's production comes from the immensely powerful and charismatic Douglas Henshall, with Nicholas Woodeson and Neil Stuke in vital support; all of them, in a junk shop on Chicago's South Side, come to the conclusion that they can really only hope to survive as a family, no matter how dysfunctional. In that sense, *American Buffalo* owes a considerable debt, one I have never seen acknowledged by author or critics, to Arthur Miller's *The Price* which was also about the detritus of the American dream and the scavenger instinct; Mamet's is much the more immediately powerful of the two scripts, but I sometimes wonder if it will live as long as, say, *The Caretaker* to which it also owes an obvious debt in both characterisation and setting.

~

On the National's Cottesloe stage, Peter Gill (as both author and director) premieres *Cardiff East*, which is that total rarity, a play about latterday Wales. It was Paul Scofield as Thomas More who queried one of his clerics selling out his principles for that particular area: 'what shall it profit a man to betray his own soul for the world, but for Wales?' and that attitude of shameful dismissal persists theatrically to this day. Plays about Ireland and Scotland are almost weekly events; for great plays about Wales you have to go back to Emlyn Williams and Dylan Thomas. But Gill's thesis is that all the world comes together in Cardiff: he has written and staged a prose update of *Under Milk Wood* in which a group of often soap-operatic characters begin to consider what if anything their Welsh identity actually means today, if they are not to be just a group of immigrant strangers who happen to have made their home there. Across an often raucous and rancid human landscape of the mind, Gill has assembled his witnesses in comedy and ultimate tragedy to reflect a cross-section of a society he evidently knows and loves intimately; and if the play doesn't completely hang together, then neither does the society it represents. A large cast led by Kenneth Cranham make of this complex patchwork both a celebration and an epitaph for Wales.

Dead Behind the Eyes

The Entertainer (Hampstead)

Death of a Salesman (National)

To Hampstead from Jill Fraser's courageous, constantly threatened (currently by a motorway, no less) but feisty Watermill in Berkshire comes a stripped-down version of *The Entertainer* which sharply challenges all our memories of Laurence Olivier as the original Archie Rice going dead behind the eyes. All Osborne texts could do with a thirty-minute cut, and this one also benefits from a quintet of equally strong performances, so we are focused throughout not just on Michael Pennington's wonderfully seedy pier comedian, Ted Ray gone rancid, but also on his wife, father, son and daughter – all of whom were originally inclined to wilt under Olivier's magnetism. This is also, of course, a play about death at Suez, the death of a son and an Empire as well as the vaudeville Empires around which Archie is still trying to carve out a meagre living, just as his nation's government was trying in an equally seedy, dismal and defeated manner to prop up its own imperial life and influence among countries which were no longer willing to applaud or even stay in the game.

Where Olivier gave us *The Entertainer* through a magnifying glass, Pennington offers an intimate downsizing, no less moving or bitter for its refusal to climb Larry's mountain of maudlin self-pity. Stephen Rayne's production allows Julian Curry as Archie's dying father, the last twice-nightly nobleman, his place in the footlights as well as that of Jane Wood as the long-suffering wife and mother disappearing into drink and darkness. More than ever does this play now emerge as the provincial English answer to *Long Day's Journey Into Night*, no less powerful and moving for running now about half O'Neill's length.

~

For around fifteen years, the stage director David Thacker has been Arthur Miller's representative on earth; all the more surprising, therefore, at least on first sight, that he should have come such a cropper with a new *Death of a Salesman* at the National.

No man dare suggest that Thacker has not been good for Miller, bringing his old and new works to a whole generation of British theatre-goers at a time when Broadway had resolutely turned its back on the old sage. The view from this stall is, however, that Miller is still the greatest post-war dramatist of them all, no matter the nationality; but it is perhaps time he found himself another director. So close is the relationship now between Miller, Thacker and Chris Bigsby (who essentially runs the estate from a centre at the University of East Anglia) that they effectively operate a cartel, one which not only precludes outsiders but also means that Thacker directs so precisely to Miller's orders that the old wizard might as well be staging his scripts himself.

Thus we are back to the old problem of the author who insists on directing his own work; as with Edward Bond at the Barbican, this can lead to a terrible kind of closed-circuit predictability. Thacker's new *Salesman* is not bad, but it is woefully undercast and unwisely set as a kind of surrealist dream sequence, with trees mysteriously floating above their own trunks, and half-finished cars and refrigerators on a revolve irresistibly reminiscent of those 'Into the Future' shows at world fairs where the wonders of modern science whizz past you on a conveyor belt.

This is a play that cries out for naturalism, however much its author may think it needs to be treated like a dream or Willy's dying vision: it only really works when rooted in the reality of post-war America, riding on a smile and a shoeshine into a future about which it is desperately insecure, despite the apparent wealth. Once you lift it up into the realms of the symbolic you lose its central grasp of reality, and Alun Armstrong's Loman is also wildly out of place, walking and looking and sounding like a defeated Scots trade-union secretary rather than the man with the case of samples forever in his trunk and on his mind.

In the half-century since the play was first seen, it is probably only Archie Rice who has ever equalled Loman's tragic glory: this remains the great American tragedy as Willy loses the race to the scrap-heap, his struggle for continued existence counter-pointed by a fantasy in which all his no-good sons are triumphant and all the world loves a seller. Miller himself once told me that in a more benevolent script Willy would have died not a suicide but of a heart attack while polishing his car one Sunday afternoon; but in forcing through the realisation that his life has been a hollow and shameful charade Miller also forces through the awareness of something nightmarish at the heart of the American dream.

We wait all through the show for Willy to die, and when he does, not even his wife can shed a tear: instead she notes simply that the last payment has been made that day on their house. In the new National cast, only Ed Bishop in the relatively minor role of the neighbour catches the right tone of small-town America in moral crisis, and only in his accent did I recall what finally makes America horribly great – the two real-life salesmen who left the Broadway premiere muttering, 'I always told you that New England territory was lousy.'

Holm Sweet Holm

King Lear (National)

In a lifetime of theatre-going I must have seen upward of fifty *King Lears,* some more majestic than that of Ian Holm at the National, some still more mesmeric and some perhaps more hauntingly destroyed by their own weakness or even their own strength; but never have I seen one more moving or accessible.

Richard Eyre's valedictory Shakespeare is on the Cottesloe stage, down the centre of which he and his designer have run a racetrack kind of ramp thereby ensuring that we watch *King Lear* as we might the Derby, wondering which if any of the characters are going to make it to the finish alive. In the event it is old Kent (David Burke, one of a trio of great supporting performances with Michael Bryant's yokel Fool and Tim West's commanding Gloucester) who in the final heartbreak of his 'I have a journey, sir, shortly to go: / My master calls me, – I must not say no' gets past the post dragging a cart on which are not only the bodies of all three daughters but also Lear himself. Father Courage could not have done it better or more tragically.

This is often a *Lear* of surprises: not entirely specific in date, it gives us for instance a Regan (Amanda Redman) who starts out as a high-society hostess, forever encouraging Lear's faintly disturbing paternal passion for her, only to disintegrate into illness and death in a journey that seems to mirror that of her father from the safety of indoors. Then again, Anne-Marie Duff's Cordelia at times appears no less manipulative, the baby daughter accustomed to being spoiled and only too late aware that she, too, has a journey shortly to go. Bryant's Fool, as old and as weary as his royal master, sets up a useful mirror in which Lear can see himself as well as his imminent downfall, while in Paul Rhys and Finbar Lynch we have, for the first time in my recollection, an Edgar and an Edmund who could in real life be bastard half-brothers, so alike are they in looks and bearing.

Beckett and Pinter seem somehow to have made their way in here, too, so that a terrible, black, bleak comedy underlines many of the key moments; if we have tears, we are told not to shed them now because in a moment or two they may be required by someone else even less deserving of them. Timothy West's magnificent Gloucester is there all the time to remind us, by example and nobility, that his is a tragedy no less moving or demanding of sympathy than Lear's, perhaps more so in that he, unlike his King, has done nothing to bring it on. Bryant is there to show us the King as Fool, but the ultimate achievement of both Eyre as director and Holm as Lear is to bring home to us the idea that this is our tragedy as well as the monarch's. Never have I seen a production of Shakespeare's most demanding play which was more willing to accommodate itself to our understanding and involvement, and less inclined to distance its hero whether on the throne or on the heath.

To call this *Lear* domesticated would be to undervalue its infinite pity and compassion; yet by allowing the intimate dictates of the Cottesloe to condition what is effectively a studio production, Eyre has managed to celebrate the space and the play and the actor without any of the modernist gimmicks which have all too often marred previous attempts at downscaling.

Going Into Labour

Tom and Clem (Aldwych)

Michael Gambon is not only one of the greatest actors in the land but one of the most fortunate; a couple of seasons ago he starred on both sides of the Atlantic in David Hare's *Skylight*, arguably the best relationship play of the 1990s, and he is now at the Aldwych in another stunningly brilliant new script, this one from a first-time dramatist.

Stephen Churchett's *Tom and Clem* is the best original drama in town; it imagines a meeting at the Potsdam Conference of July 1945 between Clement Attlee, the newly elected Labour prime minister, and Tom Driberg the gay, louche, renegade MP and journalist.

On one level this is, therefore, the old Peter Shaffer debate between the man of icy principles and his poetic-romantic alter ego, and Gambon is here matched line for line by an equally brilliant Alec McCowen as a remarkably lookalike Attlee. But *Tom and Clem* is about much more than their differences; it is a play about the birth (and death) of post-war British socialism, about gay rights, about the coming of the H-bomb and, topically enough, about Britain trying to find its way out of a long period of Tory rule.

A subplot featuring Sarah Woodward and Daniel de la Falaise about Anglo-Soviet espionage is perhaps less successful, but one can forgive a lot more than that of a drama about compromise and conscience, socialism and sex, ideas and ideals in constant conflict; McCowen and Gambon are a stunning double-act, each often given five-minute speeches with which to mesmerise first each other and then us. Next time anyone tells you the West End no longer has thoughtful state-of-the-nation plays past or present, send them speedily to this one; not that there's really any danger of missing it – *Tom and Clem*, a wonderfully comic, reflective and touching history of the roots of modern Britain, will, if there is any justice, be around here and Broadway for many, many months to come.

Bedtime

The Herbal Bed (Duchess)

The Goodbye Girl (Albery)

At the Duchess, Peter Whelan's *The Herbal Bed* is a gripping Shakespearean thriller of about two hours trying to escape from a considerably more dozy three-hour ramble around its own characters. The story is a remarkable footnote to Stratford history; at the very end of Shakespeare's life, in 1613, his only daughter Susanna, married to a respectable local doctor, brought a case of slander against a local reprobate who had accused her of infidelity and having venereal disease. On this sketchy truth, Whelan has constructed a very slow-starting but ultimately gripping courtroom drama which brings into question all contemporary notions of sin and virtue, truth and convenient fiction, religion and religiosity.

Were it not for half a dozen tremendous performances, not least from Stephen Boxer as a Machiavellian prosecutor and Teresa Banham as the equally tricky Susanna, the first half of *The Herbal Bed* would seem even more languid; but in there somewhere are all the seeds of the drama that are to come to fruition during the trial, and Michael Attenborough's agile production comes good just as the play finally gets itself together for a surprising and wholly unforeseen twist.

~

Say hello to *The Goodbye Girl*, but judging from most other reviews you may have to be quick about it. This week, as it happens, four new musicals open on Broadway in the nick of time to qualify for the Tony Awards; by the law of averages, some of these are bound to go down in flames and, in the case of *Titanic*, possibly in bubbles; yet the air around Times Square is positively promise-crammed at the thought of native territory being reclaimed after more than a decade of the British invasion.

Now compare and contrast, as they say in exam papers, the situation around the West End, where at least as many major new musicals will have opened by the beginning of June. There are few entertainments the British public enjoys more than a musical, and none that are so generally loathed by my critical colleagues. Give them a great, dark, brave masterpiece like *Martin Guerre* and they tell us it is altogether too much like hard work; give them a mindless, feel-good romp like *The Goodbye Girl* and they behave as if they have been forced to sit through child rape.

Nobody is suggesting that *The Goodbye Girl* is the greatest escapist musical in town, since that is clearly Woody Allen's *Everyone Says I Love You* even if it is on film; but what we have at the Albery is a quite remarkable retrieval job by the director Rob Bettinson and the lyricist Don Black. Twenty years ago, *The Goodbye Girl* was the Neil Simon movie for which Richard Dreyfuss won his Oscar as the unfortunate off-Broadway actor forced into an all-gay *Richard III*, while Marsha Mason (then Mrs Simon) played the largely autobiographical role of the New York single mother for whom goodbye has become a way of life after several unsatisfactory affairs have left her with nothing more than a dangerously cute daughter.

Four years ago, *The Goodbye Girl* became a gross and glitzy Broadway musical with a raucous Bernadette Peters and a somewhat bland Martin Short trying unsuccessfully to retrieve a little domestic tragi-comedy from within a vast edifice of irrelevant production numbers and chorus dancing. Its original lyrics (by David Zippel, who in somewhat churlish Soviet fashion has now been 'disappeared' from the billing) were indeed too brassily acerbic for their own good, but Black and Bettinson have now changed all that, so *The Goodbye Girl* gets reinvented for London as a play with songs, brought down in scale to an intimacy which neither the original film nor the Broadway musical ever achieved.

The result is generally enchanting; a musical of light and joy and jokes never better than in an up-on-the-roof love scene with Ann Crumb and the brilliantly versatile Gary Wilmot in a celebration of every Hollywood musical ever made, lovingly and nostalgically choreographed by Tudor Davies.

Sure, there are better and braver musicals around, but few capable of spreading such utter, simplistic delight; Black in his *Tell Me on a Sunday* mood has perfectly caught, if not Manhattan itself, then certainly the Manhattan which he and we have always loved from this safe distance across the Atlantic, and in a curious way it has been left to these two Britons, Black and Bettinson, to show Neil Simon and his composer Marvin Hamlisch the real value of what they have created.

Still Getting Fixed

The Fix (Donmar Warehouse)

Beauty and the Beast (Dominion)

At a time when the future of the stage musical is a matter of transatlantic debate, not least because almost half a dozen of them have just opened on Broadway to generally unenthusiastic reviews, while in this country Andrew Lloyd Webber is seriously thinking of abandoning all management and returning exclusively to the keyboard, it is good to have opening in the same London week two such disparate, diverse and indeed deeply opposite singalongs as *Beauty and the Beast* and *The Fix*. Clearly *The Fix* still needs some fixing, but for those who like their musicals by Sondheim out of Kander & Ebb, this is indeed a knife-edged and courageously rock-edged score by two unknown Americans, John Dempsey and Dana P Rowe, which unlike almost any other in town is totally original insofar as it has no movie, play or best-selling novel in its background. Or rather it has several: you could trace the origins of *The Fix* back to such paranoid Washington conspiracy thrillers as *The Manchurian Candidate*, or forward to any sleaze-tabloid life of the Kennedys.

Indeed, by the end of an increasingly frantic evening we seem to have a child from *The Omen*, Marilyn Monroe from *The Seven Year Itch* having that famous dress blown above her waist, and the Mafia all demanding revenge for the betrayal of their boy in the White House. As you may have gathered, the book of *The Fix* is something of a shambles; it opens with the death of a presidential candidate and the decision by his wife, played by Kathryn Evans, that if she can't be a president's wife she can at least be his mother. Aided and abetted by her own brother-in-law, a gay wheelchair victim with a stammer who forces his own nephew to have sex with him in one of the show's many moments of gala bad taste, the mother from Washington Depths gets her boy within spitting distance of the White House only to have him killed, in a Christ-like crucifixion, by the Mafia who seem to have stumbled in from some altogether different plot.

The result is a black cartoon parody of White House excess and American dreams turned into nightmares: incest, rape, murder, madness, everything that makes Washington politics so much more fun than our own are here batched into a manic musical farce about a would-be First Family so dysfunctional as to make the Borgias look like the Blairs. Sometimes a rock version of *I Claudius*, at others *Camelot* rewritten by Brecht, Weill and Harold Robbins, *The Fix* is as misshapen as its central characters and at best a *Guys and Dolls* rewritten in blood and acid: in the end it really doesn't quite work, not least because Sam Mendes' agile production drifts hopelessly into caricature. But never since the arrival of Sondheim and Kander & Ebb have I been so sure of a new American musical talent; I don't think I ever want or need to see *The Fix* again, but I can't wait to see what Dempsey & Rowe write next. On a space-restricted stage, the choreographer Charles Augins has managed some of the most breathtaking musical routines in town.

~

But if you prefer your musicals the way they used to be, then hasten to *Beauty and the Beast* or rather *Disney's Beauty and the Beast* as the posters have it. This, at £10 million the most expensive show ever staged in the West End, is essentially an old Palladium pantomime in which the scenery does most of the acting and the production is redolent of all those theme-park shows in Florida and California. On Broadway the musical has made several powerful enemies, largely because rival musical producers have neither the Disneyland cash nor the access to their own television networks for the purposes of free advertising and cross-promotion. Over here, however, there is no such problem; television has never been used to advertise London stage shows because it is national, and not even Disney would want to pour millions of dollars into ads seen very largely by audiences living five huundred miles away from their show; nor, alas, have they bothered to clean up the Tottenham Court Road the way they cleaned up Broadway.

As a result, we simply have here a huge musical hit with no political or economic significance for the West End; my ninety-year-old father-in-law reckons it the best show he's seen in seven decades, and only a cynic or a drama critic would tire of dancing soup-tureens and a magical final transformation of Beast into Prince which is only fractionally ruined by some split-second late cueing backstage. The book has one good joke about the Beast's lair ('If it ain't Baroque don't fix it') and the Mencken/Ashman/Tim Rice score is never less than relentlessly adequate. This is *The Phantom of the Opera* meeting the mad King Ludwig of Bavaria, and I see no reason why it should ever go away.

Wallis and Vomit

Always (Victoria Palace)

Closer (National)

Not perhaps the greatest of weeks for stage musicals, what with Andrew Lloyd Webber declaring losses of around £10 million for his Really Useful Group on this side of the Atlantic alone, and the new Abdication musical at the Victoria Palace already unkindly known backstage as 'Wallis and Vomit'.

What is it, I have long wondered, about musicals that brings out the absolute worst in London drama critics? No, this is not going to be a defence of *Always*, essentially because there is no real defence of it; the show is indeed very nearly as terrible as most reviews have been telling you these last few days. But imagine we had been dealing with a truly terrible *Hamlet* or *The Seagull,* and believe me I have seen a few of those in my time; would the Guardian have solemnly published a box detailing the last half-dozen classical West End disasters? Or would my revered friend in the Daily Telegraph have noted that 'it wasn't quite as bad as we had been hoping'?

Just who are 'we', and why do we sit around hoping for musicals to fail? If you were starting out to write or produce a new London musical now, my immediate advice would be to stop. The critical message is that no musical is a good musical, and what could well happen now is precisely what happened in California thirty years ago when the selfsame critical message was sent out; studios not bent on financial suicide simply stopped making musicals, and I for one still miss them very much indeed.

Even so, there is precious little to be said in defence of *Always*, written by a couple of young men who would seem never to have heard of *Crown Matrimonial* or the ITV Edward Fox series or even any of the great songs of the period from Coward and Porter to Maschwitz and 'I've Danced With A Man, Who's Danced With A Girl, Who's Danced With The Prince Of Wales'; they have cobbled together a weird little Windsor wonderland, one which neatly sidesteps the few intriguing aspects of Edward and Wallis, notably his latent fascism and her reputed sexual athleticism.

Clive Carter and Jan Hartley are thus left with a couple of cardboard cut-outs, and a supporting cast led by Shani Wallis as her aunt with even less; oddly enough I once got to know both the Windsors briefly on a Venice beach circa 1955, by which time they were a thoroughly cantankerous old couple deeply resembling their own ghastly Pekingese dogs. But even then, to a twelve-year-old child, there was something more interesting about them than is ever suggested here in a show which goes for instantly shallow stage cartoon characters when it is not dealing in waxworks. A scene in France? Right then, we'll have a bloke in a beret with a concertina; I suppose we were just lucky they didn't put him on a bicycle selling onions while doing his tacky Chevalier impression. 'This kind of stress I don't need' sings the once-and-never King, and one knows exactly how he feels as yet one more lavish production number dies on its dancing feet all around him.

Another question is where the choreographer-director Thommie Walsh has been since 1950; it is one thing to organise period pieces, quite another to stage them as if they were still current. His co-director, the infinitely more classical Frank Hauser, does what he can with a few all-too-brief political scenes, but just as any of them threaten to come to life we are hurled back into yet another fashion show, cocktail party or, worst of all, choirs of loveable Welsh miners singing of their devotion to treacherous Eddie.

But worse than the choreography, or the dialogue, or the lyrics, or the music, or the acting is the realisation that nobody involved in this whole calamity seems to have had the faintest idea of the true period details of this perennially fascinating class warfare. A visit to the current Broadway *Titantic* might have helped, but as for *Always* I fear the Cunard they have tried to recapture is not so much Lady Emerald, who puts in a shaky appearance, as one of the liners of that name which now lies well and truly sunk.

~

On the Cottesloe stage of the National, Patrick Marber's second play *Closer* not only lives up to the promise of his *Dealer's Choice* but is an even sharper and more tense account of relationships in total moral and sexual breakdown. This is *Private Lives* for the late nineties, a story of four people who can live neither together nor apart but whose electric attraction to each other finally burns all of them out in a shock ending which has in fact been very carefully prepared if only we could have seen it coming. Like Coward but precious few others, Marber has a remarkable talent for making us fall in love with appalling people, and here their fatal attraction is what drives the play across the borders of comedy and tragedy. Not since David Hare's *Skylight*, about to reappear at the Vaudeville, has there been a British play about sexual politics with such raw energy and throat-catching reality, and in Marber's own production the quartet of mismatched lovers are equally breathtakingly played by Sally Dexter, Ciaran Hinds, Liza Walker and Clive Owen. Like *Skylight*, *Closer* will also have a long West End and Broadway life when it leaves the South Bank; but catch it there while it is still fresh off the typewriter.

Acting Up

Amy's View (National)

Like his long-time director Richard Eyre, the most prolific and faithful of National Theatre dramatists this last decade or so is leaving the South Bank on a considerable high: David Hare's new play *Amy's View* is not only another triumph of his national temperature-taking, but also that still less fashionable form of drama, the backstage play.

Once upon a time, every self-respecting dramatist from O'Neill and Odets to Coward, Rattigan and even Mamet and Williams felt their portfolios incomplete without at least one look through a dressing-room glass darkly. But with the recent fear and loathing of 'luvviedom' has come the belief that plays written, however well, in greasepaint are unlikely to appeal to a non-Equity audience. So what Hare has cunningly done is to save the ritual dressing-room confrontation until the very end of a touching, chilling, hugely observant contemporary social drama, most of which takes place in an equally unfashionable and long-lost setting, a country house in the Thames Valley.

It is more than a little courageous of Hare to set his stirring defence of the live drama within the framework of what might at first seem a set vacated forty years ago by the likes of Enid Bagnold and Robert Bolt, and left derelict ever since; braver still, though I appear to be alone in noticing this, is to open *Amy's View* exactly as Coward opened his 1925 *Hay Fever*, with a celebrated if now outdated actress suddenly confronted with the arrival in her living-room of an unwelcome weekend guest in the shape of her daughter's apparently unsuitable boyfriend. The only difference, seventy years later, is that we are now in Pangbourne, whereas Coward set his play a few miles downstream at Marlow.

But having paid this ritual, and I trust conscious, obeisance to the old backstage dramas, Hare moves his swiftly forward; his play is about the victims of Lloyd's insurance crash, the supremacy of cinema over theatre for the young, and above all else Amy's view, which is essentially that love will conquer all just so long as everyone is very nice to everyone else.

Only of course they are not: around Amy (a suitably wide-eyed if sometimes inaudible Samantha Bond) are gathered her mother (Judi Dench, as the predatory old actress unable to believe in a world no longer run in her image), a drunken neighbour who turns out to be the Lloyd's villain (Ronald Pickup), and a pushy young television director (Eoin McCarthy), this last a somewhat thankless nine-pin role, though not so much of an afterthought as that of the young actor (Christopher Staines) who has come out of nowhere to sustain, with remarkably little help, the final scenes. There is also an old and later paralysed grandmother, wonderfully played in a welcome return to the stage by Joyce Redman.

In the end, this is not as powerful a Hare piece as *Skylight* or indeed *Racing Demon* or *Plenty*, largely because across the sixteen years of the play's development the author himself seems to get a little confused about his own priorities of national and personal concern. The declining respect awarded to those actors who stay away from films and television? The fact that some very nice if somewhat careless people got scorched by Lloyd's? The way that a trendy film director specialising in exploding skulls will always play to better houses than the very best dramatists?

All of that is at the heart of *Amy's View*, but her view is too clouded; her sudden, arbitrary last-act demise seems the only way Hare could get us to care at least in retrospect about her somewhat dim vision, and so when the final confrontation comes between her still self-absorbed mother and the young director who has married and then betrayed her, we know from the start that the stage lady will win out over the film guy precisely because that is what this play has been all about from the beginning.

It is only at the very last that we get the glimmering of a new thought: that, in the end, an actress is always alone because no writer, no director, no relative can go out there with her to the only place it really matters and where she most wants to be. Judi Dench conveys, as only she can, a woman who finds more life in theatre than in life, and *Amy's View* is at the last reflected in a dressing-room mirror. But that mirror is not in fact Amy's, and thus does a marvellous play lose some of its ultimate purpose and direction. For all that, hasten along: Eyre's staging of the last sixty seconds is one of the most breathtaking representations of the trick of theatre I have ever seen.

Broadway 1997

Lieber & Stoller's anthem to the Great White Way, currently to be heard at the Prince of Wales in *Smokey Joe's Cafe*, has seldom in thirty years been more justifiable. Though the patriotic news is of the four Tony Awards given recently to the Thelma Holt/Bill Kenwright production of *A Doll's House,* scoring for Janet McTeer and others a scoop equalled only four other times since the war by Brits on Broadway, the real story is of an amazing local theatrical revival around Times Square.

Next week, *Cats* replaces *A Chorus Line* as the longest-running show in the entire history of Broadway, and after fifteen years there is something very satisfying historically in the realisation that the invasion which it started from this side of the Atlantic has come to an end just as it enters the history books. For *Cats* arrived on Broadway just as the world's greatest theatrical musical-machine was in total collapse.

And now it is all over; within the last month alone, five major Broadway musicals have opened in rapid succession to crown what has been the most exciting native season I can recall there since the very early 1970s. Let's take those first; the show that most richly and urgently deserves a London transfer, preferably to somewhere as operatic as the Coliseum or Sadlers' Wells (which it would stunningly reopen) is Maury Yeston's *Titanic*. Much mocked in rehearsal and preview, largely because of irresistible headlines about icebergs and 'after *Show Boat* – no boat', this Richard Jones production is also the absolute, if as yet unsung, triumph of a Brit on Broadway.

The greatness of *Titanic* lies as much in Jones' production as in Yeston's score; it is a masterpiece of invention, especially scenically, in which the ship that hit the iceberg is understood to have also been the closing of the Victorian era and an end to its nobility, as well as the arrogance which it represented. A largely unknown cast of forty play out the tragedy for all it is historically and emotionally worth, in a score which soars with great anthem-tributes to Elgar and Vaughan Williams. Not for nothing was its American composer a music scholar at Cambridge in the early 1960s; Yeston's score is a masterpiece of Old World echoes as it crashes into the iceberg of the new, and after an initially rough crossing it is already clear, at least to me, that *Titanic* is the greatest American musical to have been written since *Cats* put the frighteners on the local form.

The other superb new musical also has a London-based (although Australian) director in Michael Blakemore, who for the second time in five years, the first being *City of Angels*, has taken a jazz-based Cy Coleman score and turned it into a considerable dramatic triumph. This time the show is *The Life*, far and away the greatest lament for the old Times Square since Damon Runyon's *Guys and Dolls*, though its aspirations are considerably greater. In telling tales of the pimps and prostitutes who have just been cleared out of 42nd Street to make the area safe for Mickey Mouse and his Walt Disney invasion (itself far more threatening than anything we brought from the West End), *The Life* reaches unashamedly towards *Porgy and Bess* as well as *West Side Story* for its frames of reference. There is, as in *Titanic*, a truly tragic dimension of grand opera here which has only lately been achieved elsewhere by Boublil & Schonberg; *The Life* deserved far more awards than it won, not least for Blakemore and a stunningly streetwise cast and choreography. It, too, should be seen over here just as soon as we can afford to transport it.

This has not, however, been a good time for Kander & Ebb, in my view still the most potent musical team to have come out of Broadway since Sondheim, who is of course a team all by himself; their revival of *Chicago* swept the awards in its category only because of what seems to me Broadway's thoroughly unhealthy choreographic obsession with the ghost of Bob Fosse, but their new *Steel Pier* is a surprisingly dim account of marathon dancers at the seaside in the 1930s, a subject vastly better handled by a movie called *They Shoot Horses, Don't They?* back in 1969. Here a desperately uncharismatic cast led by Karen Ziemba sing showstoppers which embarrassingly have no show to stop, although I have an idea that the CD may begin to sound a lot more impressive than the production it represents, one already looking as tired as the marathon dancers themselves.

The other major musical revival in town is Bernstein's *Candide*, one of those endless works-in-progress which for the last fifty years everyone from Lillian Hellman to Stephen Sondheim has tried unsuccessfully to get right; this time the director is Hal Prince, who has also been messing around with the show for several decades to no avail. He has gone this time around for a vast, sprawling carnival but unwisely refused to allow his star, Jim Dale, any leeway to perform his own brand of *commedia dell'arte*, the one that made his name back at Frank Dunlop's Young Vic in the late 1960s and would have been perfect here; instead Dale, like the rest of Prince's production, just sinks under the weight of the show's many failings, not the least of which is that, having written for it the greatest overture in all Broadway history, even Bernstein himself (who has now acquired the same uneasily God-like New York status as Bob Fosse) had not the faintest idea what to do next with *Candide*. Maybe if Voltaire had wanted it as a musical, he'd have written it as one.

So much for the musicals; in the straight theatre, this has been the Broadway year of Christopher Plummer, who has a dazzling near-solo show in *Barrymore*, and again there's a kind of historic perfection in this. Just as in the twenties and thirties the American theatre clung desperately to Barrymore because he was the only notable classic actor they'd had in the half century or so since Booth, so now it clings to Plummer, solemnly billed as 'the greatest living actor' as though Gielgud and Scofield were somehow deceased, simply because there is literally no one else around the American stage with even a fraction of his stature. William Luce's rapid gallop through the decline of the great Jack is sometimes overly sketchy, and takes weird factual liberties; but Plummer bestrides the script like the Colossus he is, and again should be booked on an early Concorde.

Also away from the orchestras, Wendy Wasserstein's *An American Daughter* is an anthology of every attitude which makes America most tiresome even to those of us who love it best and have American passport-carrying children. Like much of her earlier work, this is a drawing-room comedy shot through with a lot of agonising about the role of upper-crust female Wasps, though if every time she starts on a speech about 'American women' you were able to substitute 'Icelandic' or 'Belgian' you'd have some idea of how ludicrously introverted, isolationist and indulgent her concerns remain. At best she is a pale shadow of Timberlake Wertenbaker, and at worst a compendium of entries for any Pseuds' Corner; a distinguished cast headed by Kate Nelligan and Hal Holbrook try to convince us that there is something going on here and I guess there is, at least for those who found Enid Bagnold deeply symbolic.

Briefly and finally, *Forbidden Broadway* continues after a decade or more to be a scurrilous, libellous and wondrous parody of everything else on stage, which makes it all the more shameful that we never manage it over here without ending up in the law courts; *Full Gallop* is a compelling monologue about Diana Vreeland, the great Vogue fashion guru; and *Anyone Who Had A Heart* is a brilliantly choreographed and directed (by Gillian Lynne) celebration of the songs of Bacharach & David, the first of its kind and also eagerly awaited over here once it is out of its pre-Broadway trials.

Still Waiting

Waiting for Godot (Old Vic)

Twilight of the Golds (Arts)

The Maids (Donmar Warehouse)

Plays don't change; audiences do. The lesson of Peter Hall's new Old Vic staging of *Waiting for Godot*, which he introduced to Britain and last directed in 1955, is that, although some of us may still share the doubts of that first cast about the true genius of Beckett, there is now not a lot of doubt about where his script came from or led to; it was not the isolated experience it must have seemed at the time.

The tramps eternally awaiting the absent Godot are out of Laurel and Hardy, and they lead us to Morecambe and Wise; the Rosencrantz and Guildenstern of Tom Stoppard are their most immediate theatrical descendants, and although I am less convinced about Pinter or Orton setting out from this selfsame blasted heath, I guess what Beckett taught the whole world of dramatists was that an audience could be rather more intelligent and even tolerant than had hitherto been suspected.

Although now it is famous, alongside Pinter's *The Birthday Party* and the Boublil & Schonberg *Les Misérables*, as 'the one the critics got wrong', it is in fact surprising for 1955 how many people got it right. The difference now is one of confidence on both sides of the footlights; actors play in the knowledge they are doing a classic, and when the audience laughs it is because they have been empowered by world reaction across almost half a century to do so.

If Hall's first, ground-breaking production was, as Beckett thought, rather top-heavy on sets and sentiment, this one makes amends; Alan Howard and Ben Kingsley, back on the London stage for the first time in a decade, form the most dazzling double-act anywhere in town as this quintessentially Irish odd couple (could it be that Jack Lemmon and Walter Matthau also derive from there?) with a mix of despair and delight, panache and paranoia, which alone would be worth the price of admission. If indeed, as current reports indicate, Hall's first Old Vic season is likely to cost his splendid Canadian backers at least a million pounds more than they can hope to recoup at the box-office, one can only conclude that it continues to be money well spent; this is the definitive *Godot* if for no other reason than that Hall has had more than forty years to think about it and we have had the same period of time just to get used to the idea of a play in which, famously, nothing happens twice.

One of the many great strengths of Hall at the Vic has been his ability to command supporting casts the like of which the RSC or the Shakespeare Globe or indeed the National would kill for. And sure enough here we also get Denis Quilley as Pozzo, going from majesty to madness as a kind of miniature King Lear, and Greg Hicks as Lucky, making up in sheer theatrical energy what his one great speech still lacks in philosophic coherence. This, then, is the user-friendly *Godot*, no longer an impenetrable wasteland but a reasonably straightforward tragi-comedy about two vagrants determined to blame on their boots the faults of their feet.

~

Despite considerable success all over America, it has taken Jonathan Tolins' *Twilight of the Golds* fully four years to cross the Atlantic and I can see why; this is a curiously Manhattanesque mix of sitcom and social drama which owes rather more to such television hits as *Cheers* or *Friends* than to any more strictly theatrical source, rooted though it is in a passion for Wagner's *Ring* cycle as echoed by the title. The Golds themselves are a couple of affluent achievers (what makes me think this script was a product of the last boom of the eighties?) who discover not only that they are to be parents but that their unborn son is genetically destined to be gay.

To abort or not to abort? The wife's brother, himself a Wagner-obsessed gay, is understandably indignant that the question should ever arise, and as the whole show is written and indeed voiced from his perspective primarily, it is not surprising that we can soon guess the final outcome. Along the way, Tolins will drift down any byway that affords him a good gag or any new little insight into the problems of growing up gay and Jewish in the big city; but in the end the play seems unable to decide whether it wants to be Neil Simon or Wendy Wasserstein and therefore misses both targets. The actress Polly James, in her first directing role, though, does get some very good performances from Gina Bellman and Sheila Allen as two of the five characters still in search of an author here.

~

And, finally, the return to the Donmar Warehouse of *The Maids* which, written also in Paris only a few years before *Godot*, has also taken a half-century or so to find its true focus. Based on a celebrated murder trial of crime passionel, this erotic black mass, in which two oppressed chambermaids gear themselves up for killing through a series of increasingly creepy power games, has recently often been played by men in drag, something the playwright Genet himself suggested as early as 1947. But for this new production of an agile David Rudkin translation, the director John Crowley has gone back to basics, with Niamh Cusack and Kerry Fox in fine form as the maids of the title, and Josette Simon cascading from a great height before joining them in the lower depths as their mistress. This is not really a production which tells us anything we did not already know about the play, and even in a brisk, no-interval ninety minutes the characters still seem to be playing one or two power-reversal games too many; for all that, Genet's fantasy remains a powerful argument against going into any kind of domestic service.

Apocalypse Now

Heartbreak House (Almeida)

Chips with Everything (National)

As Britain starts to stumble back to life from a collective, Diana-inspired national nervous breakdown, this may well be as good a time as any to revisit *Heartbreak House* in a brilliant and breathtaking new staging by David Hare at the Almeida. It is even arguable that, just as Shaw was writing here the first of this century's state-of-the-nation plays, Hare has recently (in his National trilogy) written the last, so what we have here is effectively one bookend gazing back across eighty years at the other.

Shaw started to write his play in 1916, in a large country-house in Sussex, which allowed him to hear both the witterings of the Bloomsbury set who were its residents and the distant sounds of the guns in Flanders as the First World War reached its climax. In that sense this is where Chekhov meets the apocalypse; what starts as a country-house comedy of appalling manners ends in blood and bombardment and death: 'The Captain is in his bunk drinking bottled ditchwater and the crew is gambling in the fo'c'sle,' says Shotover in his last great speech;

'She will strike and sink and split; do you think the laws of God will be suspended in favour of England because you were born in it?'

It is such a good question, and eight decades on it still seeks an answer. Sure there are always problems with *Heartbreak House,* not least the fact that this Shaw-advertised 'fantasia in the Russian manner on English themes' may start out like the local *The Cherry Orchard* but very soon drifts into an Edwardian *Hay Fever* of which the real star apart from Shotover is the house itself, one where hearts and nations can be broken with equal ease while its inhabitants debate the virtues of selling your soul to the devil in Zanzibar.

It has thus always been a rambling structure, at times apparently run up in haste by an unholy alliance of Turgenev and Ben Travers, and to people it with weekend and other guests Hare has assembled one of the starriest and most impressive casts that even the Almeida has recently known. Richard Griffiths, a splendid mountain of a man getting to be very nearly as large in voice and circumference as Orson Welles, gives Shotover moments of unaccustomed tranquillity and gentleness; Patricia Hodge cascades from great and chilly heights to offer a memorable and definitive Lady Utterword, halfway from Lady Bracknell to Ottoline Morell, while Penelope Wilton as Hesione and Emma Fielding as a waif-like Ellie Dunn do their best to keep the intellectual dry rot of an already collapsing house from total disintegration.

The men are no less impressive: Peter McEnery, Harry Landis, Malcolm Sinclair and Simon Dutton have all understood that what we have here is domestic farce masquerading as social history. You might, if you were very lucky, see a more firmly rooted production of *Heartbreak House* than this one in the next half-century, but I doubt you will ever see a more quintessentially or unmissably theatrical one, richly deserving a rapid West End transfer.

~

Arnold Wesker is also a dramatist unafraid of taking the national temperature theatrically, and it is good to have his *Chips with Everything* on the National's Lyttelton stage in an energetic new square-bashing production by Howard Davies. There is, however, now a problem with Wesker, as with John Osborne; the more that their revivals improve, the shakier the plays themselves are apt to seem. This is the first major revival of *Chips* in London since it first opened at the Royal Court in 1962; at that time, the male audience divided into those who had either been through a war or done peacetime National Service and those of us born in or after 1941 who were the first generation this century never to have worn any kind of uniform. Here for the first time was a play which told us just what square-bashing was like, and what it did to the individuality of young men trying to come to terms with the complexities of adulthood. It was raw, tough and ultimately heartbreaking, and I still don't understand why it never got made into a movie.

But time has not been altogether generous to the play; though it remains a savage indictment of Air Force regimentation, and though the ever-smiling Smiler is still a tragic figure ('Can't help it, Sarge, I was born that way'), I had forgotten how much the play owed at least in the first half to *Seagulls over Sorrento* and *The Hasty Heart* and *Worm's Eye View* and all those other theatrical sitcoms about life in the mess which start out as comedy and always end in tragedy. All the cross-sectional class and social stereotypes are here, from the upper-class misfit to the barely literate hero, and although Harold Hobson once wrote that this was 'the first anti-Establishment play of which the Establishment has real cause for fear', in fact the battle had already been fought and won on other territory. National Service had been abolished two years before the first staging of *Chips*. What the play did achieve was the post-trilogy confirmation of Wesker's real genius for dialogue and dialect and dialectic, and it still seethes with a kind of angry vitality.

The new revival has some great performances, not least from Rupert Penry-Jones as the aristocrat who wants to escape down the class structure, a character later adopted in movie after movie by Dirk Bogarde and Jo Losey. In the role that made a star of Frank Finlay, James Hazeldine is a magnificently lugubrious Corporal Hill, and Julian Kerridge's Smiler could have wandered in from *Of Mice and Men*. On Rob Howell's brilliantly versatile wire-mesh set, Julian Glover is also hugely impressive as the Wing Commander who suddenly realises, almost unnoticeably, that the world is about to change even on the parade ground, but it is in the end more as a choreographed dramatic ballet of brutalisation than as a drama that *Chips* remains effective.

Epic Opening

An Enemy of the People (National)

Cyrano (Stratford)

Henry V (Stratford)

Trevor Nunn, who now formally becomes the fourth director of Britain's National Theatre, has also this week triumphantly broken the handover curse of the other three: Laurence Olivier, Peter Hall and Richard Eyre all felt the need to open their managements with a staging of *Hamlet*, and in every single case it was a mistake. Nunn by contrast, has broken at least temporarily with the Bard and opened with what he has always done best, a production where a community is in ferment and at the barricades of some kind of civic disorder. Without denigrating the equally remarkable work he has done in chamber settings, notably the Ian McKellen *Macbeth* and (with McKellen as Iago) *Othello*, it still seems to me that if Nunn's reputation is to rest on any single achievement it will be the kind of crowd control and epic stage management he brought to *Les Misérables* and *Nicholas Nickleby*.

And where better to try for the triple crown than with Ibsen's *An Enemy of the People*, one of the very few classic plays to have at its heart a sustained public meeting? By opening his regime on the Olivier stage, always the most treacherous and demanding of the three in the National complex, Nunn has fervently and brilliantly declared his hand as both director and producer. This is precisely the kind of huge theatrical adventure that the Olivier most needs, and all too seldom gets.

Christopher Hampton's new version of the text is also a revelation, taking us far away from the more simplistic adaptation by Arthur Miller in which Dr Stockmann, the enemy of the title, becomes just another variant of John Proctor in *The Crucible*, a man defiant and alone in front of the McCarthyite mob. What Hampton suggests is considerably more disturbing: that Stockmann may in many ways be as dangerously fascist as all of his crowd of opponents. And when, in Ian McKellen's breathtaking and barn-storming performance, he finally stands at the head of what is left of his family staring fiercely into the future, we are offered yet another chilling political and social image, that of the Lenin recruiting posters of the early Soviet era.

This has always been a play steeped in politics, and its plot probably lives now more famously in *Jaws*, the shark movie which I once persuaded its author Peter Benchley to accept as having been drawn almost scene by scene from Ibsen; wisely, however, he kept that information from his Hollywood masters, lest they took fright at the idea of anything quite so goddamn old and cultural. But it is hard now not to see that shark swimming across the back of John Napier's magnificently versatile set, especially when the townsfolk, who teem through and around it, are forced to choose between publicising a horrible home truth or preserving their tourist trade at the spa.

Nunn has drawn on so many influences here, from Dickens to D W Griffith, that at times there is the danger of simply having too much going on in too many corners of the community. But as the play's searchlight falls first on McKellen's mad professional evangelist, then on his corrupt brother and alter ego, the mayor and police chief (Stephen Moore in a splendidly Machiavellian turn), who, equally hungry for power, has simply chosen to go for it by more orthodox ballot boxes, we begin to realise that everyone here has a tale to tell. Only the two most virtuous characters, Penny Downie and Lucy Whybrow as Stockmann's long-suffering wife and daughter, are borderline boring because of their extreme goodness.

So this is no longer the story of the Master Builder as revolutionary hero; instead, it is the saga of a town in crisis, and the result is a topical piece, in which dialogue about press harassment, the morality of journalism and the hopelessness of the soft-centred liberal cause seems torn from the morning papers. If the test of a great play is eternal familiarity, then Ibsen has given us that; if it is a play about the communal corruption of the common good, then that is here too. *An Enemy of the People* has been reborn as a passionately current debate about the value of the individual.

~

Antony Sher's intriguing Cyrano seems to be a more radical departure from the heroic norm. Given an actor whose Richard III cavorted on crutches and whose Tamburlaine hung upside down on ropes, one might expect to have his buckles well and truly swashed, even in the relatively constrained spaces of the Swan. Instead, Sher shrugs, grins embarrassedly, hops from foot to foot, fiddles with his spectacles. His famous 'panache' looks more like innocent absent-mindedness than heroic disdain for danger. What Sher communicates is Cyrano's peculiar incompetence. His stories are always being interrupted, his poetry misappropriated and misread, his ambitions thwarted, his innate romanticism strangled by circumstances. His nose isn't just a freak of fate without which he would be another D'Artagnan (as it was in Rappeneau's film starring Depardieu); it's the inescapable sign that everything he does is tinged with ridiculousness.

Neither of these new versions of familiar plays fully explores the suggestions that their leading men provide. Greg Doran gives us an effective, well-played, rollicking *Cyrano*, rousing and moving as required, and apparently ignoring the subtle doubt that Sher brings to the central role. Ron Daniels' *Henry V* has some interesting ideas, but tends to fall back on a critique of nationalism which will surprise no one (does anyone still think the play isn't about these things?).

The characters move through time via the costume department. First World War outfits seem to signify a gentlemanly attitude to warfare, while the campaign in France switches to the messier visual language of the Second World War; Pistol and his band of profiteers are dressed up as Hell's Angels, appropriate for civilians who think it's fun to imitate the obscenities of real combat. Some of this works, but the effect is often to divide the play into a series of rather disjointed tableaux, and so to flatten the drama. The set, like the lighting, is stark and monotonous. Michael Sheen's nervy, humane Henry doesn't fit into these rather abstract meditations on warfare; the production is at its best when it leaves him to hold the stage on his own, leading us through his private anxieties rather than lecturing us about the ambiguities of his public role.

Offsetting the routine feel of both productions is the RSC's usual ensemble strength. Best of the peripheral figures in *Henry V* are Alan David's hilarious Fluellen and Campbell Morrison's swaggering, grubby Pistol. The supporting cast of *Cyrano* has more work to do, and acquits itself impressively. Alexandra Gilbreath makes a perky Roxane, clearly more suited to Cyrano than to Raymond Coulthard's plausibly dim Christian. Anthony Burgess' translation of Rostand's play, dating back to 1971, still strikes the right mix of antique romanticism and ironic modernity. The performing text of this *Henry V* has been cobbled together using the same scissors-and-paste technique as was adopted for the RSC's current *Hamlet*, and, as in that production, the pace of the resulting version is about right, although (perhaps inevitably) much wonderful material has been excised.

Shropshire Lad

The Invention of Love (National)

For those of us, maybe just those of me, who believe that Tom Stoppard has never written anything greater than his 1974 *Travesties*, there is great news at the National; by way of a leaving present, Richard Eyre has staged superbly the latest play by the man who is essentially what we on this side of the Atlantic have instead of Stephen Sondheim, and without the music.

That Stoppard is the most intellectually brilliant playwright of my half-century life-time, I have no doubt; but when that brilliance leads, as I believe it did in his last play *Arcadia*, to a series of often exclusionary mind games, there is cause for concern; the professor was in danger of disappearing up his own genius.

The Invention of Love (Cottesloe) brings him back centre stage and in total triumph; once again we are, as in *Travesties*, dealing with a group of world-class talents who might have met, though in fact few of them did, in a place where they all happened to be living at roughly the same time. Instead of Lenin and Tzara and James Joyce in 1917 Zurich, we now have A E Housman (the Shropshire Lad himself, or at any rate his creator, and how typical it is of Stoppard's quirky research that we discover only now that there were few places Housman hated more than Shropshire), and Oscar Wilde and Frank Harris and Jerome K Jerome and Walter Pater and John Ruskin, all gathered on the banks of the Oxford Isis sometime in the early 1880s.

Except, of course, that nothing in Stoppard is ever quite that simple; this river is not just the Isis, but also the Thames of *Three Men in a Boat* and the Styx of Hell, complete with a quixotically boring boatman, Michael Bryant as Charon: 'I had that Dionysus once in the back of me boat.' So this is a play about a river? Not exactly.

It is a play about Housman young (Paul Rhys in edgy undergraduate uneasiness) and Housman old (John Wood, always Stoppard's best interpreter, here in the performance of his life: 'I am not as young as I was,' he tells his younger alter ego, 'whereas you of course are'). At one level, and there are many, many more than I can only begin to excavate here, this is a play about a little known, self-torturing, closet gay poet trying to come to terms with his sexual and poetic self amid tremendous late-Victorian uncertainty; one of the many central paradoxes of the man is that he left university without a degree and was within fifteen years one of the most distinguished classical professors in the world, as acerbic in his textual commentaries as he was paralytically shy in real life, so shy that he moved house six times, on every occasion because a neighbour spoke to him on the train to work.

His life was marked only, as Stoppard notes in the play, 'by long silences', and though many dramatists might have been content just to fill in those silences, Stoppard is not many dramatists. His play veers off into the night sky like a firework display. One minute we have all the great 1870s dons at Oxford playing imaginary croquet as they debate the nature of poetry and philosophy; the next, we get Oscar Wilde cutting to the heart of the play's only problem: 'Biography,' says Tom's Oscar, 'is the mesh through which our real life escapes.'

The Invention of Love is a great play about a great deal; but in the end it is, I think, about the corruption of texts and men, and the price that the hypocritical and flawed public and private morality of the last century exacted from its greatest talents.

Balancing Act

A Delicate Balance (Haymarket)

A Letter of Resignation (Comedy)

When Edward Albee's *A Delicate Balance* first opened here, in a somewhat austere staging with Peggy Ashcroft at the Aldwych all of thirty years ago, I took its cross-references to be towards Samuel Beckett: the nameless dread which forces a married couple to billet themselves indefinitely on their best friends, and above all the bleakness of the vision of Agnes their hostess ('Finally there's nothing there, save rust and bones and the wind'), certainly seemed to point in that direction. It wasn't until some time later, when I came across a brilliant preface written by Albee to the plays of Noël Coward that I realised we might in fact be a great deal closer to home.

What, for instance, is the game of Get the Guests in his *Who's Afraid of Virginia Woolf?* if not a variant on the agonies inflicted by Coward on his weekenders in *Hay Fever*? Moreover, when we come to *A Delicate Balance*, once again we are sharply reminded of Sir Noël: an elegant house in the country, unwelcome guests, an alcoholic sister, a recalcitrant daughter, an all-knowing mother, and a father who has effectively retreated from even his own existence: all are Cowardly stereotypes from the 1920s given sharp and sinister make-overs by Albee. It is the triumph of the new production at the Haymarket to have realised these connections still considerably ahead of most Albee scholars. Anthony Page, the director, and his brilliantly elegant designer Carl Toms have come up with a hugely rich staging in which Eileen Atkins and John Standing hold the fort against their own self-destruction while Maggie Smith (as the hard-drinking, concertina-playing sister), Sian Thomas (as the four-time divorcee daughter) and James Laurenson and Annette Crosbie (as the petrified neighbours demanding refuge) fill out the best cast in London this season, maybe the best ever seen in any Albee over here.

On Broadway last season, it was Elaine Stritch who walked away with this revival as the sister: but at the Haymarket Maggie Smith faces vastly tougher competition and at the end of the evening it is the world-weary, infinitely elegant, carefully wasted husband who, in John Standing's mesmerising performance, best captures the spirit of familial and personal self-destruction that lies at the heart of this great play. *A Delicate Balance* can now be seen as the time-bombed bridge that gets us from *Virginia Woolf* to *Three Tall Women*. Where once only marriages imploded in Albee, now it is entire families passing from generation unto generation the destructive art of the dinner party gone poisonous, the hostess off her trolley, the family that only stays together to slay together, even if the victims do turn out to be themselves. There are no nearest or dearest in Albee; and if we are to take home any single message, it is perhaps that there is a surprising amount to be said in favour of the orphanage when you consider most alternatives; the relative values have long since gone into deficit.

~

At the Comedy, Hugh Whitemore's *A Letter of Resignation* takes us back to the Profumo scandal of 1963, though it is arguable here that the resignation of the title is also that, both personal and political, of Harold Macmillan whose premiership was fast drawing to a close and speeded on its way by the aftermath of the affair.

We have lately had a lot of documentary drama around the West End, and much of it focused on the politics of the post-war years; but Whitemore's interest is really only in the character of old SuperMac, as played by Edward Fox in another of his startlingly lookalike impressions. Fox's Macmillan, much like his equally impressive Edward VIII in the first Abdication drama on television some twenty years ago, is a man in retreat from any kind of reality, holed up in a Scottish castle as the news from Westminster gets worse by the hour and by the messenger. Two of the latter (one from MI5, the other from the Cabinet Office) have arrived to break the news to the old man that his beloved Jack Profumo has finally admitted lying to the House of Commons over his relationship with the model Christine Keeler, and virtually all of Act One is taken up with an unusually plodding recapitulation of their story.

Only then does it become clear that Whitemore has another interest: the affair, starting back in the 1920s, between Macmillan's wife Lady Dorothy and another wayward Tory MP, Bob Boothby. This, in an uncomfortable flashback, emerges as the prime reason for the prime minister's sexual and maybe even social withdrawal from contact with the reality of love and lust, and therefore his inability to understand or manoeuvre the Profumo affair to any real advantage. There are some uncharacteristically clumsy moments in *A Letter of Resignation*, not least a scene in Act Two where Lady Dorothy (presumably for our benefit) reads aloud to her husband the letter of the title which we have seen him on stage reading to himself an hour earlier. But at the heart of this docu-drama is Fox's ravaged, retreating premier, already aware that with Profumo goes not only his own career but also a whole way of British life which, for better or worse, at least meant that gentlemen were allowed to play with call-girls without exciting the attentions of a still docile press.

Windy City

Chicago (Adelphi)

Mutabilities (National)

Bugsy Malone (Queens)

An obsessive lover of the Broadway musical in general and those of Kander & Ebb in particular, why do I now find myself the only critic in London underwhelmed by the current revival of *Chicago* at the Adelphi? No musical of recent times, not even those of Lloyd Webber or Cameron Mackintosh, has been more expertly or carefully pre-sold, and there is no doubt that the queue will be halfway down the Strand for at the very least the next two years. We know, of course, that the production comes from the last Broadway season, where it collected several Tony awards; what we are not told so often, however, is that it began not on the Great White Way but as a one-weekend-only concert staging, similar to our Lost Musicals seasons at the Barbican.

As a result, there is very little here by way of scenery or costumes; a giant bandstand dominates the stage, while all the acting and dancing has to be done around it in surprisingly constricted spaces. The original show has thus been cut back, by its director Walter Bobbie, to its very barest essentials, and in fact we might as well be witnessing it at a Barbican concert or the Royal Festival Hall, so limited is the acting area now available at the Adelphi. The other problem, it seems to me, is the passionate reverence for the late Bob Fosse evidenced by the choreographer Ann Reinking, once his wife, so that the knees and elbows are everywhere; I have always believed that a little Fosse goes a very long way, and here it goes all through the show and then around the back of the orchestra and around again, just in case for a split-second we should forget the style of the original creator. As I have always believed of Agnes de Mille, allowing even a genius choreographer to dominate a show is rather like giving the whole thing over to the senior lighting man.

So what of *Chicago* itself? Dating from 1975 as a musical, it in fact goes back to the early 1930s as first a play and then a Ginger Rogers movie called *Roxie Hart*, which told of a publicity-seeking dancer on trial for murder and determined to bring her showbiz talents into the witness box. God has certainly been good to the current Adelphi producers, delivering them not just O J Simpson but also the more recent Boston au-pair trial to prove that in America jazz and justice, showbiz and show trials are never far apart; I still think the clue to the whole enterprise lies in a lyric from the big 'Razzle Dazzle' number which goes 'Long as you keep 'em way off balance, how can they spot you got no talents?'

Chicago has always been sleight of hand, a massive circus trick which happens so fast and so noisily that you forget to notice that there isn't really anyone up there on the high wire after all. There is certainly a good basic idea here, to show that Chicago in the Twenties got the gangsters it deserved, and that if you treat Capone or Pretty Boy Floyd as media stars, then you might as well set their murders in a showbiz circus. The result is a Death Row vaudeville, full of great big-band solos and duets and the occasional crackling dialogue: 'We broke up because of artistic differences – he saw himself as alive whereas I saw him as dead.'

But there are only so many times that you can stop a show that never really gets started, and *Chicago* suffers from divided loyalties trapped between the rival traditions of Cagney and Bogart on the one hand and Busby Berkeley on the other. The new production is certainly shorter and sharper than the originals on either side of the Atlantic, but instead of a musical play we now have a dance festival. Ute Lemper in her London legit debut is just wonderful, bringing precisely the right edge of Brecht and Weill to a Berlin-influenced score, while Nigel Planer perfectly captures the heartbreak of *Mr Cellophane*. The rest of the casting is patchier, but Ruthie Henshall and Henry Goodman certainly do not lack presence; I just wish that bloody bandstand were on a trap and could occasionally be lowered to let them get on with the non-musical action.

~

On the National's Cottesloe stage, Frank McGuinness' *Mutabilities* is a grave disappointment, all the more since it is Trevor Nunn's debut production as director there; Richard Eyre must have left him very little else in the hand-over cupboard. Set in the Ireland of 1598, this is a seriously weird and hopelessly portentous piece in which Shakespeare and Spenser slug it out among the bogs with a couple of strolling players out of Stoppard and a seriously dysfunctional family of Irish warlords led by Gawn Grainger in a mad parody of the Brian Cox *King Lear*. Nothing here makes a lot of sense, though as the mist occasionally clears it seems that McGuinness wishes us to consider issues of identity and nationhood which have haunted his native land these last 400 years; did I not know better, I would have been inclined to assume that this was the winner in a student playwriting competition or more possibly the runner-up, awarded points for nobility of intention rather than stagecraft. Patrick Malahide as Spenser and Anton Lesser as Shakespeare do their best to flesh out an imaginary meeting of the bards, and fail as dismally as the rest of an amazingly ill-conceived evening.

~

And, finally, to the Queen's, the National Youth Music Theatre have brought for Christmas a first-ever staging of *Bugsy Malone*, the old Alan Parker film about the kids and the splatter-guns; the curious thing here is that the company are really much better when stretched toward adult roles, as in their recent *Whistle Down the Wind*, than when playing and singing within their own age range. Either that, or else *Bugsy* never did have much more going for it than the one joke about kiddie Capones; whichever way, Paul Williams' score has not stood the test of a fairly brief time.

Nothing Like A Dane

Hamlet (Barbican)

We all know the economic struggles of the RSC, but this is getting ridiculous: a new Barbican *Hamlet* with no Fortinbras, no Barnardo, no Marcellus, only one Gravedigger and real-life 'Citizens of London' brought in at presumably non-union rates to flesh out a mysteriously empty court. At this rate we shall soon be getting *The One Gentleman of Verona* and *Prince Lear* – but I note the company is making no corresponding reduction in its ticket prices.

So what, apart from the cuts (which bring the show in at three hours rather than the usual four), does Matthew Warchus' new production have to offer? Modern dress for a start; the Prince wanders around the party celebrating Claudius' all-too-rapid wedding to Hamlet's mother with a camera taking mugshots of the guests, and by the time it comes for Polonius to die he does so by the bullet rather than the sword.

There have been modern-dress *Hamlets* for the best part of a century now, and some have worked very well indeed; even the Alec Guinness/Kenneth Tynan version of the early 1950s still has its defenders. But Warchus has gone further than most; from the opening and closing home movies of Hamlet's happy childhood through to the kind of 'Goodnight Sweet Prince' ending once much favoured by old Edwardian actor managers who didn't want some upstart Fortinbras ruining their big death scene, he has cut, rearranged and sometimes just messed up the text; all occasions do not inform against this Hamlet, for the simple reason that this great soliloquy has disappeared altogether; most of the others just suffer severe internal cuts.

Warchus has, I suspect, seen rather too many of the Shakespearean movies that have lately been pouring out of Hollywood and elsewhere; but whereas

Sam Mendes' recent *Othello* at the National was a brilliant attempt to convert the closet style of Orson Welles to a staging which still managed neither to lose nor to betray any of the original text, this *Hamlet* seems gimmicky and barren of any real emotion. Nor is there much context; by cutting Fortinbras and the whole world beyond Elsinore, we lose all perspective on this alter-ego figure, all action and power where Hamlet is all indecision and weakness; you might as well have Hal with no Hotspur to fight in *Henry IV.*

What's more, the cast seem, in the move from Stratford to London, to have lost all faith in whatever this original concept may have been; Alex Jennings races around the stage with guns and flashbulbs as if auditioning for the Tarantino remake, Susannah York as Gertrude seems to draw back from the proceedings as far as she decently and understandably can, and the rest of the cast is, as usual with the RSC these days, more of an undercast. So there is no engagement here, no involvement; instead of persuading local citizens to swell out their ranks, the company would do well to recruit a few professional actors who can handle the verse with at least some of the authority so lacking in a frenetic but ramshackle gallop through the text. Only Edward Petherbridge, doubling the Player King with a cocktail-party Ghost, seems to have any real command of the tragedy, but even he is left out on a series of limbs, looking and sounding as pained as if Paul Scofield had started out to play Romeo and suddenly found himself in the midst of a gang of Jets from *West Side Story*.

I have no way of knowing this, but I'd be willing to bet that somewhere in rehearsal the words 'relevant' and 'new generation' and 'attention span' were used in director's notes, yet the irony is that Shakespeare becomes most relevant to our times when, as in the recent close-up Ian Holm *King Lear* at the National, we get to hear the whole text with all its subtleties and contradictions and psychological insights. Here we get caricatures rather than characters, and an already diffuse plot becomes largely incomprehensible when taken at this pace; whatever happened to old Norway, whose illness could be said to have been one of the principal motives for the action? *Hamlet* is not only about Elsinore, nor is it only about Hamlet; indeed we learn most of what we need to know about both only when they are contrasted with an outside world which seems to be making a lot more sense and headway. That, too, has gone from here; seldom can so many babies have been let out with the bathwater.

Theatre 1997

Right then, let us just survey the battlefield, and this at the end of a year which I remind you brought us a supposedly arts-friendly government. Covent Garden: board resigned, builders in, touring and interim plans a shambles. Old Vic: for sale, Peter Hall forced out, no sign of a likely buyer. Chichester: director resigned, board told to do likewise if they wish to see their theatre open at all in 1998. Sadler's Wells: builders in residence. The Gate and the King's Head: grants slashed, likely to close in April. Greenwich: grant slashed, no longer to have any resident company. Coliseum: English National Opera may effectively be closed down, in the proposed move to Covent Garden on a time-share basis with Royal Ballet, that's if there still is a Royal Ballet.

Any other arts problems? Museum charges likely, an overall cut in the Treasury grant of £35 million, the British Film Institute cut by another million, National Heritage cut by £3 million and the British Library by £5 million. Official government forecasts now indicate that the arts will lose a further £50 million per year until at least 2001. Apart from that, Mrs Lincoln, how did you enjoy the show?

Given that a combination of Nero and Caligula would have been hard pressed to do more damage to the arts in Britain this year than Chris Smith and his merry butchers from the Treasury, it is some kind of miracle that we still have any kind of theatre at all, let alone one as strong in both plays and productions as this has been. The invasion of new Irish plays continued to be overwhelming, but this was also the year that gave us major new work from Tom Stoppard (*The Invention of Love*, a tender and brilliant account of the poet A E Housman at Oxford and after), David Hare (*Amy's View*, about to transfer to the Aldwych, a wondrous account of the loneliness of the actor from a writer who also gives us next year a new Oscar Wilde, *The Judas Kiss*, and a revival of his *Plenty*) and Patrick Marber (*Closer*, a *Design for Living* for the late nineties in which four people find themselves unable to live apart or together). The fact that all three of these modern classics came out of Richard Eyre's last year at the National gives some indication of the class act that Trevor Nunn now has to follow, though with the RSC still in meltdown and most other classical companies shuttered for lack of funds, at least he doesn't have to worry too much about the competition. In the commercial West End, it has been a year of political documentaries more notable for performance than writing: Corin Redgrave and Amanda Donohoe as the Duke and Duchess of Windsor in murderous exile, Edward Fox as Harold Macmillan at the time of Profumo, Michael Gambon as Tom Driberg and Alec McCowen as Clement Attlee at Yalta. Madame Tussaud herself couldn't have had a busier season, while in revivals the performance of the year for me was John Standing as the semi-detached husband in Edward Albee's *A Delicate Balance* at the Haymarket, one he is still giving in the face of immensely tough female competition from Eileen Atkins and Maggie Smith.

Then again there were two sterling *King Lears*, from Ian Holm in the intimacy of the Cottesloe (Eyre again), and Alan Howard in the more classical surroundings of the Old Vic, where Peter Hall had a truly wondrous year, from Felicity Kendal in *Waste* through to Howard and Ben Kingsley in *Waiting for Godot*; as I write the rumours backstage are that Bill Kenwright will take the Hall company into the Piccadilly for a residency, so all may not be lost on that one front at least.

As Broadway comes back to life for the first time in a decade with half a dozen major new musicals, the life seems fast to be ebbing out of them over here: after a valiant two-year fight Cameron Mackintosh has finally abandoned the struggle for *Martin Guerre*, though I still believe its classic status will be recognised the first time anyone has the courage to revive it, and while we await one of Lloyd Webber's best and most unusual scores (*Whistle Down the Wind*, due into the Aldwych midsummer 1998) there has been precious little else of note. *Maddie* was Coward's *Blithe Spirit* with songs but alas without the jokes,

Always was a dire attempt to do the Abdication in Ivor Novello style, and the first-ever London staging of the Hart/Weill/Gershwin *Lady in the Dark* was sabotaged by miscasting a catastrophic production.

From New York also came the hugely overrated bandstand revival of *Chicago* and a fascinating if flawed *The Fix*. Not that we can afford to be smug or critical any longer as regards our musical supremacy: a London theatre which in one year managed to give us Cliff Richard as *Heathcliff, Summer Holiday* and *The Goodbye Girl* is in no state to boast.

A good year for young directors, and I haven't even the space to do more than acknowledge the greatness of Sian Phillips in a virtually solo *Dietrich* and Clare Skinner in Sam Mendes' superbly filmic *Othello*. Oh yes, and on the night he opened a strong *Front Page* it was announced that his Donmar Warehouse would be losing its subsidy a year ahead of schedule due to a change of sponsor-management. At least 1998 can't get much worse; or can it?

1998

An Awfully Big Adventure

Peter Pan (National)

A long with no other theatre-goer I have ever met above the age of ten, I have all my life believed that J M Barrie's *Peter Pan* is the greatest British play of the century. A vast, poetic, sprawling, dark masterpiece about life and death and love and loss and crocodiles and fairies who will die unless children applaud them, it stands so far outside the regular canon, and is often so unwieldy in its ambitions, that its nearest relative would probably be Ibsen's *Peer Gynt* written only a few years earlier.

Happily, we now have 'the boy who would not grow up' on the main Olivier stage of the National, where he should have been at least twenty years ago; admittedly this version is not entirely new, having first been devised and staged by Trevor Nunn and his *Les Misérables* partner John Caird for the Barbican back in 1982. Nunn has now dropped out as co-director, to be replaced by Fiona Laird, but in essence many of their original intentions remain intact; Peter is again played by a boy (an innovation they introduced) and we now have Alec McCowen in superb form as the crusty Scots Barrie himself to lead us through the still labyrinthine plot as narrator, observer and ultimate moralist.

The set this time is the most lavish ever seen at the National, even though John Napier's designs have now gone so far over the top that his Mermaid Lagoon resembles nothing so closely as the backdrop for an Esther Williams pool movie of the early 1950s. There are, in fact, so many things wrong with this *Peter Pan*, and so much right with it, that in the end it becomes a kind of high-scoring draw between the author and the production team.

What gives the play its eternal fascination is, at least for me, the cost to Barrie of writing his only real classic: of the five 'Lost Boys' he picked up by the round pond in Kensington Gardens where Pan's statue now stands, two committed suicide and three others said that their lives were never the same after the play first opened in 1928. Barrie's motives have always been at least a little suspect in regard to his love for the young lads, and the chances are that nowadays he, like Lewis Carroll, might have found himself having a quiet word with the local child protection agency. But *Peter Pan* was undoubtedly his lifelong obsession, and Caird and Nunn have tried to wrap up most if not all of its many versions into this one three-hour extravaganza; not just the 1928 play but the 1911 novel, the New York version of 1905 and the screenplay Barrie himself wrote for an unproduced Charlie Chaplin silent of 1920.

Mercifully, they have given the Walt Disney and Steven Spielberg travesties a wide berth, but even so we get moments of unforgiveable parody and jokiness, as though the directors are beginning to lose faith not only in the play but, more disastrously, in the audience to cope with its psychological complexities and sexual uneasiness.

True, this *Pan* does restore to us the almost unknown last act, in which years after the children have flown home to their Darling household Peter returns, only to find that Wendy has done the unforgivable and got married; still, there is always her daughter to be kidnapped and flown to the Neverland which lies just beyond the second star to the right and then straight on till morning. Far and away the most heart-breaking moments in the show occur at the very end, when Alec McCowen's narrator flies us out of the past and into the future to show us the terrible things like banks and bishoprics which have befallen the boys who allowed themselves, under Wendy's influence, to grow up reasonably normal instead of flapping around Peter's lost island staging battles with pirates. As the pirate chief (and also of course the children's father Mr Darling, a double that has been traditional since the play was first staged) Ian McKellen seems oddly subdued, able neither to feel nor inspire the terror that lies behind the Hook hand; but the rest of the casting works well enough, with Daniel Evans as a charismatic Peter and Claudie Blakely as an unusually tough, feminist Wendy.

Again some very weird liberties have been taken with the text; some of Hook's great speech from the pirate ship, a parody of Irving and Tree and all the actor-managers Barrie most disliked for their histrionics, appears to have been cut heavily, and 'Oh dark and sinister man' was never intended as the cue for some cheap malapropisms. Equally shameful is the moment when McKellen, having just reverted from Hook to Darling, allows an echo of Hook to invade his nursery performance in the doghouse. These and many more are self-referential gags which chip away at the original, while the late Stephen Oliver's score still hovers uneasily between background music and full-blown operetta. Given the deviser-directors' expertise with *Les Misérables* it would surely have made more sense to allow this production to become the musical it wants to be by simply borrowing the Jule Styne/Mary Martin Broadway score which remains one of the best I have ever heard and vastly more loyal to the original Barrie plan.

But if the true heart of darkness is missing here, we still have more than enough; this must be the first *Peter Pan* ever to be stolen by a Narrator whom Barrie never intended to be on stage, but as Peter and his boys soar though the auditorium and Hook sinks into the teeth of a crocodile apparently on loan from *Jaws*, it suddenly becomes clear that, like Alan Bennett's *The Wind in the Willows*, the National has a Christmas treat to see it safely though the millennium, by which time they might even have managed to pay for it.

An Epic Civil War

Flight (National)

Macbeth (Orange Tree)

One of the requirements, indeed designations, of a national theatre that is not to disintegrate into a museum, as have so many elsewhere in Europe, is that it should introduce us to major and sometimes epic work which no other stage in the land could afford or consider. On that one, the jury is still out on the new Trevor Nunn regime on the South Bank; neither his new *An Enemy of the People* nor *Peter Pan* are exactly rediscoveries, and the announcement of a forthcoming *Oklahoma!* for the summer and a *Private Lives* to celebrate the Coward centenary next year is frankly more than a little depressing in its weary, play-safe familiarity.

But we do now, on the open Olivier stage, have Bulgakov's *Flight* and this is precisely what the National should be doing. Written in 1926 by the great Russian author of *The Master and Margarita*, this one was all too predictably banned by Stalin and only resurfaced long after the author's death in 1940. Essentially it's an epic black comedy in eight episodes, subtitled 'dreams', through which we follow a group of White Russians on the run from the 1918 civil war but still dreaming of a return to the homeland. Other playwrights and screenwriters have had their fun with White Russians in exile, but Bulgakov has the courage of a vast odyssey, so that we follow these no-hopers through Constantinople and into Paris as, increasingly desperate, they take up crime and cockroach-racing and gambling in an attempt to restore lost family fortunes.

Alan Howard in magnificent lassitude heads the troupe of losers on the run, and in Howard Davies' spectacular production the new Ron Hutchinson translation crackles with energy. Hopelessly underpowered, ill and wildly impractical, this gypsy band drifts across the democratic world trying to find lost identities, a living, or maybe just some distant relative to offer them bed and board until the next revolution, the one that never came.

Bulgakov's genius was to tell a civil war story of death and horror with an amazing amount of bleak and black humour; just as we start to feel sorry for these exiles on the run, we are shown how utterly hopeless they will always be at rebuilding any kind of a life. They have left it too late to join a winning team for which they are anyway disqualified by birth, see no point in staying with the losers, but are at the same time unable to survive outside the disciplines of Russia at war with herself. This is a pageant of retreat, about people who wander and lust but cannot deal with wanderlust.

~

We underestimate Sam Walters at our peril; what makes him special is that only Dan Crawford at the ever-imperilled King's Head in Islington has a longer record of running a pub theatre, though since Walters's Orange Tree has now moved across the road it is technically a theatre next to a pub rather than inside one.

But in the almost thirty years since he founded the Orange Tree, I can only recall one Shakespeare, which makes the *Macbeth* that opened there this week all the more intriguing. It has a cast of only ten, and is played on a bare-board stage with virtually no props or identifiable costumes; there is no precise period here, and precious few Scots accents. Indeed, Walters's production starts alarmingly neutrally, threatening a Shakespeare-for-schools effort with the director determined not to inflict any recognisable theory which might conflict with the current schools exam syllabus.

But then, in the second half, it suddenly gets fascinating: the notoriously difficult 'England' scene, always the hardest in the play to sustain audience interest, becomes an electrifying political and moral debate, and immediately after it Paul Shelley's hitherto only serviceable Macbeth starts to tear up the planking of the stage like some manic Noah bent on sinking his own ark. The subsequent battle scenes are played kabuki-style, and the last, usually dying-fall act becomes instead a centre of tension and surprise which suddenly lifts, almost too late, a low-key revival into something mesmeric and magnificent.

Pub Crawl

The Weir (Duke of York's)

I Am Yours (Ambassadors)

The Royal Court, though still several months away from returning to its Sloane Square home, has managed in exile around St Martin's Lane to fill two and sometimes three small stages with some immensely impressive work, but nothing better than *The Weir* which comes to the Duke of York's after a brief outing last summer. In the dramatist Conor McPherson, we have yet another of the young Irish brigade who have lately colonised the London stage, but what sets him apart is a unique gift for monologue.

His *St Nicholas* a few seasons ago at the Bush gave us a drunken drama critic (as if such characters exist) who falls in with a group of South London vampires; it was somewhere between a ghost and a shaggy-dog story, but one of remarkable poetry and potency. This time, in *The Weir*, he gives us four regular hard-drinkers, each with a ghostly tale to tell to the girl from Dublin who has just bought a house in the village, until, inevitably, she tops them all with her own truly terrible personal story, one far more alarming than any that the men have managed to conjure from the mists.

So we have moved on a little, from monologue to duologue and sometimes even dialogue; in that sense the similarities here are often very close to Saroyan's *The Time of Your Life*, as a group of regulars try to top each other's encounters with the unknown, until at the last they are brought up against the undeniable voice of truth. McPherson's point here, it seems to me, is that the men can only overcome their own sense of loss and failure in an Irish retreat by spinning these yarns, each of them just safely on the far side of immediate plausibility. What they are doing is essentially myth-making, whereas what the girl finally offers is a slice of real, brutal if accidental life and the death of a beloved little daughter in a drowning accident.

Suddenly the men's tales are made to seem somehow theatrical, if not downright phoney; they are admirable bar-room story-tellers but the stories have been told for so long, from generation to generation, that they have lost all reality. Whereas the outsider, the one who has kept so demurely quiet as they related their oft-told tales, is the only one of them truly possessed by a ghost, and in that realisation all the men seem almost to crumble as they go out to face the midnight air; what has held them together has been a fantasy, and now, suddenly, they have been faced with a reality, that the supernatural can and does still exist.

Ian Rickson's production is a masterclass in how to keep a fundamentally very static and talky play alive and moving, while the performances of Julia Ford as the only woman, and of Jim Norton and Des McAleer as two of the male regulars, resonate with suppressed passion and lost hopes. Only in the beyond, it seems, can they find some explanation for the here and now in all its disappointments.

~

Meanwhile at the Ambassadors, Nancy Meckler's Shared Experience company have come in with *I Am Yours*, a play by the Canadian dramatist Judith Thompson which has taken more than a decade to cross the Atlantic. And although I fervently believe that we are still not seeing nearly enough contemporary Canadian or Australian drama in this country, *I Am Yours* does not make my case any easier. This is a rambling, enigmatic family drama cut up into 36 scenes across which we come to learn of a couple of dysfunctional sisters and the boyfriends they collect along the way. But this remains really a play about the past; a kind of familial guilt hangs listlessly over the sisters, and the admirably literary Meckler, with immense elegance, has directed as though this were some vast novel of a bygone era in which very little happens.

The trouble is that it's not; rather it is a contemporary piece about the horrors facing unloved one-parent mothers, and the general air of drift and despair that would seem to characterise suburban Canadian life. There are many better plays than this hovering around the Toronto fringe, and it would be good to have a look at one which did not so determinedly resemble a day-time soap for the emotionally disenfranchised. In a cast of six, not one makes us really care what happens to them, and one ends up wishing they would cease dumping their long leftover teenage anxieties about sex and marriage on us.

Both these plays are well within the Court's remit for the discovery of challenging new writing; but what makes *The Weir* so much better than *I Am Yours* is simply its urgent willingness to draw us into the charmed circle by the pub fireside, whereas the other play constantly holds us at arm's length, as if inviting us to consider a couple of curious case histories of emotional disorder which may well have its roots in parental neglect or something rather worse. There is a deliberate lack of involvement here, and it spreads like a forest fire; at the end of the evening, one is left idly wondering what would be the hourly rate for a family therapist who had to sort out this mess.

Lights Out

The Real Inspector Hound / Black Comedy (Comedy)
New Edna: The Spectacle! (Haymarket)

What could be better than a classic farce from the 1960s? Well, try two. In putting Tom Stoppard's *The Real Inspector Hound* together with Peter Shaffer's *Black Comedy,* the director Greg Doran and the new Warehouse touring company at the Comedy have simply and satisfactorily solved a problem that has been around since both plays were first seen thirty years ago, namely what to couple with each of them.

Neither Shaffer nor Stoppard, having created these hour-long masterpieces, ever managed to get the other half of a necessary double-bill quite right, lending an awful kind of reality to the pronouncement of Moon and Birdboot, second-string drama critics caught up in the plot of *Hound*, that 'if it goes on beyond half-past ten it's self-indulgent: pass it on.'

Few of us who have been drama critics of whatever string in the life of this play have ever managed to see it without flinching, not just at that line but at the sight of Moon – or is it Birdboot? – trying without success to recall anything at all about the play he has so recently described for poster quotation as an unforgettable experience. Though the mechanics of this double-satire, in which Stoppard guns not just for reviewers but also for that whole genre of country-house thrillers still represented by *The Mousetrap* (and can he have believed, even in his worst nightmares, that the object of his brilliant attack would still be playing in the West End three decades after this demolition job?) have been overtaken in the meantime by Michael Frayn's still more complex and brilliant backstage *Noises Off,* there is no doubt that some of Sir Tom's best writing can still be found in that speech about bands of marauding understudies, twelfth men, deputies and other social outcasts rising up in great revolutionary groups to overthrow the very men they are supposed to be shadowing.

Nicola McAuliffe's definitive Mrs Drudge, the charlady employed solely to update us on plot and setting ('Hello,' she answers a mysterious telephone caller, 'it's the same, only half an hour later'), takes the honours in the first half narrowly from Desmond Barrit's massively lugubrious Birdboot and David Tennant's subdued Moon, but in the second half of this joyous evening Tennant amply redeems himself as the unfortunate Brindsley Miller, about to give a party when all the lights fuse in his apartment. Only then, by the brilliant reversal of Shaffer's *Black Comedy,* do we get to see what is going on; an old Chinese opera device allows us to see in the dark but not the characters on stage, so some brilliantly confused exits and entrances are enlivened by Miller's increasingly disastrous attempts to restore stolen furniture to its rightful owner. Only another drama critic would here take the trouble to point out that it was Kenneth Tynan, yet another drama critic, who worked closely with Shaffer on the mechanics of the plot, thereby ensuring the play's initial National Theatre triumph and, to some extent, disproving the uselessness of our trade as demonstrated by what is now preceding *Black Comedy* in this new double bill.

Others involved in both manic farces include Sara Crowe, suitably inane in the first and vindictive in the second, Gary Waldhorn and Anna Chancellor. They, like their scripts, are lethally funny, and the only really depressing aspect of a wondrously giggly evening is the realisation that in thirty years no British dramatist (always excepting Frayn) has managed to write any better or more expert mechanical comedies. Ben Travers used to achieve them annually, but that was in another universe and, besides, the wit is dead or at any rate no longer fashionable; we have allowed the theatre of pure hilarity to disappear with Moon and Birdboot, and the loss is all ours.

~

Talking of lost laughter, something has gone horribly wrong with *New Edna: The Spectacle!* at the Theatre Royal Haymarket or, to be more precise, just about everything from the choice of theatre to that of director and lyricist. The Haymarket, Alan Strachan and Kit Hesketh-Harvey are all admirable in their various ways, but those ways are not those of Dame Edna, the greatest drag act of my lifetime although now beginning to come apart at her voluminous seams.

In trying, for her first West End season in a decade, to co-opt help from the legitimate theatre, the Dame has drifted disastrously from her best anarchic and destructive territory, only to end up with a first half of interminable length and desperate inadequacy in which we are treated to a life-history of Edna before Damehood which manages to be still worse than the worst of the shows it is attempting to parody. There is nothing really wrong here which couldn't be solved by cutting a couple of hours and the choreographer's throat, but in the meantime one thought back nostalgically to that other Hesketh-Harvey masterpiece of recent years, *Which Witch?*

After the interval, realising perhaps that something unspeakably awful even by the standards of Edna's prostate obsessions had happened before it, her begetter Barry Humphries wisely returns to the monologue which has always been at the heart of his and her brilliance; but even this seems to have come curiously unstuck, as if Humphries's heart and considerable energy are somehow no longer in tune with Our Lady of the Gladioli, or her determination to humiliate her faithful attendants. It is just possible that her Massage Parlour of the Human Spirit is ripe for a takeover, and that, like the ventriloquist's dummy in *Dead of Night*, the Dame has finally strangled her creator's genius.

I trust not; on a good night, nobody plays a crowd better or makes them wish more fervently that they were some place else. But at the Haymarket first night it was suddenly the Dame herself who seemed to wish she had chosen another theatre and maybe a more responsive audience; to risk live phone calls from the stage to unsuspecting babysitters at home is only ever going to work if you ring the right people, and the final irony of a deeply misguided evening is that in soliciting, for the very first time, the aid of a lyricist and a director other than herself, the Dame has also for the first time come up with a show which badly needs both writing and staging.

If you can't get the proper staff, as Edna must have discovered early in Melbourne suburban life, better to do the job yourself. Or maybe not at all.

Ice Age

Our Lady of Sligo (National)

In a powerfully Irish time, Sebastian Barry's *Our Lady of Sligo* betrays an odd debt to O'Neill, for here too a single character takes centre stage for twenty-minute monologues of despair and disgust as she looks back on a life wasted by alcohol. Sinead Cusack, in the performance of her career, remains bedridden as she dies of cancer in a 1953 Dublin hospital. But she too is fifty-three, and it does not take us long to realise that *Our Lady of Sligo* is not necessarily the religious painting on the wall, nor even perhaps the cancer victim, desperately trying to make some sense of her tragically wasted life even as it wastes her. Not to put it too heavily, what we have here is Ireland herself in the first half of this century, condemned by de Valera to be way outside any European action and turned so far in on herself that drink and illicit sex are all she has left to occupy the passing years.

Nigel Terry gives a no-less touching performance as the army officer also drowned in drink and violence; *Our Lady of Sligo* may not ostensibly be connected to the headlines of this week, but once again in giving us Ireland's past as a poetic historian, Barry also manages to give us visionary glimpses of an essentially unchanging future. In telling with brutal clarity the story of his own grandmother, Barry has also given us the story of her nation in no less torment, and Max Stafford-Clark's production is as magnificent as its two central performances.

Old Man River

Show Boat (Prince Edward)

Musicals don't come a lot better than *Show Boat*, and indeed they wouldn't come at all had it not been for this one. Back in 1927 Jerome Kern and Oscar Hammerstein got together to write what was effectively the first Broadway score ever to have a coherent plot and integrated songs; integrated in every sense since the first one opened controversially (though it does so no longer) 'Niggers all work on the Mississippi', a lyric that has now been tactfully readjusted to 'Brothers all work' for the purposes of current racial feeling. But what was most important about the original *Show Boat*, based on Edna Ferber's great sprawling novel of river-boat life (for which she still gets far too little credit) was that it also tackled such then-scandalous themes as those of mixed-race marriages, gambling, infidelity, illegitimacy and everything else that made life upon the wicked show-boat stage such fun.

For the purposes of this new revival, which comes to us from Toronto via New York with the original touring cast, Hal Prince has treated the show with all the operatic reverence usually accorded to *Porgy and Bess* almost a decade later. Prince has seen in *Show Boat*, traditionally a light romantic musical, a dark history of America itself and has accordingly drastically rebuilt the show, tearing out the whole Chicago World's Fair which used to open Act Two and giving us instead a series of cinematic montages which get us through the First World War and most of the twenties, admittedly somewhat abruptly despite Susan Stroman's breathtakingly vital and period-accurate choreography.

There has, of course, always been a problem with the book of *Show Boat*, which is that no stage version under about eight hours could hope to encompass the scope and sprawl of the original manuscript, so it is left to each decade and director to fillet out the bits of plot which they think will make most sense to a contemporary audience, and sometimes even now the leaps in time and space are a problem: a hero like Gaylord Ravenal gets most of the first act and then nothing till the closing moments of the second. Characters appear, disappear, reappear with almost cavalier disregard for any real development of plot or personality, so that the whole show comes to resemble one of those primitive picture-wheels you held to your eyes while flicking through a related series of images in three-dimension.

But from the moment Michael Bell comes out to sing 'Ol' Man River' (something he does in this revival so often that one fears he will turn up at every single scene change, refusing like Nixon ever to go away) and the great American classical actor George Grizzard invites us aboard the steam-boat, we know we are in safe and lyrical hands. As hit after hit from 'Make Believe' through 'Why Do I Love You?' to 'Can't Help Lovin' Dat Man' and even the wildly misplaced 'Bill', a song lifted from an earlier P G Wodehouse score so that we now have a simple mixed-race river-boater regretting the absence of cricket and polo in her life, it becomes evident that *Show Boat* was not only the first American musical but also the one that made all others possible.

There is a joyous historical neatness in the fact that the young lyricist here, Oscar Hammerstein, went on to remake and rebuild the Broadway musical twice more in a single lifetime, first with *Oklahoma!* and then by becoming the tutor and mentor of Stephen Sondheim. So a direct link runs back evermore to *Show Boat* across more than seventy years, and this epic, rambling musical history of mid-century America now comes up looking as fresh as ever it could have done in 1927, thanks to a truly wonderful company which includes not only Grizzard and Carole Shelley as his sourpuss wife but also Joel Blum, far and away the greatest vaudeville comic dancer since Donald O'Connor or Ray Bolger.

If you plan to see only one musical this year (and you have still more than usual to choose from) make it this one: as a history of showbiz America it may be a little diffuse and patchy, but as a model for the construction of musicals (from the opening chorus to the very last finale) it is a master class in what the American theatre still does best – those vast sweeps of musical emotion from the depths of despair ('Misery's Comin' Aroun'', hardly ever heard in previous revivals) all the way up to the unbridled showbiz joy of 'Life Upon The Wicked Stage'.

Hal Prince has finally realised that this is above all else a show about family, and he even gives one of its greatest love ballads not to the young romantic leads but to a grandmother with a baby in her arms; yet somehow as the river-boat rolls through two acts and twenty scenes, somewhere halfway from Noah's Ark to the Titanic, she takes us with her on a journey that is nothing less than the discovery of America's greatest art form.

Citizen Kane

Cleansed (Royal Court)
Saturday Night Fever (Palladium)

Were we now to compile a profit and loss account for the director Stephen Daldry as he prepares to hand over his management of the Royal Court to Ian Rickson, there is no doubt that he has continued, notably with *Mojo* and several Irish imports, that theatre's great tradition for the discovery of new writing.

On the loss side, he has ripped out the hearts of two much-loved West End theatres (the Ambassadors and the Duke of York's) while occupying them until the new Sloane Square rebuilding can be completed, and unfathomably lent the Court's prestige to Sarah Kane, a young playwright who managed to hit the headlines three years ago with her first play *Blasted*, set in war-torn Leeds and mainly memorable for babies being eaten alive and eyes gouged out. Now she's back, at the Duke of York's, with the ironically titled *Cleansed* in which a good many more eyes get put out or forcibly injected; one suspects that as a child she must have been deeply traumatised by the Duke of Gloucester in *King Lear*.

And here it is not just the eyes which have it. Though the set resembles a concentration camp, we are surprisingly within a university campus where limbs are lopped off, tongues tortured, rats encouraged to gnaw living flesh and sex-changes conducted by force. It will doubtless be argued that the Shakespearean and much of the Jacobean theatre was equally gory, but in all those revengers' tragedies there was a kind of salvation, a kind of humanity which won through in the end against impossible odds. Kane offers none of that; like a naughty schoolgirl desperately trying to shock an increasingly bored and languid audience, she piles horror upon horror without ever bothering to give us a character or a situation to care about. Jeremy Herbert's sets are wonderfully inventive and stylised, but if even a fraction of that talent had gone into the writing we might have had a play worth serious consideration; as it is, *Cleansed* is in every sense a shocker, but the greatest shock of all has to do with neither drugs nor rats nor restitched genitals; it is that anyone at the Court thought Kane a playwright worth staging, let alone staging twice.

Cleansed will doubtless live on its own publicity as the most violent play of the season, but that alone is hardly enough; it is also a tacky, tawdry apology for a play, in which any real skill of characterisation or plotting is simply replaced by yet another bloody amputation. What we have here is a weird attempt to combine *Waiting for Godot* with *The Duchess of Malfi* and it misses both by more than a mile. *Cleansed* leaves you feeling as grubby as James Macdonald's production.

~

The passion for turning movie musicals into stage shows (this last week alone we have had *Saturday Night Fever* at the London Palladium and *High Society* on Broadway, while still to come on this side of the Atlantic are *Ragtime*, *The Lion King* and *Doctor Dolittle*) suggests either a terrible lack of new theatrical product or, more plausibly, a recognition by theatre managers that if they are now to charge upwards of £30 a ticket they had better be selling something people already know they are going to enjoy even before the curtain goes up.

Saturday Night Fever is thus a reasonably faithful recreation of the 1977 box-office winner. In place of John Travolta we have a reasonably adequate stand-in, Adam Garcia, who has clearly studied the video long enough to perfect that curious bodyline strutting with the outstretched index finger that was the hallmark of an otherwise unexciting movie. But the real Palladium star is Robin Wagner, whose immense sets give us a working replica of Brooklyn's vast Verrazano Bridge and, also in tribute to the late Sean Kenny, a huge spaceship which descends, breathing smoke and blazing floodlights, from the roof of the old nightclub where most of the action is still set.

There the good news ends: Travolta himself may have managed to kickstart his old Hollywood career back into some kind of afterlife, but the musical that made him a star is now as dead as the character who finally jumps off the bridge, presumably so as to avoid having to sing yet another wedge of the Bee Gees' cheesy muzak score. This has always been a *West Side Story* for the brain-dead, and although Arlene Phillips's frenetic choreography has a certain ghastly period accuracy, as a director she has singularly failed to give the Gibb Brothers' inane singalong any real energy or heart.

The result lurches uneasily from book musical to rock concert, still strong on flares but totally lacking the flair that might have made it a worthwhile staging. Curiously, this old dinosaur comes back to us now looking vastly more dated than the *Show Boat* which preceded it by half a century.

Shaw Thing

Major Barbara (Piccadilly)
Three by Harold Pinter (Donmar Warehouse)

In a time when dubious arms deals are back in the headlines, the everlasting topicality of Shaw's masterly *Major Barbara* once again reinforces my belief that Peter Hall's financially embattled resident company is still far and away the best classical repertoire in London this decade. True, Peter Bowles as the massively sinister Undershaft, a megalomaniac arms dealer based none too loosely on Alfred Nobel, was a little shaky on the longer speeches at the first night, and Jemma Redgrave seemed an oddly uncharismatic Barbara; but both these performances, like so many others in the Hall seasons, will soon settle down, and when they do we may well have the best production in living memory of a play written in 1906 and still quite literally firing on all its targets.

As so often, GBS has at least three separate plots going on here; there's the opening, a conventional Edwardian drawing-room comedy about unsuitable marriage, with Anna Carteret doing a memorable parody of Lady Bracknell; then we have the Salvation Army scenes, effectively *Guys and Dolls* without the score, and finally the great explosive shed at Undershaft's munitions factory where his conversion of his own children to the benefits of dynamite is infinitely more triumphant than anything achieved by the Salvationists.

It is here, in Undershaft's lyrical defence of the power of arms, that we find Shaw in his anti-Shotover mood, predicting that the world can only ever be run by men who are prepared to kill and be killed for their beliefs. Only when Hall gives us, at curtain fall, the sounds of the guns at Flanders in a world war already less than a decade away do we realise the terrible price about to be paid for Undershaft's seductive philosophy.

In a strong cast, David Yelland is an unusually pugnacious Cusins and Michael Pennington splendid as an Alfred Dolittle in embryo. With the National about to settle into a summer of *Oklahoma!* and the RSC already out of the Barbican, it is Hall's company at the Piccadilly which alone continues to give London the right to consider itself the capital of major classical revivals.

~

If one play by Harold Pinter is good, then two must be better and three best of all. That certainly is the thinking behind a new staging at the Donmar

Warehouse of *A Kind of Alaska, The Collection* and *The Lover*, and at almost three and a half hours at least nobody can complain this time about too brief a Pinteresque outing.

A Kind of Alaska dates from 1982 and is the one derived from Oliver Sacks' discoveries about patients brought back from years of catatonic lethargy by a then-new drug called L-Dopa. Pinter's patient (originally Judi Dench, now Penelope Wilton in a no less touching or memorable arousal, if perhaps a rather less petulant one) is Deborah, who fell into coma when she was sixteen and we now meet some twenty-nine years later, awakening to find her doctor and sister (Bill Nighy and Brid Brennan) trying to explain how she has come to lose three whole decades in sleep. *A Kind of Alaska* is about the unfreezing of the body while the mind remains desperately unable to thaw out quite so fast, and it remains one of the most touching and, of course, timeless of all his plays.

The other two plays here are television scripts from the early 1960s; *The Collection* is a betrayal thriller with each of the four characters (Lia Williams, Colin McFarlane, Douglas Hodge and a massively sinister, silk-dressing-gown turn from Pinter himself) caught up in what may or may well not be a series of gay and straight affairs. What matters here is the mystery, not the solution, and Joe Harmston manages to keep the tension going well enough. But *The Lover*, the last in this trio, has always seemed to me a curious series of variations on a theme by Molnar, who in *The Guardsman* first set up the idea of a married couple only ever happy in their own bed when masquerading as illicit lovers. All the same, a Pinter treble of unresolved menace is a remarkable tribute to his unique stagecraft over the last thirty or forty years.

Boys in the Band

Brassed Off (National)

The cinema routinely plunders so much of what is great about the British theatre that it is good to see something paid back at last; a couple of years ago, *Brassed Off* was Mark Herman's touching and savage account about the closing of yet another Yorkshire coal-face, and the determination of its pit band to play on regardless. The film never got its full credit, largely and unluckily because it was overtaken all around the world by the huge success of the not-dissimilar *The Full Monty*. But of the two, it was always *Brassed Off* that had the better script, and the dramatist Paul Allen has now come up with a wondrous stage version which plays the National's open Olivier stage through to the end of this month only, on a visit from its native Sheffield Crucible.

From the moment the miners flood across the open stage, trombones raised and helmet lamps lit, it is clear we are in for a good night; whereas the film harked back to *This Sporting Life* and that whole Woodfall raft of early sixties northern movies, the play suggests a still longer heritage, leaning back to Priestley and Emlyn Williams and *How Green Was My Valley* and even the pit plays of D H Lawrence, all of whom saw down the mines a metaphor for communities in some kind of peril.

Except that now, of course, it's all over; as a whole society fragments and dies, men who only get up in the morning to see if their luck has changed, and women who believe they were only put on earth to make up God's numbers, try to cope with the end of an era. So *Brassed Off* is not just about a brass band in crisis; it's about all its players struggling against the Heseltine edict of 1992 which closed down more than half their pits. Their reactions, from pragmatic through suicidal to merely stubborn, and what happens to a community when its sole purpose for existence is suddenly taken away, is what this great and terrible story is all about, and to have the band on stage gives us a very moving climax as their leader refuses the trophy for which they have worked all their lives.

The Second Wind

Whistle Down the Wind (Aldwych)

Just what is it about the British and musicals? To be more specific, just what is it about London drama critics and Andrew Lloyd Webber? By my reckoning, his *Whistle Down the Wind* has thus far had three or four good reviews and another eight or nine of such breathtaking hostility that you begin to wonder whether quite soon writing a musical in this country will become an offence punishable by a short prison sentence, or perhaps just a sizeable fine. Moreover, of the good reviews, at least two had writers who acknowledged a connection: one has a relative employed by the show as a music director, and another is writing a biography of the composer. So, present company excepted, we are now down to about one review that could claim to be wholly disinterested and wholly favourable.

One out of a dozen. Is *Whistle Down the Wind* really that terrible? No, it's not; it may not be perfect, but it does represent a major attempt by its composer to move forward, or at the very least to tackle the age-old complaint that he might be very rich, but he still isn't Sondheim. This is a dark, thoughtful, intelligent show about religious obsession; its roots are in an extremely good and successful 1961 novel-into-film by Mary Hayley Bell. For those who believe that all good musicals can be summarised in a single sentence, this one is about a trio of lost children who come upon an escaped killer in a barn and, because he curses 'Jesus Christ' upon discovery, mistakenly assume that he is simply giving them his name.

But where, nowadays, do you find kids that dumb? The problem is that you don't, so Lloyd Webber and his quite brilliant lyricist Jim Steinman have gone back to 1959 Louisiana, and a backwoods community where religion is still to do with snakes, and trains don't even stop at the local station. So this is not another Bible-belter in the old Webber tradition of *Joseph* or *Superstar*, its debts are instead to *Elmer Gantry* and John Steinbeck and *The Grapes of Wrath* and maybe even the film *Deliverance*, which dealt with a barking mad, long-inbred community of latterday savages in that same district.

I have now seen *Whistle* three times in three years; once in a kind of workshop concert (with some of the present cast), once in a lavish but again critically disastrous staging in Washington by Hal Prince, and now in its London premiere by Gale Edwards, the Australian director who did a wonderful salvage job on another hugely underrated Lloyd Webber score, *Aspects of Love*. Each time, *Whistle* has changed radically, and we now, I believe, have it about as good as it will ever get. Yes, there indeed remain some problems; the set is still causing performances to be cancelled, and I am less in love than the composer with the idea, also tried in *Sunset Boulevard*, that you have two levels on a gigantic kind of hinge so that the upper level can fold down into the lower. Not only does this cause mechanical troubles backstage, but it also plays hell with sightlines for rather too many rows of stalls and circle.

Then again, we now have rather too many children; not just the original trio, but a whole army of their friends whose anthems drift dangerously close to *Annie* or even *Oliver*. This new concept of kiddie power plays hell with the original idea, especially when they sing choruses about how life will be when they rule the world; with one bound we are back to Harry Secombe and a whole arca of ghastly British 1950s musical mistakes, whereas the real tragedy of *Whistle* as originally conceived is that these children don't rule anything, and are hostages to their parents' ill fortunes.

And yet this still doesn't explain the hostility. If you are a playwright in this country, or indeed a young director, the oft-quoted George Devine plea for 'the right to fail' is endlessly invoked; if you are a writer of musicals, you seem to have no right to fail and no right to succeed either. There is a lack of tolerance here which I think will quite soon hurt all of us as theatre-goers; people will simply stop writing new musicals in this country, because the risks and the costs of failure have become just too great. This is not unrealistic; it happened in America these last twenty years or so (as usual, Sondheim remains the exception who proves the rule), where only recently has a new generation of musical writers arrived to revive the genre.

So, all other issues aside, is *Whistle Down the Wind* worth your time and ticket money? Emphatically, yes. Unlike such current hits as *Grease* or *Saturday Night Fever*, unlike *Sunset Boulevard* from the same composer, this is not simply an old movie reheated for the stage with most of its source power long gone; it is a genuine development of the original, with a yearning intensity and a lyrical, reflective score which will I believe be recalled when many more immediately acceptable scores have disappeared forever. Above all, it remains a play with songs, and the play has a power of plot and character development which most of us had long since given up looking for outside the works of the aforementioned Sondheim plus Boublil & Schonberg.

Whistle Down the Wind is largely about growing up, and that is something the composer is also now doing, albeit maybe a little late; it is far and away the most adult of all the Lloyd Webber scores, and for that reason also perhaps the most dangerous and difficult. Its two newcomers, Marcus Lovett and Lottie Mayor, are seriously good in tricky leading roles, and it demands a great audience leap of time and space and faith. When the *Wind* listens to its own whistle, and stays true to its own dark soul, it is deeply and dramatically moving, and I think it deserves a much better deal than it has thus far had from my colleagues. From now on, it is up to you; the show will live, or very possibly die, by word of mouth and I cannot believe that will be anything like as hostile as the print reaction.

Right Show, Wrong Stage

Oklahoma! (National)

Right then, there's a bright golden haze on the meadow, the corn is as high as an elephant's eye, and the new National Theatre *Oklahoma!* is the best we are ever likely to see in the rest of a lifetime. Trevor Nunn has wisely gone back to the original play, Lynn Riggs' *Green Grow the Lilacs*, in order to find a little much-needed plot, while the undoubted star of the evening, Broadway's leading choreographer Susan Stroman, has after fifty long years finally cut through all those tired reruns of Agnes de Mille impersonators and given us a brilliantly vibrant new dance staging.

True, Maureen Lipman is a little young for Aunt Eller, thereby suggesting a new relationship with her future nephew Curly, but Hugh Jackman and Josefine Gabrielle (a real dancer, so mercifully no more doubles for the ballet) are genuine finds for the leads, while Peter Polycarpou and Shuler Hensley are no less talented in the chief character roles.

So why couldn't I join the cheering that ran through the Olivier last week as loudly as I have ever heard it? Because it makes a mockery of the idea that the National should stage shows that no other theatre can. *Oklahoma!* has no place, any more than the concurrent *Jean Brodie*, in the repertoire of a state-subsidised company with (on this occasion) extra financial help from Sir Cameron Mackintosh, who has already often toured other productions of an over-familiar classic. What of the National's past musicals, then? *Lady in the Dark* and the Sondheims could never have been seen elsewhere in such expert or lavish stagings; *Guys and Dolls* had all but disappeared locally, and *Carousel* was a redefinition of a hitherto hidden, dark heart at the centre of the piece.

Oklahoma! is neither revelation nor rediscovery; it is just a very good, endlessly played landmark musical given here an expert and expensive revival. Certainly the National should stage musicals, especially in financially hard times, and certainly a great musical can be as wondrous an experience as a great Shakespeare or Shaw play. Certainly the National should celebrate the genius of Rodgers & Hammerstein, but how much better, surely, to have given us after almost half a century the British premieres of their long-lost *Allegro* or *Pipe Dream* or *Me and Juliet*.

Nobody has ever underestimated the importance of *Oklahoma!* in the wartime rebirth of the American musical, nor its message to returning servicemen that this is what they were fighting for, as many a new day dawned. But there is nothing really new to tell us about a show which would look just fine at Drury Lane, or indeed the Lyceum which is where this revival will probably end up pre-Broadway. How long now before the National gets around to *Annie* or *A Chorus Line*, both of which could well be defended on this precedent?

In Like Flynn

Tarry Flynn (National)

The Best of Times (Bridewell)

Into the National Theatre from the Abbey in Dublin has come what seems to me quite clearly the production of the year. Even in as rich a time as this for new Irish drama, this utterly amazing and joyous rediscovery of Patrick Kavanagh and his early biography of a recalcitrant youth in the County Cavan of the middle 1930s stands out as nothing less than the *Peer Gynt* of its own time and place.

Conall Morrison's adaptation and production starts out, thanks to the equally dazzling choreography of David Bolger, with a small, backwoods, already forgotten village community stamping its feet into the unforgiving earth, and if that sounds a lot like the opening of *Martin Guerre*, well, it is, though not for any copycat reason. Two productions, starting roughly simultaneously, have simply hit upon the same metaphor for a village tale in which the earth is really all there is between the life and death of its occupants.

From there, *Tarry Flynn* heads off into an altogether different direction; those of us seeking signposts in an unfamiliar terrain will find *Billy Liar* and *Larkrise to Candleford* and especially *Under Milk Wood* of some assistance, but none of them even together adds up to the unique experience on offer here. Tarry himself is a likely lad on the make in, and eventually on the run from, a stifling community; part-Peter Pan, part-Puck and part-devil, he is an unlikely hero in that there is nothing essentially lovable or even likeable about him despite James Kennedy's mesmerising performance, the best by a newcomer (at least to me) that I can recently recall.

Around him, a cast of thirty Abbey stalwarts led by Pauline Flanagan as his equally unforgiving mother (and again, the echoes of Aase in *Peer Gynt* are at their strongest when these two are together) plays out the various villagers, hostile neighbours, girlfriends, mad priests and daughters of this lost community, though in one sense you could argue that a nearly three-hour play is really only about Tarry plucking up courage to quit for the big city, a courage he finds only through the last-minute intervention of a long-lost and equally wayward uncle.

Tarry Flynn is in no sense a tidy play, but its central theme, that of a raggedy man who will never accept his non-place in the world, nor that where he is born has to be where he is to die, has the haunting quality of a half-finished landscape, or of somewhere only half-recollected in a dream.

As in the pioneering work of Theatre de Complicite, the cast doubles as chickens, heifers, fields and fences, at times becoming a complete farmyard, at others just a hostile force for oppression and age-old enmities. The greatness of Kavanagh's original memoir, first published fifty years ago, lies in its love/hate observation of the Irish village as a force for both good and evil, and this first ever staging captures all its original power. Tarry is never a hero even in the sense of Billy Liar; he's a dour, vengeful, repressed and angry spirit who will probably come to no more good in the big city than he ever has in his native village. And yet there is just enough of a spark in him, just enough of the possibility of redemption through love, to make us care and hope for the best for him. If there was to be yet another signpost, it would I think point toward

Billy Bigelow, the fairground barker of *Carousel,* written in the same late 1940s and set again in a backwoods community from which death is often the only escape. Tarry avoids that at the last by simply packing his few belongings in a suitcase; but the suggestion is that he will never really escape his neighbours, most of whom take the dour view that hell will not be full until he is safely in it.

Like a young Hume Cronyn, Kennedy holds the centre of this picareseque, parochial, hugely inventive epic; and if some management does not now give us *Tarry Flynn* in the West End or on Broadway, the rest of the theatre-going world will have glimpsed only too briefly what may well turn out to be the Irish classic of the decade.

~

As for the music of the old Broadway, nobody does it better than Jerry Herman; his own recent anthology may have died a speedy New York death but across the last thirty years, from *Hello Dolly!* through *Mame* and *Mack and Mabel* to *La Cage aux Folles,* he has been the most assured show-song-writer of all those anthems for large ladies on even larger staircases, from Merman through Channing to Angela Lansbury, even if at the last, when it came to *La Cage,* they were really only large men dressed up as large ladies on large staircases.

So now, at the tiny Bridewell, we get around sixty of those showstoppers in two hours; sure there are problems, not least a singing American pianist who could have given Liberace a lesson or two in schmalz, and some choreography dating from ocean-liner concerts of the early 1950s. There's also a woefully uncharismatic cast, in which only Garth Bardsley and Melanie Marshall stand out as the stars they are one day going to be.

But – and it's a big one – those Herman songs remain just wonderful; for some reason he is still not given his due credit as the last survivor of the old Rodgers/Hammerstein/Berlin school of sheer joy. Somehow, in order to love Stephen Sondheim you had to be seen to hate Herman, which is rather like the notion that if you liked Cole Porter you had no reason to love Larry Hart. It is Herman who still writes all the songs we really need when we are down and out, their titles alone suggesting a kind of resilient optimism and simple courage now hopelessly out of fashion and favour – 'I Am What I Am', 'Open A New Window', 'Tap Your Troubles Away', 'I'll Be Here Tomorrow', 'I Promise You A Happy Ending'.

No musician since Irving Berlin has given the world so much to sing about from an all-American viewpoint; the difference is that, whereas Berlin's songs were essentially mindless pap, Herman's are sung by drunks, losers, gays, transvestites, all of whom find first in them and then in themselves the courage to carry on regardless. Sure, it is a sentimental and simplistic notion of survival against the odds, but it is also resilient and touching and tremendous; this is what musicals were made to sound like before they got melancholia.

Carry On up the National

Cleo, Camping, Emmanuelle and Dick (National)

Not since John Osborne's *The Entertainer*, and that has been all of forty years, have we had a play which deals as lethally or as brilliantly with the moment in a comic's life when the raised eyebrow and the fixed grin become a death mask: Terry Johnson's *Cleo, Camping, Emmanuelle and Dick* (directed by the author himself on the Lyttelton stage of the National) is the best and bleakest comedy of the year, and one which deals with the real lives, in so far as they ever had them, of the three principal stars of the *Carry On* sequence of thirty or so low-budget screen farces all shot between 1956 and 1978.

By the time we join the cast and crew backstage, at some point midway through the series, things are beginning to fall apart both on and off the set; scripts are already as tired and repetitive as the real lives of those who have to play them, Kenneth Williams is already suicidally gloomy about the work he is being forced to perform, Barbara Windsor is watching her jealous husband go to jail for armed robbery, and Sid James, he of the dirty laugh and the need to molest every girl who comes through his dressing-room door, has already seen a vision of the death that awaits him, a death already presaged by that of his old partner Tony Hancock.

Johnson's genius here, as in his earlier *Dead Funny*, has been to construct a stage farce far funnier than any of the ones that his cast are ostensibly shooting, and also once again to focus on the reality that inside every comic is a deeply sad and disturbed man or woman trying to get out and confront a world which only wants to make them as unhappy as only a comic can be.

The casting here is also just wonderful; Adam Godley's Kenneth Williams may from time to time drift dangerously close to Stanley Baxter, another comic hero of the period, but he has perfectly caught Kenneth's constantly wounded pride and that sense you had of him always sitting around waiting to be insulted. Samantha Spiro's Barbara Windsor is also an amazingly lookalike/soundalike creation, the only one of the comics that Johnson treats with any real love or respect for her genuinely good nature. Kenneth MacDonald as the heavy sent by her gangster husband to keep an eye on her affair with Sid may be little more than a thug from central casting, but Jacqueline Defferary as the dresser who can never quite manage to tell Sid she is his illegitimate daughter, and Gina Bellman as Imo Hassall are both heartbreaking in their attempt to crack Sid's armoury of despairing laughter, while as this central figure, Geoffrey Hutchings, in the performance of the evening and his own career, gives us a Sid James that is breathtaking in its accuracy of impersonation and understanding of a deeply unhappy man who would go anywhere for a laugh except into the arms of the few people who genuinely loved or understood him.

The idea of the clown with the heart of sheer misery is not exactly a new one, but what Johnson does here, watched over by the shadows of Hancock and Joe Orton and others who died violently for their laughs, is to capture that borderline moment when it all starts to come apart at the seams; as one of these desperate entertainer's notes, 'just when you're beginning to be really tired of life, you've got your sixties to look forward to.'

Nor does he ever forget that he is writing a comedy: 'Ronnie', says the gangster with the gun who has been sent by him to watch over Barbara and the assaults on her by Sid between shots, 'says it's not so much the money you owe him, nor you shagging his wife, but you shagging his wife while owing him the money what really hurts.'

There are better laughs here than in all the *Carry On* movies put together, but behind them all lies the real agony of people who were literally dying for a giggle. Johnson's play is as potent a lament for the end of the *Carry On* era as was *The Entertainer* for the end of music-hall, and in its own way manages to capture a moment in British showbiz history when it too was consumed by hatred for itself and its audience: 'Never marry anyone,' says Sid at one point, 'just find someone you really hate and buy them a house.'

Hopeless at organising their own love lives, whether gay or straight, able only to create a creaking and repetitive series of farces out of their own reality, these characters are lost forever now to a world where it is thought more important to remain politically correct than get a belly-laugh out of ancient prejudices. If you want to see how and where and why true British comedy committed its own lingering, gasping suicide, this great tragi-comedy will tell it all the way it was and never will be again.

The Ebb Tide

Cabaret (Watermill, Newbury)

Blood Brothers (Phoenix Theatre)

Sugar Sugar (Bush)

Though I would hardly go as far as my revered colleague Milton Shulman, who on his retirement last year memorably announced that in half a century of nightly theatre-going he had seldom come across a truly great play, it is true that in the reviewing business miracles don't come that often, so to get two in a traditionally slow August week calls for some sort of celebration, if only in print.

The first miracle can be found an hour or so due west of London. Outside Newbury, the tiny Watermill Theatre (alongside the Mill at Sonning, one of the two most enchanting riverside playhouses in the world) has recently been struggling for its life against a motorway and a funding gap. The motorway is alas now on its doorstep, but the local council, perhaps already feeling guilty about what it has done, has at least guaranteed the theatre's financial future through the millennium, and the show currently playing there is far and away the best version of Kander & Ebb's *Cabaret* that I have ever seen.

And I must, over thirty years, have seen at least a dozen including the original 1966 Broadway production, overblown and over-dominated by the great Lotte Lenya who kept inadvertently reminding us that it wasn't quite as good as her late husband Kurt Weill's *The Threepenny Opera*; then there was the 1969 London one, not helped by the absence of Joel Grey, and most recently the Donmar Warehouse version, still triumphing on Broadway but perhaps overly fixated on the Nazi subplot.

But what the director John Doyle has now realised is that *Cabaret* is about so much more than just the coming-to-Berlin power of the Nazis in 1934; the subplots involving Sally Bowles, and Cliff, and the Master of Ceremonies, and Herr Schultz and Fraulein Schneider all had equal importance in Isherwood's original Berlin stories, and Doyle has now restructured and realigned the show to look more like a play with songs than ever before. Most impressive of all, he has found a cast of only eight, all of whom double and treble roles while also playing all the instruments in the nightclub's pit band.

On the Watermill's already tiny stage, now converted to in-the-round with the audience sitting, as they were at the Warehouse, at nightclub tables, we are closer to *Cabaret* than we have ever been before, and the results are just dazzling.

By returning Schultz and Schneider to centre stage, so that we learn to care more about the old greengrocer and the derelict landlady than we ever have, and by running the score into the plot with no breaks for singing, and no applause allowed after any of the numbers, Doyle has revolutionised *Cabaret* and turned what was always a great musical into a masterpiece. Mike Afford and Karen Mann as Schultz and Schneider, Simon Walter as the evil MC and Jo Baird as a haunting, waif-like Sally Bowles made of silk and steel, all give performances that have never been and I believe will never be bettered. There have been a lot of *Cabaret* revivals around lately, and we are promised yet another for the autumn; but Doyle seems here to have created the first truly music-theatre ensemble I have seen in this country, and it would be heartbreaking if they did not get the chance to play to a wider audience. Come to this *Cabaret*, old chum, for you will never see another quite like it.

~

The other miracle is back in central London, where Willy Russell's *Blood Brothers* is currently celebrating its tenth anniversary. When it first opened I wrote that the show was unmissable and unbeatable, but I'm not sure that even I in my original enthusiasm would have estimated it at ten years and still counting. The wonder of *Blood Brothers* is that, like *Cabaret*, it is essentially a play with music rather than a musical, and indeed its author Willy Russell (more famous for *Educating Rita* and *Shirley Valentine*) has only written one other, the Beatle parody *John, Paul, George, Ringo and Bert*.

And although it now enters the London long-run musicals chart behind only the trio of eternal Lloyd Webbers (*Cats*, *Phantom of the Opera* and *Starlight Express*) and of course *Les Misérables*, *Blood Brothers* was originally a sleeper which kept coming and going to and from London before eventually settling at the Phoenix. Its roots are deep in the myth about twins separated at birth, the one that always served the Greeks and Shakespeare well enough; and although it is unmistakeably set in the Liverpool of the early 1980s, *Blood Brothers* remains almost alarmingly topical since none of its central issues of poverty, unemployment and class warfare has gone away in the meantime.

This is, in fact, the closest we shall ever get to an English *Threepenny Opera*, a harsh folk tale about love and death with up to a dozen brilliant, brittle numbers which the producer Bill Kenwright and his director Bob Tomson have kept as sharp as ever they were a decade ago; Lyn Paul now leads a wondrous new cast.

~

And finally, at the Bush, Simon Bent's *Sugar Sugar* is a weird mix of Joe Orton and Harold Pinter, with a bit of Rattigan thrown in for good measure. Set in a Scarborough seaside boarding house out of season, it consists of some marvellously funny characters all in search of some sort of a plot. Some of these characters are stock (the sex-starved landlady for instance, wonderfully played by Sue Johnston) while others are genuinely new comic creations, like the misanthrope who could fill supermarkets with the people he wants dead.

The plot, when it does come in Act Two, all seems to happen at once in a kind of rush, but there's no doubt (on this evidence and his earlier *Goldhawk Road*) Bent is that rarity, a new comic dramatist of considerable promise in characterisation if not storytelling.

Round and Round La Ronde

The Blue Room (Donmar Warehouse)

I have somehow failed to catch the Nicole Kidman fever currently rampant among my critical colleagues. In the first place, as she was a talented and hardworking Australian stage actress long before she made the Cruise marriage or some of the very few good Hollywood movies to have emerged over the last decade, it seems to me curiously patronising to express such amazement that she can skip lightly through the half-dozen very sketchy playlets to which David Hare has reduced Schnitzler's once-great *La Ronde* in what is now *The Blue Room* at the Donmar.

Second, her achievement in doing this, such as it is, can scarcely be compared (though it has been) to the very much greater risks successfully run by other Hollywood movie stars who have lately turned up on the London fringe, such as Kevin Spacey in *The Iceman Cometh*, or even Juliette Binoche in a long-lost Pirandello. Though written at the end of another century, *La Ronde* has never really been lost, given the great Anton Walbrook-Simone Signoret movie of fifty years ago, and in his current update Hare has, presumably intentionally, abandoned one of its greatest strengths.

As I have always understood it, what links the short blackout scenes in the Schnitzler original is that, as we follow ten social-stereotype characters through two sexual encounters each, what they are in fact passing on to each other is venereal disease; if that now seems somewhat medically dated, surely AIDS would have been an almost exact contemporary parallel.

But Hare doesn't bother with any of Schnitzler's subtext, despite the fact that it has hitherto been the most interesting thing about *La Ronde*, and was presumably the reason why it had to wait twenty years for a public performance, and was even then the subject of a six-day obscenity trial in Vienna as late as 1921. Instead, he contents himself with some very minimalist sketches, stripped of any supporting characters; in ninety no-interval minutes we get Kidman and her widely overlooked but rather better co-star Iain Glen quick-changing into cab-drivers, playwrights, aristocrats, call-girls, models, actresses and housewives in what are now inevitably rather repetitive brief encounters, not so much a battle of the sexes as some desperately inconclusive skirmishes.

Kidman is not remotely as interesting in any of these roles as would have been an actress like Felicity Kendal or Jane Asher, though in all fairness to her the sketches inevitably allow for no real plot or character development; Hare simply hasn't given them space or time to breathe, and as a result we have lost any sense of the original sexual carousel. The whirligig of time has not here brought in any of its revenges, and we are left with a kind of architect's redrawing of the original, without any of its interior decoration or furnishings. Less is not, in the instance of *The Blue Room*, more, despite some valiant attempts by the director Sam Mendes to make us believe that every time they start a new sketch the rabbit may finally be about to emerge from the hat. Sadly it never does.

All of a Rushdie

Haroun and the Sea of Stories (National)

It is perhaps a little ambitious of the publishers of Salman Rushdie's *Haroun and the Sea of Stories*, now in its first-ever staging at the National Theatre, to advertise it as 'a children's classic in the tradition of *Alice in Wonderland* or *The Wizard of Oz*.' In the first place, that kind of classic status usually takes a half-century or more to achieve, and, in the second, these stories are not now, or perhaps ever going to be, as accessible to children of all ages. If you know of the fatwa, and of the terrible self-imprisonment from which Rushdie is still only tentatively emerging (there were police guards and metal detectors all around the theatre on the first night), then indeed there is a fearful relevance in the villainous Khattan-Shud, arch-enemy of stories, foe of all language, prince of silence, who has his followers sew up their own lips.

Clearly and unsurprisingly Rushdie sees the story as both democratic and subversive, and storytelling from generation to generation as one of the last great freedoms: even in most prisons, there are still tales to be told. The more you know of his own story, the more heartbreakingly relevant his stories become; and (as at the Young Vic on his work with Grimm and Kipling tales) Tim Supple has given them a marvellously inventive staging, with a largely Eastern orchestra and actors willing to turn themselves into monsters of all kinds.

Melly Still, who designs and co-devises with Supple, has surrounded her ever-fluid set with an entire library of books, but here, as with the orchestra and the East/West stage games of the players, there are clashes of styles that never quite settle down into a coherent evening, If you could imagine Ali Baba rewritten by C S Lewis, you would have some idea of the weird mix of academic satire and Far-Eastern magical mystery tour that lies at the heart of Haroun's determination to restore his father's lost narrative arts.

An extremely socially and politically aware twelve-year-old might just get all this, but even then there are references and traditions here which require rather more careful study and thought than is expected of the usual Christmas treat for children of all ages, preferably on this occasion between about twenty-five and dead.

Supple has done some breathtaking stage wizardry on a tight budget, and the wheelchair-bound star Nabil Shaban manages to be as mischievous and endearing as ever; the rest of the company, whether fighting off sea monsters or shadow-duelling with themselves, are a tribute to the years of Cheek By Jowl and Theatre de Complicite, which have finally brought the arts of mime and mimickry and magic back into mainstream theatre.

West End

West Side Story (Prince Edward)

The imminence of a recession can often be forecast in direct proportion to the number of old musicals around; it's about as reliable an indicator as any other, though it is not usually necessary to run for the bank until they announce a revival of *42nd Street*. By that token, so far so good, though we do already have *Annie* and *Oklahoma!* and *Chicago* and *Grease* and *Saturday Night Fever*, with *Fame* and *The King and I* and *The Sound of Music* just waiting in the wings. We also have *West Side Story* back at the Prince Edward some forty years after it was first seen here, though, by the look of it, in the same production and with the same now somewhat tacky sets.

One of the great advances in musical revivals this last year or two has been the final destruction of the power of the original choreographer. While nobody would have dreamt of reviving, for example, the Rouben Mamoulian *Oklahoma!*, though he was indeed its first director back in 1943, it was until recently considered perfectly respectable to leave Agnes de Mille's name on the credits, despite her original routines being restaged by dance directors probably not even born when she first took her Second World War rehearsals. Mercifully all that has changed, and the new National *Oklahoma!* (soon to move to the Lyceum and then doubtless New York) has been brought to totally new life by Susan Stroman, just as the current Broadway *Cabaret* has precious little to do with Bob Fosse or even Hal Prince.

For some unfathomable reason, however, *West Side Story* is still being revived in its original version, despite the fact that of the original creators Jerome Robbins, Leonard Bernstein and the designers are all dead, leaving only an octogenarian Arthur Laurents, who has this month been openly denying Robbins' claim to his 'original concept' credit, and Stephen Sondheim who has often denigrated his own first Broadway lyrics.

So why now bring into the West End, after months on the road, this weary retread instead of taking the opportunity to have a new team look at the original classic? Even that was not, after all, what Robbins originally wanted; his idea had been to set the whole thing in California, have it written by Betty Comden and Adolph Green and concern a battle between Catholics and Jews, a kind of musical *Abie's Irish Rose*. The fact that what emerged in 1957 had a great deal more to do with Laurents and Sondheim and Bernstein than Robbins himself is only now, a few months after his death, being generally admitted; but we are still stuck with his second-act 'dream ballet', or a handed-down version thereof, even though its convention was already looking tired back then.

What is going on now at the Prince Edward is little short of disgraceful, though I think it must be some tribute to the everlasting power of *West Side Story*'s immortal soul and score that precious few of my colleagues have bothered to record the fact. Nobody seeing the show for the first time in this exhausted road-revival could have any idea of the power of the original, nor what it meant in the history of the American musical; you might as well go to see the movie, which at least has the virtue of showing us what New York looked like before they built the Lincoln Centre and bulldozed the alleyways where the Sharks and the Jets first snapped their fingers in that historic gesture of defiance at just about every musical that had gone before it.

In the era of *Rent* it is simply not good enough to pretend that forty years of musical theatre have never happened; whoever thought that *West Side Story* would end up as a museum piece, as firmly set in concrete as any of the buildings which have replaced its original mean streets? This is a show, and a score, which desperately needs to be reconsidered for the millennium; not just because a number like 'I Feel Pretty' would now sit more happily in a revival of *Flower Drum Song*, but because nobody is ever going to know why *West Side Story* mattered so much if it goes on getting revived like this. It was the first show to use dance and song to further the plot instead of interrupt it; it was the first to have almost no adults in the cast unless you count the wise old bartender, last seen as Friar Lawrence in *Romeo and Juliet*, or the cops who are there to remind us just how oppressive the land of the free really was to its Puerto Rican immigrants. Above all, it was the first great Broadway hit after *My Fair Lady*, only a few months earlier, lowered the final curtain on the old book musical which had then been around for the best part of a century. *West Side Story* was where the modern stage musical started, and it is just awful now to see it looking so arthritic and lame and lacking in any real theatrical energy or pace. Better surely to bury it for a while until some new director or choreographer has the courage to reconsider it for a new generation.

Murder on the Nile

Antony and Cleopatra (National)

Given how much is wrong with the National's new *Antony and Cleopatra*, it might be as well to start with what is right, and that is essentially the casting of Helen Mirren. Having played Cleopatra three times in a thirty-year career, she is now in total charge of the role, and exudes a confidence and control of the ever-changing moods of the play which is elsewhere sadly lacking. True, Sean Mathias' gimmicky production is not exactly helped by Tim Hatley's sets, which incarcerate the Romans in a kind of grubby Perspex greenhouse, while allowing Cleopatra herself to die in what looks like a cut-price candle warehouse.

We also get, somewhere in Act Three, a repeat of the weird line-dancing with which Mathias also opened his *A Little Night Music* on this stage a couple of years ago, not to mention an Enobarbus who, so far from the usual grizzled warrior, seems to have wandered in from a gay bar somewhere in downtown Alexandria. We also, on the first night, were treated to the unhappy spectacle of a large cast having to bend double in order to enter or escape one particular set which had clearly failed to rise to sufficient height, as well as an Antony from Alan Rickman so patently exhausted and dispirited, presumably from rehearsals, that his defeat at the hands of the Romans and Cleopatra herself, when it did come some three hours later, also came as no surprise.

Whether Alan Bates, the original casting here, would have survived the sets and the production any better is debatable; what is clear is that Mathias has so little faith in the play or the poetry that he is finally reduced to sprinkling fairy dust on his players, thereby all too aptly summarising what has already gone so wrong. Given that the National is now run by one of the best of all Shakespearean directors, Trevor Nunn, it seems amazing that this production was ever allowed to open on its main stage; but then again, all tickets for a brief run were sold out in advance on the strength of Mirren's television fame, so presumably the thinking was that they had nothing to lose. The trouble is that, having established with a recent *Othello* and *King Lear* that the National could indeed overtake the RSC at its own game, this production has put them back to zero.

Unhappily Ever After

Into the Woods (Donmar Warehouse)

Guiding Star (National)

Troilus and Cressida (Barbican)

Christmas has come a little early to the Donmar Warehouse this year; Stephen Sondheim's dark anti-pantomime *Into the Woods* is back in the West End less than a decade after it folded somewhat abruptly in a glitzier staging over here, though on Broadway it remains the second-longest running of all his scores.

Once again, as so often with Sondheim at home and abroad, we started with the long-shot and now we get the close-up; in the intimacy of the Donmar, on a wonderful set by Bob Crowley which looks like an exhibition of Christmas trees, we are taken deeper into these woods than ever before, and theoretically we should be in very secure surroundings, given that this is the third festive-seasonal Sondheim at this address.

But Sondheim is not, of course, notably festive, and nor is he likely to make us feel secure; *Into the Woods* is a multi-level deconstruction of the old pantomime stories, a frequently grim look at the Brothers Grimm. Essentially it deals with what happened unhappily ever after; Cinderella and Rapunzel and their respective Princes ('I was brought up to be Charming, not necessarily sincere,' notes one of these), and Little Red Riding Hood and assorted other fairy-tale figures are reassembled in James Lapine's brittle, often brilliant book some years after their stories were supposed to end in eternal happiness.

Except, of course, that they didn't; what is now stirring down in the forest is the realisation that even for these legendary figures, perhaps especially for them, the future is full of doubt and divorce and death. Again, as so often with Sondheim, the problem is the second half; the first act is a magically funny retelling of old tales ('There's no possible way to describe what you feel,' sings Red Riding Hood's Wolf, 'when you are looking at your meal') which gradually interweaves half-a-dozen panto plots of apparent happiness. But listen carefully to those lyrics; already Jack (of Beanstalk fame) is singing of Giants in the Sky, and the wicked witch is already cursing. Sure enough, after the break, a deadly mother Giant is there to seek revenge by destroying the woods and all who now live there; in the quest to slay her, most of our first-act heroes and heroines die horribly, and we are left with the few survivors looking as though they have just come through the holocaust, grimly starting out again with far more self-awareness and even cynicism than they ever had before. And yet no synopsis does justice to what is going on here; in constant counterpoint, Sondheim also wants us to know that life can be magical, that (in the words of the last and most haunting lyric here) 'No One Is Alone', and that even a mother Giant has a right to a private life devoid of murder.

The problem with the present production is that (unlike the Warehouse's last Sondheim revival *Company*) it is very undercast, so that only Nick Holder and Sophie Thompson (as the Baker and his Wife) and Clare Burt as the Witch seem to have the full measure of this immensely tricky score. In the end, *Into the Woods* is about self-deception and the final, terrifying discovery of who we really are and what we are capable of doing; it is generational but ungenerous, fanciful but unforgiving, magical but murderous, and it needs an absolute security of staging which is not yet apparent in John Crowley's new production. Things are likely to be better by Christmas, which is more than you can say for what *Into the Woods* has to tell us about the possibility of a festive season.

~

Jonathan Harvey is the dramatist who made his name with a touching account of gay teenagers coming to understand themselves (*Beautiful Thing*), but the play he brings now to the National from Liverpool is something both chillier and more ambitious. *Guiding Star* tells the story of a father who can never forgive himself for the fact that he and his two sons survived the Hillsborough soccer-stadium disaster, which killed nearly a hundred of their friends and neighbours almost ten years ago. Harvey still writes a good soap-opera, in which his characters variously get involved with shipwrecks, London call-girls and depressive illness; but you can all too often see the joins where several self-contained confrontations have to be framed into a coherent drama and then linked back to the after-effects of Hillsborough. Gemma Bodinetz's agile production is not helped by some remarkably tacky sets, the National's scenery budget having apparently been used up for the season by their appalling *Antony and Cleopatra*.

The star of this evening is Samantha Lavalle as the girlfriend from hell, unstoppably chatty and attired in a range of Dayglo clothing; yet even she manages to grasp that Hillsborough has done something terrible and total to Liverpool, which will show its scars well into the next generation.

~

And, finally, a *Troilus and Cressida* at the Barbican which seems to me all too symbolic of the Royal Shakespeare Company's current nervous breakdown; we are maybe in Bosnia, maybe in some Greek civil war. Wherever, all is confusion, from costumes to casting; can there be any reason other than weird gimmickry to have Achilles's lover Patroclus played by a woman and then shot by his/her own side merely to get Achilles back into armour? As is now all too common at the RSC, the cast are catastrophically unused to Shakespearean verse-speaking and Michael Boyd's production betrays a deep lack of faith in the play, which he allows to drift aimlessly along with Irish accents adding to the general confusion. Amazingly, this production is scheduled to tour at home and abroad; it does the RSC no service anywhere.

Anna and the King

The King and I (Battersea Arts Centre)

Killing Rasputin (Bridewell)

If you want to see what a real Rodgers & Hammerstein rediscovery looks like this Christmas, go over the river to the Battersea Arts Centre where Phil Willmott has a breathtaking small-stage *The King and I*. Often undercast, hopelessly underfinanced in a set looking like the back room of a Thai take-away restaurant, this is nevertheless a brilliant reminder of how it all started, with a book of memoirs and then a non-musical film called *Anna and the King of Siam*. Now, stripped of its widescreen glitz and the haunting presence of Yul Brynner, you suddenly see why the show remains banned in Thailand, where they have recently also refused to allow the movie remake; Thai beer firms in London have even declined to be involved here as sponsors.

Why? Because, seen once again but for the first time in half a century as a play with music, this *King and I* emerges as a bitter attack by Oscar Hammerstein on Siam/Thailand's age-old chauvinism and all-powerful monarchy. While the rest of the world treats the Rodgers & Hammerstein score as harmless and now dated showbiz, Thailand's rulers recognise it for the timeless time-bomb it remains.

I was only ten where Gertrude Lawrence created the first *King and I* on Broadway in 1951 with Yul Brynner way down below the title; but from all I have learnt and researched of that production, I believe that fifty years later Willmott has, maybe inadvertently in a no-cash situation, got us back to first base. This is a radical, angry story about a savage autocrat and a rebellious nanny (Rodgers and Hammerstein were to write it again ten years later as *The Sound of Music*), and although I have seen many richer and some better productions of *The King and I*, I have never seen one so ultimately heartbreaking or true to its roots.

Willmott (well self-cast as the supercilious British envoy who was Anna's first love) stages the death of the King at unusual dramatic length, and ensures that our final memory is not the customary 'Shall We Dance' but instead the moment when Anna effectively kills her King by denying his right to horsewhip a rebellious subject. We also get the full measure of the King's handover of his powers to a faintly more liberal son, while the usually turgid *Uncle Tom* ballet is acted rather than danced, now much after the fashion of the play in *Hamlet*, giving us the full foretaste of what is to come in the rest of the story. Lindsey Danvers is a fine, feisty Anna, and Alan Mosley seizes the chance to play her King as a full tragic hero rather than the usual bald despot.

~

From old American to new British; if we are to have any kind of a local musical theatre into and beyond the millennium, then we may have to do something more encouraging and pro-active than sit around awaiting the next Lloyd Webber or Boublil & Schonberg on their roughly five-year cycle, while casting nervous eyes across the Atlantic to see what missile Sondheim plans to hurl at us next.

All of which is, I guess, one way of saying that although *Killing Rasputin* (at the Bridewell) still has its problems, it arrives there with all the right credentials, having been premiered four years ago at Lloyd Webber's Sydmonton Festival and then developed at the Sondheim masterclasses at Oxford and through his Mercury workshop for young musical writers.

Shows like this are famously not written but rewritten, and the killer monk has come a long way since his first appearance; so too has his lyricist Kit Hesketh-Hervey, of *Kit and the Widow* fame, who now wisely deletes all reference to his London musical-writing debut with *Which Witch?* even from his own programme-note, while composer James McConnel has happily also overcome his recent disaster with Dame Edna Everage at the Haymarket.

Rasputin is a courageous show, given us now in a spare kind of chamber production by Ian Brown. True, the old drama queen still takes a long time to be killed and even longer to die, which essentially is all that happens here; around the periphery, the complete and utter history of Russia in first world war nervous breakdown is apt to look a little sketchy when performed by a dozen actors on a bare stage.

Tolstoy and Chekhov and Dostoyevsky are hard acts to follow in this minimal context, and at times one even starts to long for the movie of *Nicholas and Alexandra* which at least had a budget and some snow. So we're not talking *Dr Zhivago* here, while from a *Les Mis* kind of choral opening the score leaps bizarrely in the second half to a weird kind of *Cabaret* parody. Nevertheless, it's all rather interesting in a dark and soulful way, and I for one remain eager to hear what McConnel and Hesketh-Hervey write next; perhaps *Rasputin* needs the full opera, and preferably by Tchaikovsky.

Directing the Redgraves

Song at Twilight – a rehearsal diary

1 December 1998

This has been an unusually high-profile year for my friends and colleagues in the Critics' Circle. Four of them directed plays at the Battersea Arts Centre in the spring, while in the autumn another four got caught up in a distinctly hostile Channel 4 television series about the role of the reviewer. Having stayed unusually well clear of all that, what am I now doing in a derelict and disused saloon bar down the Goswell Road directing Corin Redgrave, Kika Markham, Nyree Dawn Porter and Matthew Bose in Noël Coward's last play *Song at Twilight*, due to open at the King's Head in Islington on 4 January?

We need to go back a bit. I once asked Kenneth Tynan why, as the most powerful and brilliant drama critic of my lifetime, he had thrown it all up at the *Observer* to become Olivier's literary manager at the National, a job which (though Ken begged for it) really only existed in wily Larry's view to keep Tynan well away from a theatre column in which he could prove vastly more dangerous.

'Because,' Ken said simply, 'I got fed up with eating night after night in restaurants where they would never let me write the menu.' And that in essence is our theatrical fate; it is also why we are regularly told that a critic is someone who knows the way but can't drive the car, and that nobody ever raised a statue to a reviewer (not true, incidentally; there are at least two in America).

It is therefore not surprising that, somewhere in early or late middle age, most of us critics take to teaching or broadcasting or writing books; we can't all be Bernard Shaw, but it nevertheless is not enough to spend your entire professional life doing nothing but trying to evaluate the work of others. In my case, I began writing about Noël Coward in 1965, and that first biography, his and mine (*A Talent to Amuse*), led me on to his lifelong partner Gertrude Lawrence and a mini-musical called *Noël and Gertie* which I have sometimes directed, and which Twiggy is happily now about to open in New York to mark the Coward Centenary over there.

5 December

This, however, is my first attempt to direct a play, and I have been more than lucky in my casting; Corin and Kika are doing their first-ever Coward, and Nyree has been off the London stage for far too long, not unlike her character in the story. The play itself is something of a revelation; if you didn't know the authorship, you might well guess Rattigan or even J B Priestley. In essence it's a blackmail thriller, loosely built around Somerset Maugham in old age, and I do not propose to give away any more of the plot than that. Noël himself was getting very fragile when he played it briefly in London in 1966, and since then it has had only very rare road revivals here and in America. The version of *Song at Twilight* we are now doing is a British premiere, a heavily cut (by Noël himself in 1972, just before his death) variant on the original which runs barely ninety minutes.

10 December

I have begun to realise that Noël left this play ticking behind him as a sort of posthumous time-bomb; essentially it's about the outing of homosexual celebrities at a time when the word 'outing' had yet to be coined, and of course it is to some extent autobiographical, though in the character of the veteran novelist Sir Hugo Latymer are also strong echoes of both Maugham and Max Beerbohm.

The brilliance of Corin in this role, quite apart from his tact and talent in rehearsal for making me believe I have something to teach him, is in wrapping all those troubled literary ghosts into his performance but then creating a wholly new character with no trace of Noël at all. In my view he has also built in a certain amount of his father Sir Michael, though he would probably deny that it was done consciously; Redgrave relatives are now understandably bored of family connections still beloved by the press.

12 December

An all-too-short rehearsal period is not helped by a prior engagement whereby both Corin and Kika have to try out new work in America, so I lose them both for ten days. My other main problem is that an already fragile Noël wrote himself an almost entirely sedentary character and play, so if I'm not careful this whole staging will look like a Radio Four readthrough. I am however now vastly helped by a set by Saul Radomsky which, on the usual King's Head budget of about £15, nevertheless manages to suggest an elegant lakeside hotel in the Switzerland of the 1960s.

20 December

Redgraves now safely home from America, and we are moving swiftly into our last few days before previews. Nyree, though physically frail, is extraordinary as Carlotta, the movie star who threatens to demolish Hugo's public life; she somehow links her straight to Elvira and Amanda and all those other Coward heroines who were versions of his beloved Gertrude Lawrence.

28 December

Minimal Christmas break and, to my amazement, a first preview for which they are already standing at the back of the theatre. Something about the Coward Centenary, the Redgraves, Nyree and an 'unknown' Coward play seems to have spread the word with, as yet, no advertising of any kind, and this in a Christmas break.

I realise that, as a critic, I have spent far too much time watching the stage and not enough looking at the audience; they in the end are the ones who teach us all we need to know about a play and its performance.

4 January 1999

Tonight we open to my colleagues in the press, or at least those kind enough to turn up in Islington on the first day after the long holiday. How do I feel? Bloody terrified, since you ask, but fairly sure I have now done all I can for and with this amazing cast. Real (that is, full-time) directors often note how devastated they feel when their production starts to take on a life of its own and they are no longer needed, especially in the dressing-room; I have to note a kind of relief, and that I am almost looking forward to getting back to the usual Radio Two arts programmes and the books and the reviewing of other people's productions.

Whatever happens tonight, we know that we are already more than half sold for the run at the King's Head, and that we just might even achieve an afterlife. This does not, in the end, have a lot to do with me, though I might just possibly have become a fractionally better critic by seeing what happens to actors before they get to a press-night. If we have a hit, it will be entirely because of Noël Coward and this great cast; if we have a flop, I shall have nobody to blame but myself.

(*Song at Twilight* later transferred, with Vanessa Redgrave as Carlotta, to the Gielgud Theatre in the West End, where it ran for six months.)

1999

Mothers from Hell

Perfect Days (Hampstead)
The Memory of Water (Vaudeville)
The Merchant of Venice / The Tempest (Barbican)

If 1999 carries on the way it has started, theatrically this new year is going to be a rough one for the male of the species; five of them turn up in the first two plays of the season, Liz Lochhead's *Perfect Days* and Shelagh Stephenson's *The Memory of Water*, and all are a complete and utter waste of space.

In that sense, I guess both new productions are 'women's plays', but intriguingly neither is any kind of feminist tract; both are written within well-defined comic guidelines, both are traditionally well-made, and both are clearly destined for some kind of after-life on television, which is where either could have started as something halfway from a serial drama to a sit-com.

Most Edinburgh Festival hits make the long trek south in the following months looking distinctly hungover, and often very fragile in the colder light of a London winter; the wonder of *Perfect Days* is that it is every bit as good as we were told from Scotland last August.

In an elegant Glasgow loft lives Barbs (the feisty and fiery Siobhan Redmond in what will clearly be one of the performances of the year), who has her own day-time television slot and a highly successful hairdressing salon. What she doesn't have is a baby and, approaching forty, she decides this has to be sorted. An ex-husband of remarkable if hopeless tolerance, a gay boyfriend, a college-age lover and a mother from hell are soon on the scene to aid and abet her quest for motherhood, and Lochhead's hugely vital, funny and charming comedy looks at times as if Neil Simon had rewritten *Shirley Valentine* north of the border.

No, *Perfect Days* is not perfect, but in John Tiffany's production what saves it from being a dire morality play is Lochhead's evident enjoyment of her characters and their various social and sexual predicaments. If it weren't to sound like a sexist insult, I'd say she was a new Willy Russell in drag.

~

The other 'new' play dates still further back, to the July of 1996, and also features a mother from hell, though in this case she does have the grace to be dead, albeit omnipresent. This one comes from Hampstead, where Shelagh Stephenson's first script, the patchily brilliant *The Memory of Water*, was first seen in a production by Terry Johnson. Nearly three years later, after a long regional tour, a new production comes into the Vaudeville, again directed by Johnson but with an all-new cast starring Alison Steadman, Samantha Bond and Julia Sawalha as the three sisters gathered at their old family home on the north-east coast of England to bury their cantankerous mother (Margot Leicester), who reappears periodically from beyond her shiny new coffin to make all their lives still more troublesome.

The Memory of Water is no *Blithe Spirit*, but it is an intriguing throwback to all those plays of the early 1950s by Wynyard Browne and N C Hunter, 'English Chekhov' as they were then termed, in which at some kind of family reunion skeletons would tumble from every closet. Sure enough these three sisters, all of whose lives have in their individual ways gone horribly adrift, turn out to have been bruised beyond belief by a maternal upbringing somewhere between Alan Bennett and Joe Orton, and the genius of Johnson's production is the way that once again it ends up in bleak, black humour, not waving but drowning in its various admissions of familial guilt and relative failure.

~

At the Barbican, the RSC has long had an intriguing habit of wrong-footing its critics in the very nick of time; just as The Sunday Times, across three pages, finally takes up the message I have been trying to deliver for almost two years here, that the company is in some kind of artistic breakdown, hey presto! two productions come into London looking very sharp indeed, while out at Stratford on the home stage a new *A Winter's Tale* is also hailed.

The Philip Voss *The Merchant of Venice* has a sinewy strength and speed, while also on the main Barbican stage Adrian Noble's *The Tempest* has a powerfully unusual Prospero in David Calder, who philosophically drives this staging through to new discoveries and map-readings of an island which has always been as sinister in its magic as the Neverland of *Peter Pan*. There are also strongly comic turns from Barry Stanton (Stephano) and Adrian Schiller (Trinculo) in two of the unfunniest jester roles ever written even by Shakespeare.

Nobody, not even me, has ever doubted Noble's talent as a director; the question still open is whether he is also the producer who can, in these last pre-millennium months, pull the RSC back into some kind of overall shape before it fragments entirely into individual productions on a wide variety of London and regional stages. These two Barbican transfers indicate that there is still a problem with talent in the middle and lower ranks of the company, and still another with verse-speaking and even sometimes understanding; but they are the most encouraging start to a new year that the RSC has had in a very long time, and the hope must be that once again the company can pull itself together in the very nick of time.

Crookback Capers

Richard III (Savoy)

Bad Weather (Barbican)

For longer than I care to remember, I have been suggesting that what most ails the current Royal Shakespeare Company is a discernible lack of the old star power which once dominated and even dictated the repertoire. Stars, it seems, are now much happier closeted in brief runs on small studio stages, or away from the theatre altogether, than clambering up the old cliff-faces of the major tragedies, though on that note we do soon get (albeit not from the RSC) a *King Lear* from Sir Nigel Hawthorne, and a *Macbeth* from Rufus Sewell.

But it will doubtless seem churlish to note that, now the RSC do at last have a major box-office name in Robert Lindsay as Richard III (at the Savoy), that doesn't solve their problems either. For instead of returning to the old RSC star system of the 1960s, whereby you had two or three great stars and several great character actors in any one production, the director Elijah Moshinsky has with one bound gone way back to the star system of the 1940s and Sir Donald Wolfit, whereby one actor gets to chew up the scenery and all the rest get to stand around watching politely and respectfully from an upstage distance while he does it.

True, this production, though starting at Stratford, was evidently built for touring and then the West End, rather than the RSC's traditional Barbican home, but that still doesn't explain the heavy textual cuts, all of which have been made to give the old hunchback villain even more time centre stage. And, again in the Wolfit tradition, Lindsay declines to play scenes with other actors; instead, he plays them with the audience, giggling and smirking at us across the footlights like some vaudeville comic who has suddenly discovered the classics. If his performance is reminiscent of anyone, it is not Olivier or Sher or any of his great predecessors in the role, but instead the old Cowardly Lion himself, Bert Lahr, when he took in late life to tackling Samuel Beckett instead of *The Wizard of Oz.*

The Moshinsky staging makes a strange bargain with the devil of declining regional audiences, which is basically that if you come to see Lindsay as Richard III you will have at least as enjoyable an evening as you would sitting at home with a television sitcom. Accordingly, every light joke in the text is underlined as if for theatre-goers who have already left their brains with their coats in the cloakroom and are eager to get out in under three hours, and the production is therefore fatally and utterly devoid of the two things that the play is centrally about, history and power.

Denied the prequels of this great history cycle about an age of kings, we get no real sense of where this Richard is coming from or why; equally, because he seems to regard his mass murders as some kind of pathetic joke, we too fail to take them very seriously, In his own butch way, Lindsay is here as camp as a row of tents; David Yelland as an unusually elegant Buckingham does his best to remind us that there is a play as well as an over-the-top star performance to watch, but he and such distinguished others as Anna Carteret and Robert East lose that battle as surely as Richard finally loses his last. He has lost his kingdom not so much for want of a horse, as for yet another hoarse cry of isolated stardom run riot. Which is sad, because with tighter direction Lindsay is one of the best actors in the land.

~

Meanwhile, it might be wise to stay home out of the rain rather than venture down to the RSC's Barbican Pit in search of yet more *Bad Weather*. Robert Holman's new play makes a somewhat needless journey into London, since none of the problems that were flagged when it first opened at Stratford last summer seem to have been solved or even addressed in the meantime. Holman is an odd throwback to Christopher Fry and T S Eliot, poetic dramatists in whose plays not a lot happened and then happened again after the interval.

The story of a youngster (Ryan Pope) wrongfully locked up for a crime committed by his best friend (Paul Popplewell), the play soon drifts off from downtown Middlesbrough to rustic France, where various characters loosely tied to the main storyline sit around consuming salads and chuntering on about innocence and guilt and ethics and pregnancy and how strange life can be; it then rains a bit, and they mostly go home to carry on with their uneventful lives and loves in varying degrees of satisfaction or despair. In an unusually brilliant review of the play, one of its characters notes that 'It's all degrees, a bit of knowledge here, a bit of understanding there. It's all a mess.' And so say all of us.

Children's Hour

Goodnight Children Everywhere (Barbican)

I find myself out on something of a limb in regard to the Royal Shakespeare Company at present; while most of my colleagues seem less concerned than I am about the possibility that the company is in a serious midlife artistic and managerial breakdown, they still find it hard to credit the RSC with what I believe is still their greatest achievement in contemporary theatre, their sustained support over ten plays and twenty years of the American dramatist Richard Nelson.

He remains, even in his own country, without much other honour; very few Nelson plays (unless you count *Two Shakespearean Actors* and the revisions he did to the American book of the Tim Rice/Abba musical *Chess*) have ever had a Broadway life, and even over here we seem happier with the more immediately obvious and identifiable work of a David Mamet or Sam Shepard.

Like his great contemporaries Terrence McNally and A R Gurney, Nelson often gets becalmed in mid-Atlantic; unlike them, he writes almost exclusively about Anglo-American attitudes and his latest work, *Goodnight Children Everywhere* (into the Barbican Pit from Stratford) starts in classic Nelson style with an English teenager returning home to south London in the spring of 1945 after a five-year wartime evacuation to Canada. But as the play develops, it becomes clear that Nelson is for once not interested in the culture shock or social clash that usually arises in his plays when groups of American tourists try to make their way around the classical landmarks of Britain (*Some Americans Abroad*), or when latterday British settlers try to make some sense of modern America (*New England*). Instead, he seems to be revisiting J B Priestley's *Laburnum Grove* through the eyes of a post-war Chekhov and, if that ambitious plan doesn't entirely succeed, Nelson's semi-failures are, as always, far more intriguing than the hits of many of his rivals.

Not a lot happens in *Goodnight Children Everywhere*, a title taken from a classic BBC wartime signature tune; the boy, hauntingly and hesitatingly played by a hugely impressive newcomer, Simon Scardifield, returns home to discover that his three sisters have been changed by the war as much if not more than he has; one (Sarah Markland) has become a nurse, another (Cathryn Bradshaw) has married an unfaithful doctor old enough to be her father, and the third (Robin Weaver) has become an actress desperate to trade her sexual favours for any kind of stage role.

Nelson's belief here is that surviving the peace could be as difficult as surviving the war; his on-stage characters may not have been bomb-damaged, but they are psychologically and sexually disturbed to such an extent that incest, infidelity and discreet prostitution have all taken over a household which, pre-1939, was a bastion of moral virtues.

Ian Brown's production (on a set by Tim Hatley) wonderfully captures what Moss Hart once called the dark-brown taste of genteel poverty; these people are not starving in any gutters, they mostly have jobs, but there is still a tin bath in the living-room and they have to pool their ration coupons to make a welcome-home cake for the prodigal son. Priestley and Coward, in their thirties plays about suburban households in revolt, are the ghosts who haunt Nelson's Clapham flat, but his central interest is in lost souls who were destroyed because the crucial years of their crossover from childhood to maturity were denied them on account of the war. The lights have been out all over Europe for a long time, but now the shadows on the stairs are lengthening and darkening; a play about incest still retains a curiously shocking power, but *Goodnight Children Everywhere* is about much more than that, and having just seen it for the first time I am as usual shocked but not surprised by the way that its initial Stratford staging fifteen months ago was greeted with such lukewarm enthusiasm.

I have long believed Nelson to be among the greatest dramatists of his generation, but he does not always make it easy on an audience; his concerns with Anglo-American attitudes date back to the simplicity of Winston Churchill's 'two nations divided by a common language', but he is always ready to explore yet one more wave, one more tempest sometimes, on the transatlantic crossing. There is a remarkable kind of poetry here which is not to all tastes; but if you want a complete postwar history of what has gone wrong with the hands across the sea, you can start and end it with the Nelson touch.

Star Quality

Macbeth (Queen's)

To be or not to be a permanent company? Just as we lose the Peter Hall company at the Piccadilly, just as Trevor Nunn launches, on all three stages of his National Theatre, the first residential season to play on the South Bank for almost twenty years (with a group of actors on year-long contracts in everything from *Troilus and Cressida* to *Candide*), and just as the RSC faces up to the agonising choice it has to make between big stars on necessarily short-term contracts for one show each, or a team of lesser players willing to stay longer, we get two useful West End reminders of the dangers of the old star system in the classics.

First the Robert Lindsay *Richard III* at the Savoy, a weird music-hall turn in which the star seems to prefer working with the audience rather than his fellow players, and now the Rufus Sewell *Macbeth* at the Queens where again the effort to get his name on the poster seems to have exhausted all other thoughts about how and why the play should be conceived for the contemporary West End. With one big star doing his thing centre-stage, there seems to be precious little money left over for scenery and costumes, or a supporting cast who appear to have been instructed to watch politely from the sidelines. Essentially it becomes ego-Shakespeare, and we are all the losers.

For his Shaftesbury Avenue debut as a director, John Crowley has chosen to give us a minimalist, regional studio-staging which might just about get by somewhere miles from anywhere and starved of Shakespeare, but looks decidedly cheap at West End prices. Rufus Sewell is indeed charismatic as Macbeth, recalling an odd hybrid of the young Oliver Reed and the young Albert Finney, but he gets very little backing, even supposing he were willing to look for it, from Sally Dexter's curiously wan and underpowered Lady Macbeth, and a supporting cast of catastrophic weakness, many of whom seem to have strongly Irish rather than Scots accents.

As for Jeremy Herbert's set, virtually non-existent in the first half, it gradually comes to consist in the second of an indoor swimming-pool for Macduff's castle, and a black cardboard box which entombs Macbeth until, intentionally or not, he puts his foot through its cardboard side in a fit of rage, though whether at the production or his imminent defeat is not entirely clear.

~

Over in New York, in the closing months of the century in which Broadway first acquired its name as a theatre district, the streets around Times Square are as lively as at any time I can recall in the last thirty years. Virtually all theatres are open, and the role-call of stars, movie and otherwise, now playing eight shows a week or in rehearsal is as impressive as it has ever been in post-war memory.

From the National come Corin Redgrave in Tennessee Williams' first play *Not About Nightingales* (vastly stronger now than when it first opened at the Cottesloe a year ago), his niece Natasha Richardson in *Closer* and Judi Dench in *Amy's View*, of which the author David Hare is also giving his solo *Via Dolorosa*. Surprisingly, neither Redgrave nor Dench has been on Broadway in almost forty years, but joining them there now are Sian Phillips as Marlene Dietrich, Zoë Wanamaker as Electra, Alan Cumming in *Cabaret*, Judy Parfitt in *Night Must Fall*, not to mention teams of the Irish in *The Weir* and *The Beauty Queen of Leenane*. So we can't exactly complain of an Equity barrier, though it is true that they have banned the National *Oklahoma!* unless its American choreographer Susan Stroman be allowed to take it over from Trevor Nunn: not a likely eventuality.*

Unusually, though, the 'new' musicals are very disappointing: *Fosse* merely serves as a reminder of the late Bob Fosse's very limited repertoire (the tilted

* This situation was eventually resolved in 2002.

bowler hat, the angular elbow, the foot on the chair); while in trying to make *Annie Get Your Gun* politically acceptable, and thereby not offend the thousands of Red Indians doubtless still queuing for tickets, Bernadette Peters turns it into a sub-Sondheim lament rather than the old Irving Berlin anthem.

Better news just across 44th Street, however, where *Band in Berlin* is the best new musical in town: a unique, intimate, six-man revue about the real-life Comedian Harmonists who in the 1930s toured Germany with a bizarre entertainment, often a cappella versions of Bing Crosby hits, while (as we see on a video screen behind them on stage) the Nazis came to power. All six had their careers changed and ruined by Hitler, though none ended up in the concentration camps which at least half the troupe, being Jewish, must have feared.

Penny Perfect

A Penny for a Song (Whitehall)

Of all the playwrights who were lamentably and needlessly killed in the crossfire of the Royal Court revolution of 1956, the one I have always missed most is John Whiting. True, by the time he died of cancer at only forty-five, half a dozen years later, he had to some extent made it back with the success of *The Devils*, but even now he remains shamefully ignored by the National Theatre (unlike another great lost dramatist of the period, Rodney Ackland). We therefore owe a huge debt of gratitude to the Oxford Stage Company at the Whitehall for giving us the first London look in more than forty years at his joyous *A Penny for a Song*.

Written in 1950 for a Scarborough theatre which had not yet heard of Alan Ayckbourn, this is a strange, lyrical fantasy set in an English country garden in 1804. Rumours are spreading of a monster bridge over the Channel, or possibly even a primeval Eurotunnel, via which Napoleon is imminently expected to invade us, probably in some fiendish foreign disguise. A group of manic, eccentric aristocrats and their household decide that he has to be stopped, preferably by hot-air balloons or fire engines or faithful old retainers sitting up trees wearing saucepans on their heads by way of protection from possible air attack. If you can imagine Shaw's *Heartbreak House* entirely staffed by the cast of *Dad's Army*, and then made over as an Ealing Comedy by the producers of *Passport to Pimlico*, you will get some hazy idea of what is on offer here.

You also have to remember that Whiting originally thought of the play in an English country garden in 1940; the idea was then of a very real enemy invasion, but one that could be countered by all the bizarre virtues of hazy summertime cricket, and picnics on the lawn at which there was plenty of honey still for tea.

A Penny for a Song is in my view one of the greatest British stage comedies of the century, and though I am sad that the current director Paul Miller has gone for Whiting's revised version, written when his confidence had been destroyed by a hostile press, rather than the classic original, he has at least assembled the best collection of vintage comic character actors in town, from Charles Kay as the Squire whose Napoleon impersonation is regrettably indistinguishable from his Lord Nelson, through Jeremy Clyde as the besotted fire-fighter to Julian

Glover as the weary, elegant Hallam who is surely going to be the diarist of these weird and wonderful proceedings.

Only the young lovers have trouble here, and there again the problem is largely that of the revised text; Oberon Books has, however, published the original, along with a collection of Whiting's critical writing from the 1950s, and here now at long last is just the chance that we might get back to a dramatist of comic genius and heartbreaking sentiment who was wrongly destroyed by a critical community which, tiring of the T S Eliot and Christopher Fry plays from where Whiting drew his original poetic inspiration, either could not or would not give him the credit paid by the French to his only real contemporary equal, Jean Anouilh. And there's another writer of whom the current British theatrical establishment seems never to have heard, and whom the Oxford Stage Company have happily brought us back in their vintage residency at the Whitehall, a residency which all too predictably now ends abruptly in yet another government-inspired cash crisis.

In his bleak way, Whiting has had the last laugh: *A Penny for a Song* is, even in this second and weaker version, a defiant reply to those who believed that great theatre could never be set in the garden of an elegant country house, or concerned with the activities of those on private incomes.

Malta Cross

The Jew of Malta (Almeida)

The Pajama Game (Victoria Palace)

Your starter for ten: in which play is an entire convent of nuns poisoned by a rice pudding? Who says "Twas in another country, and besides the wench is dead'? Who ends up drowned in a vast vat of boiling oil, bubbling to the surface even as the final curtain falls? The answer to all the above is the 1589 *Jew of Malta*, Christopher Marlowe's wonderfully politically incorrect alternative *The Merchant of Venice*, a play hardly ever revived nowadays, not least because it has something to offend just about every special-interest minority in the business. Marlowe makes Joe Orton (another radical, bleakly comic gay playwright who was untimely murdered almost four centuries later) look about as threatening as Winnie the Pooh.

True he was not Shakespeare, though there are moments in this his greatest play when the verse rises to Shakespearean heights. What makes Marlowe interesting is his readiness to offend everyone and anyone. Whereas Shakespeare had good guys and bad guys, Marlowe reckons to hell with the lot of them, so that a hitherto virtuous friar, suddenly faced with the mutilated corpse of a young girl, regrets only that she was still a virgin at the time of her murder.

At the Almeida, Ian McDiarmid, playing the title role in which Donald Wolfit was not so much a tour de force as forced to tour for several decades either side of the war, lacks the madly murderous passion of this Jew and is, ironically, just too good an actor to go for the full, ludicrous, overblown theatricality demanded here, while the rest of the company is either undercast or desperately eager to make us believe that this is a good play instead of just sharing with us its magnificent awfulness. Not so much a black comedy as a black tragedy, *The Jew of Malta* cries out for an over-the-top director like Joan Littlewood or the late great Sir Tyrone Guthrie or Orson Welles, or even Simon Callow, who would have celebrated its glorious bad taste. Michael Grandage's cool staging on a splendid set by Christopher Gram too often wants to rehabilitate the play instead of just revelling in its gothic, gruesome, ghoulish grandeur.

~

Talking of Simon Callow, the only real problem with his new revival at the Victoria Palace of Adler & Ross's *The Pajama Game* is essentially the 'why bother?' problem. It is as difficult for us on this side of the Atlantic now, as on the show's first and last West End outing back in 1954, to care about the story of the strike for seven-and-a-half cents in a pajama factory in the American Midwest; and like this team's only other hit, *Damn Yankees*, its essence remains oddly untranslatable into a local idiom.

More than forty years on, history has repeated itself, in that we now have understudy Jenny Ann Topham dancing in (as did Shirley MacLaine on Broadway) for an injured Alison Limerick, but the truth is the show still doesn't really work over here. This is not the fault of Callow's versatile direction, nor of the brilliantly minimalist artist Frank Stella whose sets represent the most stylish use of black-and-white I have ever seen on a musical stage.

Callow's programme-note claims for *The Pajama Game*, as one of the greatest Broadway musicals ever, are in my view simply misplaced. I would not put it even in the top twenty, largely because the songs in no way advance the story, which is ramshackle at best; quite apart from that, they seem to be in a curious running order, so that a would-be showstopper like 'Steam Heat', coming at the very top of Act Two, merely stops the interval.

Nor am I altogether convinced that David Bintley of the Birmingham Royal Ballet has entirely managed the Broadway crossover: his West End hoofers look distinctly uneasy in some of his routines, while the cast is oddly uncharismatic. Graham Bickley and Leslie Ash have trouble establishing their passion for each other; Anita Dobson is wasted as a secretary though clearly a great stage-musical hoofer, and it is left to the eccentric comedian John Hegley to try to fill shoes originally worn over here by the late, great Max Wall.

The Pajama Game yearns to be another show altogether: the picnic scene is ripped off from the Clambake in *Carousel*, and elsewhere the influences are clearly of *Guys and Dolls*; a vast amount of talent and money has been lavished on a show which, in my view, at best now deserves one of those Sunday-afternoon concert stagings in the Lost Musicals series at the Fortune. I don't think it would be possible, give or take one or two casting mistakes, to do this show better now than Simon Callow has in fact done it. I just wish he had focused all that time (the revival first opened in Birmingham six months ago and has been reworked in Toronto) and talent and energy on a score which really deserved it.

Musical Chairs

Quartet (Albery)

Drummers (New Ambassador)

One of the major surprises, and there are not many, in Ronald Harwood's *Quartet* at the Albery is that it is not a revival. Not so much well written as well remembered from other well-made dramas of the last forty years, this is a defiant end-of-century return to the kind of plays they are supposed not to be writing any more. Back in about 1955 this one would have been directed by John Gielgud with a cast headed by himself, Ralph Richardson, Wendy Hiller and perhaps even Sybil Thorndike; it would have gone to the Theatre Royal, Haymarket after a successful season in Brighton, and at matinees it would still have been possible to get tea served on a tray in the stalls. This is not necessarily to denigrate the new play, even if it does seem to have been made up largely of leftover scenes from Rattigan's *Separate Tables*, David Storey's *Home* and above all Noël Coward's *Waiting in the Wings*.

As in all three of those, we are in some sort of rest home, this one exclusively reserved for musical old players who have somehow fallen on hard times. Again as in all of those, the parts matter more than the whole and sometimes threaten to get bigger than the play; here, as the title might suggest, we have a stellar foursome made up of Donald Sinden's fruity old baritone, Stephanie Cole as the requisitely dotty old bat, Alec McCowen as the clenched recluse and Angela Thorne as the late arrival, the one with the faintly mysterious past who triggers what little plot we then get.

Of this unashamedly over-the-top foursome, only McCowen and Thorne give actual performances, while Sinden and Cole do the comic turns that their individual fan clubs have long come to expect. In his vastly better *The Dresser*, Harwood has established his backstage territory and here he is best when writing the Sinden character, the only one of the four who seems to have no regrets about a life spent belting out the Verdi standards and fantasising about a series of romantic entanglements.

Cole is already in early stages of Alzheimer's, Thorne has for largely psychological reasons lost her voice and with it her career, and McCowen gets the speech in which Harwood really defines his message, the one about artists having a greater duty to their talent than to their own peace of mind. Sure enough, this quartet ends up miming to the *Rigoletto* quartet that they once recorded when in better voice, and, since the playwright has no idea how to follow that touching if bizarre spectacle, he simply leaves his querulous foursome there to drift into an increasingly unattractive old age.

The problem with *Quartet* is not that it won't give a great deal of ancient enjoyment to ancient audiences, who have largely stopped going to theatres where this sort of elegant charade was once more available, but that Harwood is too intelligent and occasionally waspish a writer not to realise that he really hasn't got a play here, just a collection of characters in search of an author. Nothing much happens in Act One, and then again after the interval; at least Rattigan and Coward and Storey gave us a few surprises along the way, as well as a dark heart to their dramas. Harwood seems to have set out with something sad to say about the ravages of age on a profession which largely depends on staying young, but then to have been sidetracked into a sort of Three Tenors concert celebration without the Three Tenors. So his play doesn't end, it just stops, and we are left with nothing more than the memory of four performances desperately trying to make bricks despite a distinct lack of straw; if Harwood has anything new to tell us about singers who have for different reasons lost their voices and yet are now going unquietly into that good night, he seems like many of his characters to have abruptly and irretrievably forgotten what he was going to say. And the rest is a kind of silence.

~

At the New Ambassador is precisely the kind of play which was supposed to be the death of what is still going on at the Albery, although it too has its construction problems. Simon Bennett's *Drummers* is not, you understand, another musical evening; drummers in this case are housebreakers, and the drum is the target house. The playwright is himself a convicted burglar turned dramatist, and his first play is a darkly comic account of a prisoner returning after three years inside to settle some old and new scores, not least amid his own south London family.

Halfway from *The Krays* to a local version of the current American television *The Sopranos*, this is a short and brutal piece written in a quickfire dialogue that might be called English Mamet; sharp encounters between father and son, brother and brother, as a family which knows everything about housebreaking and the second-hand gold market but precious little about anything else gradually turns inwards and starts destroying each other.

In that sense *Drummers* is an insider story: raw, angry and sometimes very touching, Max Stafford-Clark's minimalist production is wired and wiry, with a cast led by Ewan Hooper and Callum Dixon, and it soon sets out on a nationwide tour which should not be missed.

Roaring Disney

The Lion King (Lyceum)

Spend Spend Spend (Piccadilly)

Since I seem to be the only critic, or indeed human being (the two are not necessarily synonymous), who deeply disliked *The Lion King* on Broadway and still deeply dislikes it at the Lyceum, I had better spell out my objections. Sure, it is visually brilliant; Julie Taymor is a conceptual artist of genius, and if the whole show were on view at the Serpentine Gallery, or some puppet playhouse, it would be a wondrous sight. But it remains in my view deeply untheatrical; all the tricks and trappings of Bunraku and traditional Japanese and African masks and masques are here, with actors on stilts playing giraffes, and weird and wonderful bicycles kitted out to resemble a herd of antelope.

The Lion King might also work as a kind of show-and-tell lesson in anthropology or geography or wildlife studies (David Attenborough with singing) but as a musical it still seems to me stillborn: lousy score, plot nicked from *Hamlet*, and dull landscape scenery as if to emphasise the gimmickry of the special effects. Indeed there is a moment when they unwisely quote 'Be My Guest' from Disney's infinitely superior *Beauty and the Beast*, and you suddenly recall the real stage-musical values that are missing here.

The Lion King is chilly, repetitive, uninvolving emotionally, and at times little better than the kind of guided tour of the African outback which the Commonwealth Institute would offer its school parties if only they had the $15 million that this cartoon travelogue has reputedly cost. The Tim Rice/Elton John score was composed for the original animation movie, and nobody seems to have thought about inviting them back to make it work on stage, while there is no chance for any actor to reach out to us across the complex trappings of wires and stilts and head-dresses they are all forced to wear.

The result is a feast for the eye but nothing much for the ear, or the mind, or the heart, or the spirit; this one should have gone straight from Disney cinema to Disney theme park, avoiding the theatre altogether, since down in old Savannah nothing at all is stirring.

~

If you want to know what a great musical should look and sound and feel like, head for the Piccadilly and *Spend Spend Spend*. True, this one has been mercilessly ripped off from Willy Russell's wonderful *Blood Brothers*, still in the West End after almost fifteen years; it even has the same original star, Barbara Dickson, in the same original role as the singing storyteller. But this time the story is a real one, that of Viv Nicholson who in 1961 won (in today's terms) around £3 million on the football pools. Money did not buy happiness; her beloved second husband died in the car she had bought him, and Viv was eventually made bankrupt.

A new composer/lyricist team (Steve Brown and Justin Greene) have found in Viv's memoirs a moralistic musical about greed and retribution, but in their grainy score they, like Russell, have managed to get as close as this country has ever come to Brecht & Weill: bitter, cigarette-stained songs of love and loss in the shadow of the pits that are already closing. If you can imagine a musical by D H Lawrence, then *Spend Spend Spend* is it; on a budget several million pounds lower than *The Lion King*, the director Jeremy Sams has come up with a show which has heart and soul rather than heat and dust. He also introduces to London two musical newcomers of considerable talent, Steven Houghton and Rachel Leskovac, and a dozen or so songs which brilliantly capture a mining community about to lose their proud heritage as Britain goes over the brink of Thatcherite greed. These people never had it so bad, even when a fortune fell into their laps.

2000

Coward's Century

Cavalcade (Glasgow Citizens')

Honk! the Ugly Duckling (National)

T he best of all New Year's Eves came a little early this year: at the financially embattled Glasgow Citizens', Philip Prowse ended the twentieth century with a characteristically inventive and breathtaking production of Noël Coward's *Cavalcade*, one which I fervently hope can soon be brought into London by any of the many managements which chickened out of staging this greatest of all theatrical chronicles during its author's just-ended centenary. Not that Prowse has needed the hundreds of extras without whom *Cavalcade* has hitherto always seemed incomplete and unstageable.

Working with barely twenty actors, he has managed to capture the dark heart of Coward's summary of the turn of the last century, from Mafeking by way of the Titanic and First World War to the Depression, while maintaining in a series of brief encounters the essence of Coward's historic chronicle as it moves upstairs and downstairs (for this is also where that TV series began) inexorably from New Year's Eve 1899 to New Year's Eve 1929. Where Declan Donnellan destroyed the recent *Hay Fever* simply by losing faith in the play, Prowse as designer and director has always understood why Coward matters, and how best to keep the faith on a low budget; here, Jennifer Hilary and Stephen MacDonald are simply definitive as the parents, while Michelle Gomez takes us from Gertrude Lawrence to Sally Bowles in the course of her 'Twentieth Century Blues'. This production cannot, if there is any theatrical justice left, be allowed to die after barely three weeks in the Gorbals.*

~

Back in London, the National has its seasonal hat trick: another hit which can be flown on to the Olivier stage as an annual Christmas-season present for Honk! family audiences of all ages, and amazingly, has the rare distinction of being the first home-grown musical ever to have been seen on the South Bank.

What that says about the state of the new British musical, or the National's obsession with long-lost Broadway classics, is not a question for this forgiving time of year; what matters is that the director Julia McKenzie, who has herself starred in more National musicals than most, has come up with a wonderfully agile and comic and touching account of the old Hans Andersen tale of the ugly duckling who grows up into an elegant swan. True, there isn't a single number in the show to touch the brilliance of Frank Loesser's song of the ugly duckling as sung by Danny Kaye in the film of *Hans Christian Andersen* half a century ago, but the score by George Stiles and Anthony Drewe is gentle and winning in an early Rice/Webber *Joseph* kind of way, and an energetic young cast features Gilz

* In fact, it was.

193

Terera, a talented black newcomer barely out of drama school, which cleverly makes this a tale of racial as well as cosmetic intolerance.

Broadway 2000

Broadway is finally out of intensive care. Ticket prices may have crashed through the dreaded $100 barrier, but more theatres are open (and playing to capacity) than at any time since the 1960s, while shows on the road are hovering around like vultures awaiting any sudden box-office collapse which would let them move into town.

True, it is not such a good time for the Brits on Broadway as a year or two ago, but the Australians are doing just fine; the director Michael Blakemore has the biggest hit of the season with a definitive new revival of *Kiss Me Kate*, while Barry Humphries' *Dame Edna*, who was effectively driven out of town a decade or so ago for mocking minorities, is playing to standing-room-only local audiences who have at last, and none too soon, managed to overcome their political correctness.

Even straight plays are back in fashion: Donald Margulies, whose *Collected Stories* Helen Mirren is now playing at the Haymarket, has a much better new script called *Dinner with Friends* which is in one sense Sondheim's *Merrily We Roll Along* without the songs, since it too moves backwards in time to chart the rise and fall of two marital relationships. But this is also a play about the rights of a man (or woman) to abandon a twelve-year marriage simply because it is not working as well as the next one just might, and about the way in which a divorce can destroy a friendship as well as a marriage. Precisely the kind of play which would sell out at Hampstead, in fact.

A R Gurney has gone back to his *Love Letters* format and written a recital for five actors to read at lecterns: *Ancestral Voices* is another of his many laments for the old white, Anglo-Saxon Protestant community of upstate New York, one that somehow vanished as more strident minorities took charge of the American melting-pot after the second world war. As always, Gurney writes with an elegiac elegance which is nowhere else to he found in contemporary playwriting, but there is a terrible lack of energy here as well as a curious feeling that the performers have somehow never read the lines before.

The rumour around 42nd Street is that it is another major Broadway dramatist, John Guare, who has done the brilliant editing and, yes, sometimes rewriting of *Kiss Me Kate*, but his name is not on the credits (although Cole Porter's 1948 classic has a couple of songs and even one or two scenes that were never there before). Unlike the *Annie Get Your Gun* around the corner, which has been destroyed by cack-handed updating, this is always true to Cole, and, although I admit I was only seven when I saw Alfred Drake in the Broadway original, I think this may well be the first revival of a major American score to come up half a century later looking rather better than it did the first time around.

I only caught the first preview of Noël Coward's *Waiting in the Wings* which, after a tricky Boston try-out opens in New York on his actual centenary, and it would be unfair to prejudge it here; of the central casting, both Rosemary Harris and Barnard Hughes have caught the Chekhovian melancholy of the piece, while Lauren Bacall in the old Sybil Thorndike role looks as if she has come to visit an elderly relative in the retired actors' home rather than moved in there herself.

But I have saved the best until last. At the Palace, scene of so many of her mother's Broadway comebacks, Liza Minnelli has a breathtaking new celebration of her father's movie songs: *Minnelli on Minnelli* tells the story of Vincente's career in clips and dance routines and songs from all his classics, not least *Gigi* and *An American in Paris* and, of course, *Meet Me in St Louis.*

Reza Sharp

Life x 3 (National)

Kenneth Tynan once said that in a hundred years' time everyone will still know exactly what is meant by 'a very Noël Coward sort of person'; will they, I wonder, still know what is meant by 'a very Yasmina Reza sort of play'?

The worldwide triumph of *Art* (coming up for five years and twenty complete cast changes in London alone) has defined a new category of popular theatre. Reza writes brisk, brief, chic and cutting-edge: she attracts an elsewhere longed-for audience of the kind of rich, fashionable people you would otherwise now be more likely to see at an art-gallery private view or a starry charity fund-raiser than in a theatre. Her plays are to a degree intellectually challenging, but she raises no issues so deep that they cannot be totally discussed and even maybe dismissed over a post-theatre dinner, which can start reassuringly early for those who have to work the next day, usually about ninety minutes after the curtain has first risen.

Reza is intellectual theatre lite, and she has plugged in to an entire generation of disaffected playgoers, those who found serious dramas too long and often boring, and light comedies too trivial to occupy their busy schedules. She is, to revert to Tynan, perhaps the first writer since Coward to have a direct line to the readers of *Vogue*; her plays count as high fashion in a world where you simply have to have seen them if you are to qualify for conversation at the next cocktail party or charity banquet. She is neither threatening nor obscure; her themes (modern art, true or false, the tricks of time, the inconvenience of small children) are universal, and her way of dealing with them is as dry as a dry martini.

Her latest, *Life x 3* (which she herself is also playing in Paris), is again translated by Christopher Hampton, he of the *Dangerous Liaisons*, and again it is a conversation piece, though this time square rather than triangular as in *Art.* We see, in true Alan Ayckbourn style, three separate versions (all in ninety minutes) of one singularly awkward dinner party for which the two all-important guests have arrived a night too early, thereby discovering their hosts in the midst of childminding quarrels. The parallels with Ayckbourn's *How the Other Half Loves* are remarkable, right down to the fact that the male guest is a man in control of his host's career, so the dinner party that never happens (the guests are left snacking on crisps and chocolate fingers) takes on a still more nightmarish dimension.

There is also a considerable debt to Albee's *Who's Afraid of Virginia Woolf?* as we watch a marriage in disintegration with an unseen (though here all too noisily real) child pushing it over the edge; but Reza is careful not to go in too deep, and always to leave us with the possibility of renewal and revival against a starry night sky. Nothing here to spoil our dinner, even if theirs has been ruined. A starry quartet (Mark Rylance and Harriet Walter as the frantic hosts, Oliver Cotton and Imelda Staunton as the glacial guests) are under the direction of Matthew Warchus; but, in Reza, the parts are always vastly better than the whole.

Heston Horror

Love Letters (Haymarket)

There is something monumentally terrible about the acting of Charlton Heston, and of course there always has been; having brought us the tablets as Moses but alas never taken them, having won the chariot race in Gore Vidal's gay Rome (loved Him, hated Hur), he now appears live on stage with all the brisk, charismatic energy of a man carved into Mount Rushmore. To the Theatre Royal Haymarket he comes with his wife, a lady also suffering from a tragic talent bypass, and there they solemnly sit centre stage reading the *Love Letters* that are at the heart of A R Gurney's ancient and creaky epistolary romance.

Gurney has elsewhere established himself as one of the best American playwrights of his generation, and it is ironic that his most commercially successful script should be a two-hander beloved of very ancient Hollywood television and movie stars because it can be read aloud, never apparently has to be learnt or directed, and is therefore ideal for dinner theatres, ocean liners or anywhere that nobody can be bothered with a real production.

You will have gathered that *Les Liaisons Dangereuses* this is not; indeed the most exciting thing you can watch here are the potted plants which have been neatly arranged, as at a funeral parlour, around the Hestons' feet. There is at least the chance that they might grow, or change colour, or start talking to us, or just wither and die in sympathy with this whole misbegotten shambles.

Anything here would be better than having to watch the Hestons still inefficiently reading, despite having trailed it around the American and British regions for some years, a script of such terminal boredom that even they seemed to be having trouble staying awake through it. Nothing at all happens in the first half, nothing happens again in the second, and then Mrs Heston commits a graceful little suicide, one she signals with a sort of well-bred whimper rather as though she were trying to attract the attention of a salesperson at Harrods on a busy afternoon.

As for Heston, the most moving thing about him is still his hairpiece; better perhaps to have had the Reagans, or even Ike and Mamie back from the grave to plough through this sloppy and cynical marketing exercise. No director is credited, presumably because if named he or she would never work again; the Hestons alas probably will, but with luck not over here.

Mamet Remade

American Buffalo (Donmar Warehouse)

Back to the Donmar Warehouse comes the play which (in 1975) first established the international reputation of its author David Mamet; since then, *American Buffalo* has been played and filmed by the greatest American actors in the business, among them Dustin Hoffman, Robert Duvall and Al Pacino, while Mamet himself has become the touchstone for a whole generation of new dramatists worldwide.

The energy of his writing, and the speed at which it needs to be played, condition and control this manic morality play. And on Kevin Rigdon's magnificently cluttered junkshop set, it is now William H Macy, a co-founder with Mamet of the Atlantic company and one of his very earliest players, who leads the cast as Teach, the poker buddy who muscles in on an underplanned robbery and reduces the other two characters (Philip Baker Hall as the proprietor and Mark Webber as his hapless assistant) to a state of total warfare.

Mamet's theme is America, and the way that crime in that country has always followed the instincts of big business; not for nothing is the Buffalo of the title a coin, but the currency here is sheer criminality. All three of these men are losers, but with such lifetimes of suppressed pain and loss that when they each finally explode, the fall-out is appalling.

In that sense, Mamet's *American Buffalo* is Arthur Miller's *The Price* on speed; two of the major American dramatists of the century have seen, in the buying and selling of junk, a metaphor for a country in moral disintegration. What makes Mamet distinct in this three-card trick is the way he deals in danger, with the suggestion that mayhem and murder are never more than minutes away; the play rattles like a snake, but there's a street poetry here, as well as an awareness that all three of these men are playing an unending game of power poker in which relationships can turn quite literally on a dime.

Hello Dolly

Baby Doll (National)

The turn of this century is proving an amazingly rich time for the National Theatre to prospect for gold down in old Tennessee. After Vanessa and Corin Redgrave's breathtaking rediscovery of *Not About Nightingales*, the long-lost first major Tennessee Williams script at the Cottesloe, we now have on the Lyttelton stage something equally enthralling: the first-ever staging of his 1956 screenplay *Baby Doll.*

This was the Carroll Baker/Karl Malden/Eli Wallach movie which carried the proud boast 'Banned by Cardinal Spellman' on just about the last occasion that the Catholic Church forgot how its bans had a habit of misfiring. What is fascinating about the new Lucy Bailey production, into the National from the Birmingham Rep, is the way in which she has managed to take an often sketchy and fragmentary screenplay and turn it into a drama of real substance, able now to stand alongside the best of Williams' plays.

Bunny Christie's set has a brilliant, dolls'-house quality, with individual rooms opening up in darkness to give you the sense that you are peering into them; and in one of them of course is the child bride, Baby Doll herself, the character who gave her name to millions of knee-length night-dresses. As played by Charlotte Emmerson, she no longer comes across as the Lolita of the Deep South, but instead as another of Williams' bruised angels forever hoping, like Blanche duBois, to depend on the kindness of strangers.

In this case the stranger is Silva Vaccaro, broodingly well played by yet another comparative newcomer, Jonathan Cake; but his interest goes beyond the sexual. He needs Baby Doll to sign a statement proving the criminality of her husband (Paul Brennen), who, in the third great performance of the evening, has agreed not to sleep with his bride until their repossessed furniture has been reclaimed. At times this is almost a parody of the world of Tennessee Williams; yet so hauntingly is it played, on a set which also manages to feature a rusting Chevy and great bales of cotton as high as the eye can see, that by the end you are totally caught up in yet another sweaty saga of the sweet bird of youth being brutally awoken to a world of rape and revenge.

Fiennes Time

Richard II (Gainsborough Studios)

Blue/Orange (National)

Lautrec (Shaftesbury)

North London's Gainsborough Studios (a difficult theatre to get into, harder still to get out of, given local Shoreditch transport arrangements) may have come back to performance-space life for only six months, but it is undoubtedly the star of the new Almeida *Richard II*. This was once the studio where Hitchcock made *The Lady Vanishes* and Margaret Lockwood starred in all those 1940s snobbery-with-violence pictures; now, stripped back to its crumbling walls, it allows for a vast stage covered in real grass and orange trees in front of a still more vast auditorium on a rake similar to that of Riverside Studios.

Ralph Fiennes and the director Jonathan Kent rekindle their old Almeida partnership in an immensely impressive, epic staging which includes the usually cut Aumerle and Gage subplot, thereby allowing Oliver Ford Davies to give one of the major performances of the evening as the cranky old Duke of York. Elsewhere, and surprisingly, given the Almeida's cutting-edge modernity, this is a staging redolent of Anthony Quayle at the Stratford of about 1955: clearly spoken verse, a constantly shifting power balance between Fiennes as the doomed poet-king and Linus Roache as the icy usurper Bolingbroke, equal attention to poetry and politics, a gorgeously vacuous Queen from Emilia Fox, and all in all the widescreen version of a play too often now given us only in close-up.

~

Good news for the National at the Cottesloe, where Nunn's long run of bad luck with new plays has been broken by the premiere of Joe Penhall's *Blue/Orange*. Not since *Duet for One*, Tom Kempinski's barely disguised study of Jacqueline du Pre and her psychiatrist, and that's almost twenty years ago, has there been a better or more enthralling drama about the world of mental health. We are in a hospital somewhere in England now; of the only three characters, one (Chiwetel Ejiofor) is a black schizophrenic in imminent danger of being returned to the farcical 'care in the community' system, except that in his case there is no care and no community outside the hospital wall. A young, idealist psychiatrist (Andrew Lincoln) has been assigned to his case, but there is also his apparent mentor, an older and infinitely more political doctor (Bill Nighy in the performance of the night), whose interests are really only in his own career advancement and the research fodder, or at least the much-needed empty bed, that the unfortunate and lonely patient might provide.

What starts as a case history of schizophrenia and its current treatment possibilities rapidly develops into a battle between the two doctors, both flawed and finally both unable to deal with the patient, so obsessed have they become with their own survival and supremacy within the system. Joe Penhall has come up with a cynical, savage but brilliantly argued account of what has gone wrong with a mental health service now bound up in its own internal battles for survival, as budgets are slashed and patients are hurled back onto the unforgiving streets to fend for themselves.

~

At the Shaftesbury, something about Toulouse-Lautrec and the can-can and Montmartre circa 1890 has once again brought out the very worst; who now recalls Jose Ferrer stumbling about on his kneecaps in a truly terrible John Huston movie of the mid-1950s, or that Cole Porter's *Can-Can* was one of his few really dud scores?

Undeterred by showbiz history, let alone art history, Charles Aznavour has come up with *Lautrec*, a musical which is not by any means a catastrophe on the *Tess* or *Which Witch?* scale; it just really isn't very good. A large cast of amazingly tall women manage to make Stevan Stephan look about the right height for little Lautrec, while the book by Shaun McKenna touches all the right buttons about the painter's dysfunctional family, disastrous parenting, nervous breakdowns and obsessive interest in leggy showgirls flashing their frilly knickers at an audience. But the musical fails to make us care about Lautrec or his work because we never really get to meet the man, just a lookalike with some good songs.

Flying High

The Witches of Eastwick (Drury Lane)

Who really knows anything about new musicals? When *Oklahoma!* opened on the road in 1943, a Boston critic thought it had 'no gags, no girls, no chance'; when Lerner & Loewe played Mary Martin their score for *My Fair Lady*, her only comment was 'You poor dears have lost all your talent'; Noël Coward, not exactly a newcomer to the musicals business, turned down leading roles in both *My Fair Lady* and *The King and I*; and more recently most London critics underestimated the run of *Les Misérables* by about fifteen years.

So what do we know about *The Witches of Eastwick* at Drury Lane? First, it is that real and precious rarity, a musical comedy; we haven't seen one of those in the West End for about a decade, since *City of Angels* in fact, and to find one actually created over here you would have to go back another decade to *Windy City*, a brilliant but commercially disastrous musical of Hecht & MacArthur's *The Front Page*. For that reason alone, we should already be cheering these Witches. Why else? For a start, or rather a first-act finale, there's the flying; not just up and down as in the old *Peter Pan*, but way out into the auditorium, and achieved not by a network railway on the roof of the Lane, but by a revolutionary, new, locally invented system involving a series of interlinked winches.

Then again there's the casting: as the witches, there are Maria Friedman and Joanna Riding (arguably the two greatest British music-theatre talents of their sex and generation) and from Broadway Lucie Arnaz, who has learnt a thing or two about being a funny and yet also dazzling leading lady in musicals from her mother, Lucille Ball, one of the very few others in that curiously tricky line of show business. As the randy devil who erupts into their small-town lives, Ian McShane is no less impressive.

Redgrave's Chekhov

The Cherry Orchard (National)

Though he is himself a master of the masses on a wide stage, one of Trevor Nunn's major achievements at the National (and there have been more of those than his critics would currently credit) has been to encourage the close-up rediscovery of major classics within the more confined studio space of the Cottesloe, originally conceived for new and experimental work.

Thus we now get *The Cherry Orchard* there, and instead of the usual rambling country estate in meltdown crisis, Maria Bjornson gives us a kind of dusty doll's house through whose imaginary windows we see an outside world moving from dawn to dusk. Sometimes this goes a little over the top: I am not entirely convinced that in Act Three the precious cherry trees should be strung with fairy lights, much after the fashion of a New York restaurant at Thanksgiving, but that remains a minor fault in a major production. Though Bjornson alone seems in charge of the greater landscape beyond the doors, what Nunn finds inside them is a series of character studies in desolation and isolation, led by Roger Allam as the peasant Lopakhin who buys the estate, and Corin and Vanessa Redgrave making their first appearance together at the National as, suitably enough, the brother and sister Gaev and Ranevskaya.

Corin Redgrave brilliantly suggests a misplaced life, only recaptured now in memories of the billiard tables where he once had his early triumphs; while Vanessa is as usual all over the place, at moments heartbreaking and at others so eccentrically mannered that you wonder how for so long she has managed to give this doomed pre-revolutionary family some sort of leadership and focus, albeit usually by remote control.

These and other performances will doubtless mature during the winter; on a slightly edgy first night, the winners were William Gaunt as the Rasputin-like neighbour Pischik, and Michael Bryant, the first Firs in my theatre-going lifetime to offer up a real challenge to the memory of Sir Ralph Richardson.

Elsewhere the female casting is weak, with only Suzanne Bertish as the dog-clutching conjuror Charlotta able to make much of an impression. At the moment, a vintage collection of primarily comic character sketches have yet to find their way into a coherent exhibition, and some are as yet far from completed portraits, but that too will change. In Chekhov, all things, both good and bad, come to those who only seem to be waiting for them to happen elsewhere; life is merely what occurs during their long wait in the antechambers of reality.

Time and the Ayckbourns

House/Garden (National)

The Graduate (Gielgud)

Almost forty years ago, Tom Stoppard made his name by wondering what happened to Rosencrantz and Guildenstern when they weren't actually on stage in *Hamlet*. On two of the National Theatre stages, Alan Ayckbourn now goes one further, though not altogether one better, by giving us all the on-stage and the off-stage action of his *House/Garden* across a six-hour day, complete with foyer fête to end it all. The result in Stoppardian terms would be like having to watch all of *Hamlet* and then all of *Rosencrantz and Guildenstern Are Dead* with only a short tea interval.

What happens in the end here, as so often in Ayckbourn, is that the stage engineer overtakes and severely damages the playwriting genius. *House* alone is in many ways one of his best plays, a brilliant retread of all those country-house-party comedies of the 1950s by Hugh Williams or William Douglas Home in which we still get the stock characters of the comic cook and the silly-ass husband and the long-suffering wife, except that now of course they are rewritten in blood and sweat and tears, for there are precious few happy endings in Ayckbourn these days.

'Sooner or later,' as someone says early in *House*, 'life pays you back,' and across the rest of this play Ayckbourn shows us, hilariously and tragically, precisely how the paybacks are to be arranged. The trouble starts when we get to the second play (*Garden*), which involves the same characters when they are not actually indoors playing the *House*. In the first place, by the time we get to the end of *House* there really isn't a lot left to say about any of them; we kind of know, from the troubles they encounter indoors, the nature of their likely troubles outdoors.

The greater problem is that *Garden* has to accommodate *House*, to the extent that not even Ayckbourn characters can be on two stages at once; so despite the brilliance of the stage-management here, there remain some ugly pauses in the actual writing where Ayckbourn himself, as author and director, is clearly having to play for time. A character we urgently need to see in *Garden* can't appear at precisely the right moment because he or she is needed indoors, so some other character (usually the unlucky Sian Thomas) is left hanging out to dry, with neither enough to say or do until we can lurch forward to the next entrance.

But there are some great moments here, and some equally great performances: David Haig as the bemused, chronically unfaithful husband; Jane Asher as his glacial wife; Michael Siberry as the genially cuckolded local doctor; and above all Malcolm Sinclair as a wonderfully sinister Downing Street power-broker with an unhealthy predilection for very young girls in school costumes; not to mention Zabou Breitman as a barking-mad French film star bearing a remarkable resemblance to Jane Birkin. All manage to create another gallery of Sir Alan's misbegotten misfits, each and every one of them trying to get a life where there seems to he nothing but living death.

In the end there are rather more than two plays fighting for our attention here, and some wondrous comic notions. But 'less is more' is not a phrase that hangs anywhere near Ayckbourn's Scarborough workshops, and in his curious belief that five plays are better than one, even within the same production, some very good ideas and even one or two very good characters are getting lost, or at least underdeveloped, in this needlessly complex, albeit intermittently hilarious, escapade.

~

Here's to who, Mrs Robinson? Can we establish at the outset, beyond the hype and the features and the flashguns and the amazing stage-door crowds, just what is going on at the Gielgud Theatre? A middle-aged former fashion model, in admittedly a remarkably good state of repair and upkeep, who was once married to a rock star, has taken over the leading role in a six-month-old West End comedy based on a thirty-year-old Hollywood movie called *The Graduate*.

It is not that Jerry Hall is actually bad as Mrs Robinson; true, she's not as good as Kathleen Turner who originated the role of the predatory sex-starved mother on stage, but then again Turner wasn't really as good as Anne Bancroft in the original movie, and nobody has ever been as good in the title role as Dustin Hoffman back in the late 1960s.

Jerry Hall does seem to have slowed the show down, however, and she has a curious habit of draping herself around the minimal set rather vacantly, as if awaiting a photographer to line her up for the next shot. But she is no worse than she was in *Bus Stop* a decade ago, and I don't recall then the obsessive fascination which now seems to surround this rather undistinguished takeover; indeed she seemed rather happier and sparkier in the earlier role.

It must then be because this time she takes off all her clothes, albeit only for about thirty seconds, and then in a tactful kind of stage twilight. But even now, some poor hack out there is still trying to find a way of getting Jerry and Viagra into the same headline, where the truth is that she is oddly unarousing in the role. Clearly she has considerable sex appeal, but it is the appeal of one of those Hitchcock ice maidens; what she lacks is any kind of stage energy, and without that Terry Johnson's brilliant adaptation of the old movie now lacks a certain zest.

Of the other newcomers, both Josh Cohen in the title role and Lucy Punch as the daughter for whom he abandons the mother are charming enough, but this is no longer really a play at all. It has become a spectacle, rather like Madame Tussaud's or *The Mousetrap* or the Tower of London, and doubtless it will soon be starring Edna Everage, or alternate members of the Spice Girls and the Beverley Sisters.

Court Circular

Dublin Carol (Royal Court)

Three years, £25 million (give or take a bob or two) and hallelujah! the Royal Court is back in business. Twice last century, first when Bernard Shaw and Harley Granville Barker took it over in 1905, and then again when George Devine moved in fifty years later, the Court was the crucible in which British theatre was burnt and reborn. In terms of new writing, there has never been a playhouse this influential, and its restoration is nothing short of a miracle. Reconstruction is always a high-risk business; it destroyed Bernard Miles' once-great Mermaid Theatre forever, made the Old Vic dangerously expensive to maintain, and rendered the Lyceum a gothic nightmare of bad taste, while there are those who will tell you that neither Sadler's Wells nor the Royal Opera House have really achieved, even now, all that was promised by their new architects, certainly not in terms of acoustics, or access, or value for money.

In sharp contrast, what is so simple, and so brilliant, about the rebirth of the Court is that the theatre has been stripped back to basics; the walls no longer plastered, timber where once there was old carpet, girders and beams where once there were false ceilings. Instead of being reconstructed, it has been deconstructed. True, we now get vastly more comfortable seating, made of leather; and the stall-backs have little lights to read by, and a rack for your programmes – how come nobody ever thought of those before? Instead of trying to make the place look new, they have simply reminded us how old it is, and the result is the most intelligent, sensitive and triumphantly right rebuild I have come across anywhere in world theatre.

Somewhere in those newly exposed walls are held all the memories of Olivier's *The Entertainer* : don't clap too loudly, lady, it's a very old building. But now it is a very old building above a great new subterranean bar-restaurant with all the newspapers and, even better, a staircase leading up into the middle of Sloane Square; all too typically, the resolutely reactionary Cadogan Estate is refusing to unlock its upstairs gate lest, God forbid, pedestrians discover there is a theatre beneath their feet, and start making of the square something more attractive than the current dogs' public toilet. Were Sloane Square in Paris, or anywhere but here, that staircase would already be crowded day and night with eager playgoers.

So much for the theatre; what of the opening play? It comes from Conor McPherson, the young Irish writer whose *The Weir*, still in the West End, has already become here and in New York one of the most awarded of all new scripts. Once again the director is the Court's new resident manager Ian Rickson. McPherson is the ancient mariner of dramatists, whose characters fix you with a glittering eye and then, at first deceptively, start to tell you the more and more terrible story of their lives. In this case it is a Dublin undertaker, Brian Cox in tremendous and tragic form, brought on Christmas Eve to the final realisation that he is already as dead as those he buries; alcoholic, unfaithful, distanced from his children and a wife dying of cancer, raw with self-pity which is never less than totally understandable, he remains a character in search of a play.

Like Archie Rice, McPherson's undertaker is dead behind his eyes; and yet there is a moment at the end, when he starts to put decorations back on a Christmas tree he has earlier stripped, when you think, who knows, given the luck he has always been denied, this Christmas it might still all turn out better. It is not by any means a great play, but in its desperation for a new beginning, in its faith that against all odds the miracle of rebirth can still be made to happen, it is hard to think of a more suitable or symbolic start for the third era of the Royal Court than *Dublin Carol.*

Elsewhere, though, London theatre news is not so hot; while the regions are slowly starved to death, both of cash and of touring productions, so that at a conservative estimate at least half a dozen local theatres will have gone the way of Leatherhead and Farnham and Ipswich (with the admirable Glasgow Citz and Birmingham Rep the latest to join the danger group) by the time this millennium is a year old, the West End's problem is somewhat different. Within the last three months, something like eighty per cent of its commercial theatres have changed landlords. The old Stoll Moss group (twelve theatres, including virtually all on Shaftesbury Avenue plus such musical houses as the Palladium, Drury Lane and Her Majesty's) now belongs to Andrew Lloyd Webber, while a further nine (the old Wyndham/Albery chain plus such add-ons as the Phoenix and the long-troubled Playhouse) have just come under the control of the Ambassador group who paid around £16 million for the lot, cheap at the price considering that Lloyd Webber had to find nearly £90 million from the banks. Then, again, some outlying barns of the old Apollo chain now find themselves run by a Las Vegas consortium called SFX.

So what? Does it really matter who owns a theatre, any more than who really owns a hotel? Well, now it does. First, nearly all West End theatres were built a century ago, to coincide with the coming of the electric light; since that time, they have scarcely if ever been adequately maintained, so that backstage conditions are often appalling and rooves are starting to leak on upper-circle patrons, if there are any left up there with no sightlines and appalling acoustics. No theatre without a resident company ever has the time or the urge to carry out maintenance, and the managers who hire them feel no more obliged to look after the fabric of a theatre building than a hotel guest feels obliged to wallpaper the bedroom before checking out.

Paradoxically, the long runs of the last twenty years have made everything worse; because a show like *Cats* can occupy a building for close to twenty years for eight shows a week, structural maintenance is virtually impossible, while the interests of a theatre landlord seldom coincide precisely with that of his tenant unless they are one and the same person. To their credit, all the new owners (except SFX) have said they will in future take much more than just a landlordly interest in what happens on their stages.

The Wright Stuff

Cressida (Albery)

Nicholas Wright's *Cressida* is a brilliant backstage idea gone faintly adrift, but retrieved by Michael Gambon, whose eccentricity on stage now begins to rival that of his great mentor Ralph Richardson. He plays John Shank, a real-life figure of the just post-Elizabethan theatre who was for want of a better word (mine, not Wright's) the Childmaster, a man responsible for recruiting, training and then selling off the boy actors who were central to the still all-male theatre of good King Charles' golden days.

Like *Shakespeare in Love*, *Cressida* trades heavily on the notion that backstage jokes, actors' neurotic insecurities and the shadier impresarios of show business never really change, even across almost 400 years. But Wright is a researcher, unable to soar into the Stoppard comic stratosphere; his play is constantly historically fascinating, and galvanised by Gambon in the scene where he teaches his latest pupil how to be *Cressida*, one oddly reminiscent of that involving the old actor in Brecht's *The Rise and Fall of Arturo Ui*.

If there is a problem here, it is that we never really get to care enough about the boys, or why Shank, an old trouper with memories of working for Shakespeare, is now in such career and economic troubles as he heads for his place in the clouds, one we are shown in an uneasy prologue and epilogue. Like April de Angelis in *Playhouse Creatures*, Wright has become understandably fascinated by what the convention of all-male casts meant to the sexual and economic and even political realities of mid-seventeenth-century London theatre; but *Cressida* somehow stays buried in his research, relying on the great Gambon's old actor-laddie to get us off the page and onto the boards. In that sense there is also a debt here to *The Dresser* and *The Country Girl* and all those other backstage dramas involving an old thespian trying to deal with new realities; but Michael Legge's initially hopeless Hammerton and Malcolm Sinclair's all-too-timeless dodgy arts administrator are strongly directed in Nicholas Hytner's agile staging.

In the end, *Cressida* is about stardom; what it has to say, via its title, about women and betrayal is ultimately sacrificed with very good reason to the more traditional dressing-room dramas. Somehow there are two plays here; the scholarly one that, historically, Wright seems to have wanted to write and the other one that, theatrically, has been rightly overtaken by the grease-painted instincts of Hytner and Gambon.

Calculating Culkin

Madame Melville (Vaudeville)

Napoleon (Shaftesbury)

At the Vaudeville *Madame Melville* is *The Graduate* for grown-ups; here, too, a likely young lad is seduced by an older woman, but in this case it is not Mother from the Midwest. Instead, she's a gorgeously glamorous thirty-something Parisian schoolteacher, who finds herself in day (and indeed overnight) care of a gawky, gangling young American teenager who is about to be sexually and socially awakened, whether he likes it or not.

True, if we didn't have Iréne Jacob, Desdemona in the last movie *Othello* and the best thing to have come out of Paris since Leslie Caron, as the teacher and Macaulay Culkin (superbly typecast) as the perennial teenager, there would not be much of a play here. Richard Nelson, the RSC's resident American dramatist (and now director, most recently, of a brilliant Broadway musical version of James Joyce's *The Dead*), has written many better studies of the Atlantic gap, that sea-change which overcomes Americans in Europe, but this one has, like its narrator-hero, an odd kind of lovability in a fundamentally sleazy situation.

There is, as Nelson realises, a good deal to be said for the passage of time; set this play in the here and now, and we would wonder why the teacher was not up before some sort of sexual-abuse tribunal, charged with the corruption of innocents in her care. But put it back thirty or forty years, to Paris a year or two before her 1969 liberation, the Paris of *Jules et Jim* and *Les Cousins* and all that Truffaut and Chabrol, and presto you've got a rite of romantic passage instead. Not a lot happens: the boy gets lucky when his teacher has a bust-up with her lover, another of his teachers at an international school, and she takes him to her bed while explaining a good deal of what else Paris has to offer him.

True, this nostalgic tale of the awakening teenager and the two women (there's also a wacky, vaguely flower-power neighbour) who form part of his dream and its subsequent reality, is not *The Catcher in the Rye*, nor even *The Go-Between*; Nelson's writing and directing are sketchy and low-key and moody. But in a rapidly deteriorating West End it is good to have a play to think about instead of merely gawp at – a play with a lot more to say than *Art*, but the same kind of chic, triangular style and resonance.

~

As for *Napoleon*, it is the most lavish, luxurious, loopy extravaganza since Ivor Novello dropped dead during his *King's Rhapsody* all of half a century ago. You may not instantly take to the idea of the little Emperor being interrupted on the battlefield of Waterloo by Josephine, back from the dead in a white nightdress to point out somewhat tactlessly that everything has been going wrong for him since their divorce; but Francesca Zambello the director, faced with a score by two newcomers already gainfully employed at the theme-park end of the Disney empire, has wisely decided to throw everything she's got at it, and the result is like a double-act of *Tosca* and *La Traviata* on speed.

The set alone looks as though not just Napoleon and Josephine but also Mad King Ludwig have been let loose in a furniture warehouse where there was a special offer on chandeliers, while the songs sound as though they were written for Michael Ball and Sarah Brightman to sing at Wembley before the Cup Final.

For this is *Les Mis*–lite: no starving orphans, but a two-hour race through French history, from the Revolution by way of Elba to Waterloo. Despite its savage reviews, Napoleon should have a long coach-party life; Zambello is aiming for those who wish to see precisely how their forty quid per ticket has been spent, and she has borrowed such classics as the balcony scene from *Evita* and the Gillie Lynne 'Masquerade' from *The Phantom of the Opera*. If you are going to borrow, always borrow from the best; and if in doubt make it look and sound (at least to those who have never seen one) like an opera.

Country Matters

Another Country (Arts)

The best news around the West End this week is the rebirth of the Arts Theatre, handsomely repainted, after years of occupation by the Unicorn Children's Theatre; their move to new Islington premises means that the Arts can now provide what we most need, a kind of English off-Broadway house, somewhere central, and filling the gap between the fringe and Shaftesbury Avenue, with about 400 seats. Still better news is that the new Arts management is giving us, for the first time in almost twenty years, a major revival of Julian Mitchell's *Another Country*; like Simon Gray and Ronald Harwood, Mitchell is one of those well-made playwrights shamefully ignored at trendier or subsidised premises, and this was the 1930s public-school play that made the reputations on stage or screen of Kenneth Branagh, Colin Firth, Daniel Day-Lewis and Rupert Everett. It tells the story of how Guy Burgess first became a Communist spy, inspired by the treachery and gay intolerance of his schooldays.

Another Country is about the way in which modern Britain still strangles itself in old-school ties, and it has lost none of its original strength; moreover Patrick Ryecart, in the brief role of the only adult in the play, a camp pacifist lecturer, gives one of the best performances anywhere on the London stage at present. Shades of the prison house are beginning to close around these golden 1930s lads, and Stephen Henry's production is a sharp reminder yet again of how many great plays are shamefully ignored by mainstream companies; hopefully the reborn Arts could take care of that, too.

Theatre 2000

'Everything's different, nothing's changed; only maybe slightly rearranged.' Stephen Sondheim of course, whose seventieth birthday is currently being celebrated in a long-delayed London premiere of his *Merrily We Roll Along*. So what have been the slight rearrangements of this theatrical start to the new century?

Mainly it seems to have been a year of farewells; in a Buckinghamshire garden on a late-spring Sunday afternoon, Sir John Gielgud died quietly, a few weeks after his ninety-sixth birthday and his last screen appearance in a short Samuel Beckett play: the classicist was a modernist after all. With him he takes the century of which he was clearly the greatest actor, one moreover who had seen Bernhardt and Duse and his own great-aunt Ellen Terry; Gielgud's career was not only the history of twentieth-century theatre, but also our last surviving link to the nineteenth.

His last public appearance was to have been at a memorial for his old friend Ralph Richardson's widow, and only a few weeks after that his greatest discovery, the actor Alec Guinness, also went quietly offstage. Asked how he would like this event to be recorded, Alec had once murmured, 'Thick fog, and people walking into a railway station at night. Dimly through the gloom one sees an evening-newspaper headline: Actor Dead.'

John was always Prospero to Alec's Ariel, Oberon to his Puck; only Scofield now lives on, albeit in self-imposed exile, to remind us what great acting was once all about, and never will be again. Television and the movies and the new supremacy of directors and even designers all have conspired to dethrone the player kings and queens; never again shall we see a generation of actors to equal that of which Gielgud and Guinness were the last survivors, and the British theatre, indeed world theatre, will always be the poorer.

Elsewhere, a year of other new departures, happily less permanent: Ian McDiarmid and Jonathan Kent bade farewell to the Almeida and eventually their own management there with *The Tempest* as the theatre goes into a marathon rebuilding project; Cameron Mackintosh threatens never again to produce a new musical; the Old Vic bids farewell to Shakespeare as it gets reborn as the permanent dance home of Matthew Bourne's Adventures in Motion Pictures. Meanwhile Jeffrey Archer, forced out of politics and into the theatre, stages his own courtroom thriller ahead of the real-life one which still awaits him; presumably if found guilty in that, he could always be replaced at the Haymarket by Jonathan Aitken.*

We also start now to bid farewell to the Hollywood movie stars who have been swamping our stages: Macaulay Culkin and Jessica Lange go home in triumph, which is rather more that can be said for Donald Sutherland or Darryl Hannah or indeed Jerry Hall, who at least had the grace never to pretend to be an actress in the first place. Nevertheless, the New Year still promises (or threatens) Calista Flockhart and Farrah Fawcett, while there could be many more if the imminent Hollywood strike proves long-term. And even in exile the Almeida still promises Anna Friel as Lulu, Oliver Ford-Davies as King Lear and a new David Hare *Platonov*.

Performances of the year? Simon Russell Beale's chubby, unusually endearing Hamlet, Corin Redgrave's weary, wasted Oscar Wilde, Bill Nighy in the brilliantly psychiatric *Blue/Orange*, imminently into the West End from the National, Felicity Kendal and Frances de la Tour and Tilly Tremayne as Coward's *Fallen Angels* and their infinitely superior maidservant, Patrick Ryecart as the cynical author in a hugely welcome Arts revival of Julian Mitchell's *Another Country*, Louis Dempsey and Sean Sloan as the entire cast of Marie Jones' *Stones in His Pockets*, Michael

* He was and he wasn't, if you see what I mean.

Gambon as *The Caretaker* and the childmaster in *Cressida*, Ralph Fiennes as *Coriolanus* and *Richard II*.

Musicals? Three unusually courageous ones: *The Witches of Eastwick*, shortly to move to the Prince of Wales, thereby clearing Drury Lane for the new National *My Fair Lady* if it works; *The Beautiful Game*, Ben Elton and Andrew Lloyd Webber's haunting account of the soccer children of the Irish 1960s; and, out at Stratford, a brave RSC attempt to penetrate *The Secret Garden*. Then there were three unusually terrible ones from France and Spain (*Lautrec*, *Notre Dame* and *La Cava*), while from Canada came a weird and wonderfully gothic *Napoleon* which often had to be seen not to be believed.

Out at the Newbury Watermill there was a war-weary, small-scale *Carmen*, just as good in its own bloodsoaked, Civil War way as the infinitely better-funded Matthew Bourne *Car Man* at the Old Vic, while both the Bridewell and Jermyn Street continued to deliver small scale treats of an often cabaret nature.

At the National, Trevor Nunn survived a bruising year only to clean up at awards time; his successes still outnumber his defeats, but the second attempt to form an ensemble was wildly misguided, and he is still in urgent need of a team of heirs apparent. His succession problem, as he is the first to acknowledge, is simply that, in the wake of Sam Mendes and Stephen Daldry and Nicholas Hytner, anyone qualified to run the National would rather be directing in Hollywood, an option that was simply not open when Nunn built his original team at Stratford twenty or so years ago.

Peter Hall and Peter Brook continue to be considerably more honoured abroad than at home, though Brook's Paris *Hamlet* at the year's close (later seen in Britain, America and Japan) was somewhat fragmented and low-key.

So what does all that mean for 2001, a year in which mercifully nobody has yet thought of a timely musical of the classic movie of that title? It means pretty much business as usual, though the King's Head and the Orange Tree are still dangerously underfunded, the touring situation is as bleak as ever, and to get a new play with an unknown cast into the West End without a previous existence in subsidised houses or the fringe is no longer difficult. It is now impossible.

Let's end on a more cheerful note; the autumn West End audience figures have been little short of terrible, as the trains and the rains took their toll. They are bound to get better as and when the climate does; meantime, anyone for a British premiere of *Two by Two*, the old Richard Rodgers musical about Noah's Ark?

Award Winners during the 1990s

1992 for 1991

Evening Standard

Best Play *Dancing at Lughnasa* by Brian Friel
Best Musical *Carmen Jones* by Oscar Hammerstein II
Best Comedy *Kvetch* by Steven Berkoff
Best Director Trevor Nunn for *Timon of Athens*
Best Actor John Wood for *King Lear*
Best Actress Vanessa Redgrave for *When She Danced*
Most Promising Playwright Rona Munro for *Bold Girls*

Olivier

Best Play *Death and the Maiden* by Ariel Dorfman
Best Musical *Carmen Jones* by Oscar Hammerstein II
Best Comedy *La Bete* by David Hirson
Best Entertainment *Talking Heads* by Alan Bennett
Best Revival *Hedda Gabler*
Best Musical Revival *The Boys from Syracuse*
Best Actor Nigel Hawthorne for *The Madness of George III*
Best Actress Juliet Stevenson for *Death and the Maiden*
Best Actor in a Musical (or Entertainment) Alan Bennett for *Talking Heads*
Best Actress in a Musical (or Entertainment) Wilhelmenia Fernandez for *Carmen Jones*
Best Comedy Performance Desmond Barrit for *The Comedy of Errors*
Best Actor in a Supporting Role Oleg Menshikov for *When She Danced*
Best Actress in a Supporting Role Frances de la Tour for *When She Danced*
Best Supporting Role in a Musical Jenny Galloway for *The Boys from Syracuse*
Best Director of a Play Deborah Warner for *Hedda Gabler*
Best Director of a Musical Simon Callow for *Carmen Jones*
Best Choreographer Rafael Aguilar for *Matador*
Best Set Designer Mark Thompson for *Joseph and the Amazing Technicolor Dreamcoat* and *The Comedy of Errors*
Best Costume Designer Mark Thompson for *The Comedy of Errors*
Best Lighting Designer Mark Henderson for *Murmuring Judges* and *Long Day's Journey Into Night*
The Observer Award Gate Theatre for a season from the Spanish Golden Age

1993 for 1992

Evening Standard

Best Play *Angels in America, Part One: Millennium Approaches* by Tony Kushner
Best Musical *Kiss of the Spiderwoman* by John Kander, Fredd Ebb, Terrence McNally
Best Comedy *The Rise and Fall of Little Voice* by Jim Cartwright
Best Director Stephen Daldry for *An Inspector Calls*

Best Actor Nigel Hawthorne for *The Madness of George III*
Best Actress Diana Rigg for *Medea*
Most Promising Playwright Philip Ridley for *The Fastest Clock in the Universe*

Olivier

Best Play *Six Degrees of Separation* by John Guare
Best Musical *Crazy for You* by George and Ira Gershwin
Best Comedy *The Rise and Fall of Little Voice* by Jim Cartwright
Best Entertainment *Travels with my Aunt* by Graham Greene, adapted by Giles Havergal
Best Revival *An Inspector Calls*
Best Musical Revival *Carousel*
Best Actor Robert Stephens for *Henry V*
Best Actress Alison Steadman for *The Rise and Fall of Little Voice*
Best Actor in a Musical Henry Goodman for *Assassins*
Best Actress in a Musical Joanna Riding for *Carousel*
Best Comedy Performance Simon Cadell for *Travels with my Aunt*
Best Actor in a Supporting Role Julian Glover for *Henry V*
Best Actress in a Supporting Role Barbara Leigh-Hunt for *An Inspector Calls*
Best Supporting Performance in a Musical Janie Dee for *Carousel*
Best Director of a Play Stephen Daldry for *An Inspector Calls*
Best Director of a Musical Nicholas Hytner for *Carousel*
Best Choreographer Susan Stroman for *Crazy for You*
Best Set Designer Ian MacNeil for *An Inspector Calls*
Best Costume Designer William Dudley for *Heartbreak House, Pygmalion* and *The Rise and Fall of Little Voice*
Best Lighting Designer Howell Binkley for *Kiss of the Spiderwoman*
Lifetime Achievement Award Sir Kenneth MacMillan
Special Award Almeida Theatre

1994 for 1993

Evening Standard

Best Play *Arcadia* by Tom Stoppard
Best Musical *City of Angels* by Larry Gelbart, David Zippel, Cy Coleman
Best Comedy *Jamais Vu* by Ken Campbell
Best Director Terry Hands for *Tamburlaine the Great*
Best Actor Ian Holm for *Moonlight*
Best Actress Fiona Shaw for *Machinal*
Most Promising Playwright Brad Fraser for *Unidentified Human Remains*, Simon Donald for *The Life of Stuff*

Olivier

Best Play *Arcadia* by Tom Stoppard
Best Musical *City of Angels* by Larry Gelbart, David Zippel, Cy Coleman
Best Comedy *Hysteria* by Terry Johnson
Best Entertainment *A Christmas Carol* adapted and staged by Patrick Stewart
Best Revival *Machinal*

Best Musical Revival *Sweeney Todd*
Best Actor Mark Rylance for *Much Ado About Nothing*
Best Actress Fiona Shaw for *Machinal*
Best Actor in a Musical Alun Armstrong for *Sweeney Todd*
Best Actress in a Musical Julia McKenzie for *Sweeney Todd*
Best Comedy Performance Griff Rhys Jones for *An Absolute Turkey*
Best Actor in a Supporting Role Joseph Mydell for *Perestroika*
Best Actress in a Supporting Role Helen Burns for *The Last Yankee*
Best Supporting Performance in a Musical Sara Kestelman for *Cabaret*
Best Director of a Play Stephen Daldry for *Machinal*
Best Director of a Musical Declan Donellan for *Sweeney Todd*
Best Choreographer in Theatre Luke Cresswell and Steve McNicholas for *Stomp*
Best Set Designer Mark Thompson for *Hysteria*
Best Costume Designer Gerald Scarfe for *An Absolute Turkey*
Best Lighting Designer Rick Fisher for *Hysteria, Machinal* and *Moonlight*
The Times Award Peter Brook for outstanding contribution to British theatre
Society of London Theatre's Special Award for Lifetime Achievement Sam Wanamaker

1995 for 1994

Evening Standard

Best Play *Three Tall Women* by Edward Albee
Best Musical No Award
Best Comedy *My Night with Reg* by Kevin Elyot
Best Director Sean Mathias for *Les Parents Terribles* and *Design for Living*
Best Actor Tom Courtenay for *Moscow Stations*
Best Actress Maggie Smith for *Three Tall Women*
Most Promising Playwright Jonathan Harvey for *Babies*

Olivier

Best Play *Broken Glass* by Arthur Miller
Best Musical *Once on this Island* by Ann Ahrens, Stephen Flaherty, Rosa Guy
Best Comedy *My Night with Reg* by Kevin Elyot
Best Entertainment *Maria Friedman by Special Arrangement*
Best Revival *As You Like It*
Best Musical Revival *She Loves Me*
Best Actor David Bamber for *My Night with Reg*
Best Actress Clare Higgins for *Sweet Bird of Youth*
Best Actor in a Musical John Gordon-Sinclair for *She Loves Me*
Best Actress in a Musical Ruthie Henshall for *She Loves Me*
Best Comedy Performance Niall Buggy for *Dead Funny*
Best Actor in a Supporting Role Ken Scott for *Broken Glass*
Best Actress in a Supporting Role Dora Bryan for *The Birthday Party*
Best Supporting Performance in a Musical Tracie Bennett for *She Loves Me*
Best Director of a Play Declan Donnellan for *As You Like It*
Best Director of a Musical Scott Ellis for *She Loves Me*
Best Choreography David Atkins and Dein Perry for *Hot Show Shuffle*

Best Set Designer Stephen Brimson Lewis for *Design for Living* and *Les Parents Terribles*

Best Costume Designer Deirdre Clancy for *Love's Labours Lost* and *A Month in the Country*

Best Lighting Designer Mark Henderson for his work during the year

1996 for 1995

Evening Standard

Best Play *Pentecost* by David Edgar

Best Musical *Mack and Mabel* by Jerry Herman, Michael Stewart

Best Comedy *Dealer's Choice* by Patrick Marber

Best Director Matthew Warchus for *Volpone* and *Henry V*

Best Actor Michael Gambon for *Volpone*

Best Actress Geraldine McEwan for *The Way of the World*

Most Promising Playwright Jez Butterworth for *Mojo*

Patricia Rothermere Award Richard Eyre for services to the theatre

Olivier

Best Play *Skylight* by David Hare

Best Musical *Jolson* by Francis Essex, Rob Bettinson

Best New Comedy *Mojo* by Jez Butterworth

Best Actor Alex Jennings for *Peer Gynt*

Best Actress Judi Dench for *Absolute Hell*

Best Supporting Performance Simon Russell Beale for *Volpone*

Best Director Sam Mendes for *Company* and *The Glass Menagerie*

Best Actor in a Musical Adrian Lester for *Company*

Best Actress in a Musical Judi Dench for *A Little Night Music*

Best Supporting Performance in a Musical Sheila Gish for *Company*

Best Choreographer Dein Perry for *Tap Dogs*

Best Set Designer John Napier for *Burning Blue*

Best Lighting Designer David Hersey for *Burning Blue, The Glass Menagerie* and *Twelfth Night*

Best Costume Designer Anthony Ward for *A Midsummer Night's Dream, La Grande Magia* and *The Way of the World*

Special Award Harold Pinter for services to the theatre

1997 for 1996

Evening Standard

Best Play *Stanley* by Pam Gems

Best Musical *Passion* by Stephen Sondheim, James Lapine

Best Comedy *Art* by Yasmina Reza

Best Director Katie Mitchell for *The Phoenician Women*

Best Actor Paul Scofield for *John Gabriel Borkman*

Best Actress Dame Diana Rigg for *Who's Afraid of Virginia Woolf?* and *Mother Courage*

Most Promising Playwright Martin McDonagh for *The Beauty Queen of Leenane*

Olivier

Best Play *Stanley* by Pam Gems
Best Comedy *Art* by Yasmina Reza
Best Musical *Martin Guerre* by Alain Boublil, Claude-Michel Schonberg, Edward Hardy, Stephen Clark
Outstanding Musical Production *Tommy*
Best Actress Janet McTeer for *A Doll's House*
Best Actor Anthony Sher for *Stanley*
Best Actress in a Supporting Role Deborah Findley for *Stanley*
Best Actor in a Supporting Role Trevor Eve for *Uncle Vanya*
Best Actress in a Musical Maria Friedman for *Passion*
Best Actor in a Musical Robert Lindsay for *Oliver!*
Best Supporting Performance in a Musical Clive Rowe for *Guys and Dolls*
Best Director Des McAnuff for *Tommy*
Best Theatre Choreographer Bob Avian for *Martin Guerre*
Best Costume Designer Tim Goodchild for *The Relapse*
Best Lighting Designer Chris Parry for *Tommy*
Best Set Designer Tim Hatley for *Stanley*
Laurence Olivier Award for Outstanding Achievement Richard Eyre
The Special Award Margaret Harris

1998 for 1997

Evening Standard

Best Play *The Invention of Love* by Tom Stoppard
Best Musical *Lady in the Dark* by Kurt Weill, Ira Gershwin, Moss Hart
Best Comedy *Closer* by Patrick Marber
Best Director Richard Eyre for *King Lear* and *The Invention of Love*
Best Actor Ian Holm for *King Lear*
Best Actress Eileen Atkins for *A Delicate Balance*
Most Promising Playwright Conor McPherson for *The Weir*
The Patricia Rothermere Award Judi Dench and March Rice-Oxley
Special Award Richard Eyre for his directorship of the Royal National Theatre 1988–97

Olivier

Best Play *Closer* by Patrick Marber
Best Comedy *Popcorn* by Ben Elton
Best Entertainment *Slava's Snowshow* created by Slava Polunin
Best Musical *Beauty and the Beast* by Alan Menken, Howard Ashman, Tim Rice and Linda Woolverton
Outstanding Musical Production *Chicago*
Best Actress Zoë Wanamaker for *Electra*
Best Actor Ian Holm for *King Lear*
Best Performance in a Supporting Role Sarah Woodward for *Tom and Clem*
Best Actress in a Musical Ute Lemper for *Chicago*
Best Actor in a Musical Philip Quast for *The Fix*

Best Supporting Performance in a Musical James Dreyfus for *Lady in the Dark*
Best Director Richard Eyre for *King Lear*
Best Theatre Choreographer Simon McBurney for *The Caucasian Chalk Circle*
Best Costume Designer Tim Goodchild for *Three Hours After Marriage*
Best Lighting Designer Rick Fisher for *Chips with Everything* and *Lady in the Dark*
Best Set Designer Tim Goodchild for *Three Hours After Marriage*
Special Award Ed Mirvish, David Mirvish for their contribution to restoring and operating The Old Vic Theatre

1999 for 1998

Evening Standard

Best Play *Copenhagen* by Michael Frayn
Best Musical *Oklahoma!* by Richard Rodgers and Oscar Hammerstein II
Best Comedy No Award
Best Director Howard Davies for *Flight* and *The Iceman Cometh*
Best Actor Kevin Spacey for *The Iceman Cometh*
Best Actress Sinead Cusack for *Our Lady of Sligo*
Best Stage Designer Richard Hoover for *Not About Nightingales*
Most Promising Playwright Mark Ravenhill for *Handbag*
Theatrical Achievement of the Year The Almeida Theatre
Special Award Nicole Kidman for *The Blue Room*

Olivier

Best Play *The Weir* by Conor McPherson
Best Comedy *Cleo, Camping, Emmanuelle And Dick* by Terry Johnson
Best Entertainment The Right Size for *Do You Come Here Often?* by Sean Foley, Hamish McColl, Josef Houben
Best Musical *Kat And The Kings* by David Kramer and Taliep Petersen
Outstanding Musical Production *Oklahoma!*
Best Actress Eileen Atkins for *The Unexpected Man*
Best Actor Kevin Spacey for *The Iceman Cometh*
Best Supporting Performance Brendan Coyle for *The Weir*
Best Actress In a Musical Sophie Thompson for *Into The Woods*
Best Actor In a Musical The cast of *Kat And The Kings* (Salie Daniels, Jody Abrahams, Loukmaan Adams, Junaid Booysen, Alistair Izobell, Mandisa Bardill)
Best Supporting Performance in a Musical Shuler Hensley for *Oklahoma!*
Best Director Howard Davies for *The Iceman Cometh*
Best Theatre Choreographer Susan Stroman for *Oklahoma!*
Best Costume Designer William Dudley for *Amadeus* and *The London Cuckolds*
Best Lighting Designer Hugh Vanstone for *The Blue Room* and *The Unexpected Man*
Best Set Designer Anthony Ward for *Oklahoma!*
Special Award Peter Hall

2000 for 1999

Evening Standard

Best Play No Award

Best Musical *Spend Spend Spend* by Steve Brown, Justin Greene, Viv Nicholson, Stephen Smith

Best Director Trevor Nunn for *The Merchant of Venice* and *Summerfolk*

Best Actor Stephen Dillane for *The Real Thing*

Best Actress Janie Dee for *Comic Potential*

Best Stage Designer Tim Hatley for *Suddenly Last Summer, Sleep With Me* and *The Darker Face of the Earth*

Most Promising Playwright Rebecca Gilman for *The Glory of Living*

Best Newcomer Eve Best for *'Tis Pity She's a Whore*

Theatrical Event of the Year *The Lion King*

Patricia Rothmere Award Simon Callow

Olivier

Best Musical *Honk! The Ugly Duckling* by George Stiles, Anthony Drewe

Outstanding Musical Production *Candide* by Leonard Bernstein, Hugh Wheeler and others

Best Play *Goodnight Children Everywhere* by Richard Nelson

Best Comedy *The Memory of Water* by Shelagh Stephenson

Best Entertainment *Defending The Caveman* by Rob Becker

Best Actress Janie Dee for *Comic Potential*

Best Actor Henry Goodman for *The Merchant of Venice*

Best Supporting Actor Roger Allam for *Money*

Best Supporting Actress Patricia Hodge for *Money*

Best Actor in a Musical Simon Russell Beale for *Candide*

Best Actress in a Musical Barbara Dickson for *Spend Spend Spend*

Best Supporting Performance in a Musical Jenny Galloway for *Mamma Mia!*

Best Director Trevor Nunn for *Summerfolk*

Best Theatre Choreographer Garth Fagan for *The Lion King*

Best Set Designer Rob Howell for *Richard III, Troilus and Cressida* and *Vassa*

Best Lighting Designer Mark Henderson for *Plenty, Spend Spend Spend, The Forest The Lion, The Witch and The Wardrobe, The Real Thing* and *Vassa*

Best Costume Designer Julie Taymor for *The Lion King*

Outstanding Achievement Award Peter O'Toole

2001 for 2000

Evening Standard

Best Play *Blue/Orange* by Joe Penhall

Best Musical Event *The Car Man* by Mathew Bourne

Best Comedy *Stones in his Pockets* by Marie Jones

Best Director Michael Grandage for *Passion Play* and *As You Like It*

Best Actor Simon Russell Beale for *Hamlet*

Best Actress Paolo Dionisotti for *Further than the Furthest Thing*

Best Stage Designer Bunny Christie for *Baby Doll*

Most Promising Playwright Gary Mitchell for *The Force of Change*
Outstanding Newcomer Chiwitel Ejiofor for *Blue/Orange*

Olivier

Best Play *Blue/Orange* by Joe Penhall
Best Comedy *Stones in his Pockets* by Marie Jones
Best Musical *Merrily We Roll Along* by Stephen Sondheim, George Furth, George S Kaufman, Moss Hart
Outstanding Musical Production *Singin' In The Rain*
Best Actress Julie Walters for for *All My Sons*
Best Actor Conleth Hill for *Stones in his Pockets*
Best Supporting Actress Pauline Flanagan for *Dolly West's Kitchen*
Best Supporting Actor Ben Daniels for *All My Sons*
Best Actress in a Musical Samantha Spiro for *Merrily We Roll Along*
Best Actor in a Musical Daniel Evans for *Merrily We Roll Along*
Best Supporting Performance in a Musical Miles Western for *Pageant*
Best Director Howard Davies for *All My Sons*
Best Theatre Choreographer Bob Fosse and Ann Reinking for *Fosse*
Best Set Designer WIlliam Dudley for *All My Sons*
Best Lighting Designer Hugh Vanstone for *The Cherry Orchard*
Best Costume Designer Alison Chitty for *The Remembrance of Things Past*

Index